V. good

Pasta With Walnuts and Peppers

2 Tbs. olive oil
4 large garlic cloves, thinly sliced
1/2 cup coarsely chopped walnuts
10 cherry tomatoes, halved
2 medium bell peppers — green, red,
  yellow or a combination — cored,
  trimmed and cut lengthwise into
  1/2-inch-long strips
1 1/2 medium yellow onions, thinly sliced
1 1/2 cups coarsely chopped parsley
Freshly ground black pepper to taste
3 cups cooked penne or rotelle
  (about 6 ounces dry)

Heat olive oil in large skillet over medium heat. Sauté walnuts and garlic till lightly browned, about 5 minutes. Add tomatoes; cook till soft, about 5 minutes. Put onions and peppers in large bowl; cover. Microwave on high power till tender. Transfer peppers, onions to skillet. Add parsley; stir to combine thoroughly. Put pasta in large shallow bowl and cover with walnut-pepper sauce. Serves 4.

Per serving: 367 calories, 9.6g protein, 46.4g carbohydrates, 4.7g fiber, 17g fat (1.9g saturated), 19mg sodium.

SOUTHERN ITALIAN COOKING

JO BETTOJA

with Jane Garmey

Wine Suggestions by Angelo Bettoja

SOUTHERN ITALIAN COOKING

Family Recipes from the Kingdom of the Two Sicilies

BANTAM BOOKS

NEW YORK · TORONTO · LONDON · SYDNEY · AUCKLAND

SOUTHERN ITALIAN COOKING

A Bantam Book / May 1991

BOOK DESIGN BY MARIA CARELLA

Library of Congress Cataloging-in-Publication Data
Bettoja, Jo.
  Southern Italian cooking : family recipes from the kingdom of the
two Sicilies / Jo Bettoja with Jane Garmey : wine suggestions by
Angelo Bettoja.
        p.   cm.
  Includes index.
  ISBN 0-553-07287-0
  1. Cookery, Italian—Southern style.   I. Garmey, Jane.
II. Title.
TX723.2.S65B48   1991
641.5945'7—dc20   90-25283
                                                        CIP

Published simultaneously in the United States and Canada

Bantam Books are published by Bantam Books, a division of Bantam Doubleday Dell Publishing Group, Inc. Its
trademark, consisting of the words "Bantam Books" and the portrayal of a rooster, is Registered in U.S. Patent
and Trademark Office and in other countries. Marca Registrada. Bantam Books, 666 Fifth Avenue, New York,
New York 10103.

PRINTED IN THE UNITED STATES OF AMERICA

RRH   0   9   8   7   6   5   4   3   2   1

Ai tanti amici del sud d'Italia
che mi hanno generosamente aiutato

ACKNOWLEDGMENTS

I would like to thank Jane Garmey, who not only wrote the introduction but also researched the subject and expanded my garbled recipe notes. Thank you to Christine Benton, copy editor, who, fortunately for me, was severe and thorough. Thank you to my husband, Angelo, who chose the wines. Thank you to my friend and agent, Irene Skolnick, but the biggest thank you of all to Fran McCullough, my editor, for her patience and understanding.

There would be no book without the contributions of these people: Antonio and Maria Antonietta d'Alì, Michi Ambrosi de Magistris, Paola Amodio Pettini, Lina Alferi, Maria Anzon, Irene Bettoja Speciale Piccichè, Silvia Cereo, Giuseppe Corleone, Toti Corleone, Agata Curcio, Ippolita Gaetani d'Aragona, Francesca Gagliardo di Carpinello Marchello, Giovanni and Assunta Grossi, Carlo Hassan, Anna Maria Lombardi, Ersilia Lucibello, Letizia Maione, Mareste Massimo, Francesco Mollo, Anna Maria Monticelli, Adele Nunziante Diana, Vera Panzera, Ada Parasiliti, Nino del Papa, Giacomo and Gabriella Rallo, Natalia Ravidà, Maria Cristina Savona, Violetta Speciale, Franca Tasca d'Almerita, Pasquale Vuilleumier.

CONTENTS

Contents

Una Passeggiata dopo Colazione nel Giardino Savona
A WALK AFTER LUNCH IN THE SAVONAS'
ORANGE AND LEMON GARDEN

Cena sulla Spiaggia da Zia Irene
ZIA IRENE'S PICNIC ON THE BEACH

Contents

Cena sulla Terrazza di Toti
DINNER ON TOTI'S TERRACE

Cena a Marsala alla Villa Rallo
DINNER IN MARSALA AT VILLA RALLO

Picnic nel Vigneto
PICNIC IN THE VINEYARDS

Una Cena in Famiglia a Messina
A FAMILY DINNER IN MESSINA

Cena a Casa Tasca
DINNER AT CASA TASCA

Una Colazione del Sabato al Palazzo
A SATURDAY LUNCH AT THE PALAZZO

Contents

Una Colazione Siciliana Informale
AN INFORMAL SICILIAN LUNCH

Una Colazione Vegetariana Data da Ada
A VEGETARIAN LUNCH GIVEN BY ADA

Cena a Palermo
DINNER IN PALERMO

Contents

Contents

Buffet Invernale
A WINTER BUFFET

Un Grande Buffet Estivo
A BIG SUMMER BUFFET

Contents

Una Cena Autunnale a Napoli
A FALL DINNER IN NAPLES

Cena Invernale
WINTER DINNER

Contents

Panza cuntenti
Cori clementi
Panza dijuna
Nenti pirduna

Contented belly
A clement heart
Empty belly
Heart of stone
SICILIAN PROVERB

INTRODUCTION

South of Rome people eat marvelously well. Southern Italian food, contrary to popular opinion, is not at all like what we know as Italian-American: spaghetti and coarse meatballs followed by dense cheesecake, etc. This vivid cuisine has its roots in North Africa and Greece and is quite unlike that of the north of Italy. Imaginative, exuberant, and often sumptuous, it's not just one but a variety of cuisines, inspired by an extraordinary history.

Southern Italy stretches south from Rome into the regions of Abruzzi, Puglia, Molise, Campania, Basilicata, and Calabria, and on across the Strait of Messina into Sicily. The terrain is often rugged and mountainous, much of the land being unsuited to farming. Archaic religious rituals and superstitions persist, and local dialects hold strong. The landscape is dotted with the remains of Norman fortresses and genuine Greek temples, towns have ancient Greek names, and Arab words have been incorporated into the local language. Not only are there significant differences between the North and South—they were not even part of

the same country until the unification of Italy in 1861—but Naples and Sicily themselves were once two separate kingdoms with separate legal and judicial systems, even though at times they were united under one sovereign in an uneasy peace.

Even today the South remains distinct from the North both geographically and culturally. What began as an ethnic boundary dividing the Etruscan North from the Greek South and later became a political division has now become what Waverley Root calls a gastronomic Mason-Dixon line.

Poverty plays a strong role in southern cuisine. Southerners eat less meat because the land is not well suited to cattle farming, and the beef tends to be tough since cattle are not raised for milk. It must be cooked for hours, which accounts for the marvelously thick, steaming southern ragouts. What pork there is tends to be made into rough, spicy, garlicky sausage. Lamb is popular in the mountainous Abruzzi region, but chicken is a great luxury. (In fact pasta in the South is made often without eggs.) Since cow's milk is scarce, butter is rarely used for sautéing but does appear in crusts and brioches; olive oil and lard are much preferred. Cheeses, except for *ricotta* and *mozzarella*, tend to be of the hard variety, usually made from sheep's milk.

Southern culinary traditions have both aristocratic and humble roots. In common with most good cooking, they take advantage of what is locally available: trees in every garden laden with the sweetest and most delectable lemons and oranges; succulent figs; multitudes of fresh vegetables that begin arriving in the markets while most of the North is still blanketed in snow; plentiful fish, including pungent anchovies, soft, meaty sardines, and the best swordfish and tuna in all of Italy. Then there is the genuine buffalo *mozzarella* from the plains of Campania, the succulent lamb, tasty olives, fragrant almonds, forest pine nuts, feathery wild fennel, and robust dandelions growing as weeds on the hillside. There is the sweetest honey, the tiniest capers, and even cultivated saffron in Abruzzi.

Most dishes are composed of a whole range of ingredients, often flavored with anchovies and seasoned with pungent spices. Fish is frequently rolled and stuffed, and vegetable dishes are often wildly imaginative. Pastry-covered savory pies are layered with elaborate fillings and are *de rigueur* on festive occasions. There are infinite variations of pizza, not only the *mozzarella* varieties we know but also two-crusted versions and many that are not savory but sweet. There are also wonderfully distinctive touches, like a bit of rum in the piecrust. However, the real culinary signature of the South comes at the conclusion of the meal: the rich, colorful, and irresistibly exuberant sweets and desserts. Here all restraint is thrown to the wind, for the South has an insatiable sweet tooth, gladly indulging in the fruits of the East, of Byzantium and Greece.

Not only is the array of sweets and desserts at any meal quite dazzling, but many of them still hold a deep religious symbolism—elaborately decorated *cassata, cannoli, pastiera*, desserts known as "Triumphs of Gluttony," pastries with wonderfully irreverent names such as "St. Agatha's Breasts" and "Virgin's Nipples." The ice creams are endlessly various, and the sherbets, candied fruit, quivering jellies, nougat, and marzipan all recall the Orient. Of all the influences on southern food it is the Arab that has been the most pervasive, making southern Italian and Sicilian cooking so original, so spirited, and so different from what we usually think of as Italian food.

The Arabs were not, in fact, the first visitors to reach the South. The Greeks had come many centuries earlier, arriving in Sicily in 415 B.C. and quickly infiltrating the mainland. In addition to architecture, they introduced wheat farming, wine making, and a passion for bread. (Athenaeus of Naucratis refers to one talented baker who regularly made 72 different kinds.) But the Greeks also brought olives, honey perfumed with flowers and sweets made with it, almonds, and lamb roasted on the spit.

The Roman rule that followed left much less of a culinary legacy. There is *maccu*, that sustaining dish made of fava beans cooked in water that has been perfumed with wild fennel, then mashed with a fork and dressed with olive oil and pepper. Fava beans had always been plentiful, but the Greeks had been reluctant to eat them, believing that the spirits of the dead used the hollow stalks of the fava plants as a pathway to the underworld. The Romans were not so superstitious, and during their occupation of Sicily the fava bean became the mainstay of the Roman soldier's diet. *Maccu* is still popular in many parts of Sicily (see the somewhat more appealing fava bean soup on page 221).

But then came the Arabs! Sicily is barely 90 miles from the coast of Africa, and at the beginning of the ninth century A.D. the Arabs invaded and conquered it, in time also establishing themselves on the mainland. Their culinary tastes were as foreign as their architecture. Rice, nuts, and saffron, and such exotic dishes as sherbet and couscous were introduced and soon became an accepted part of the Sicilian diet. Citrus trees were planted all over the island, and a whole new taste for sweet and sour combined began to flourish, creating a hallmark of the region to this very day. It was the Arabs who introduced the cultivation of sugarcane and bequeathed to successive generations of Sicilians a passion for the overpoweringly sweet, which still thrives 11 centuries later.

Many Sicilian towns and villages have their own special sweets and desserts, and a great number of them still bear Arab names. The most famous is *cassata*, from the Arabic word *qas'ah,* meaning a round pan or bowl. This pudding-cake has a sponge cake base filled with a creamy *ricotta* mixture, iced and decorated elaborately with orange and lemon peel. Many ancient desserts were later renamed for saints and are still prepared and eaten with great ceremony on religious feast days. Rich, colorful, and intensely sweet, they have assumed a symbolic stature and are often eaten with a conscious sense of ritual.

Although the Arab influence was felt most in Sicily and dishes such as couscous never reached the mainland, the taste for the foreign and exotic is discernible in many mainland dishes. A Neapolitan cookbook published in 1634, for instance, describes a dish of meat and vegetables being cooked with oil and garlic, raisins and pine nuts.

Two centuries of Arab rule came to an end when the Normans, led by Count Roger I, successfully invaded Sicily in the 11th century. These conquerors, an unsophisticated lot, appear to have been dazzled by the sophistication and luxury of Arab ways. They took to dressing in Muslim attire, established their own harems, adopted a Saracen style of architec-

Introduction

ture, and read Arab literature. Roger I surrounded himself with an Arab court and even kept an Arab cook.

In fact the Normans appear to have left little of their own imprint on the cuisine of the region. Their only major contribution was the art of drying, salting, and smoking fish. Under Norman rule, however, the South reached a degree of affluence and strength scarcely matched elsewhere in Europe at the time. The secret of this regime was crushing taxation, which reduced the population to extreme poverty and led to the Sicilian revolt of 1282. The independence movement lasted only a few months, however, and soon the Sicilian nobles were offering the crown to Pietro d'Aragona. Sicily became a part of Spain and was cut off from the political and cultural life of the rest of southern Italy.

The Spanish, of course, soon wanted more, and in 1442, referring to it as "my other Sicily," Alfonso V of Aragon drove the Angevins out of Naples, uniting Sicily and Naples under a single ruler. Following the Treaties of Blois, the South was ruled for two centuries by Spanish viceroys—one in Palermo and one in Naples. Heavy taxation filled the coffers of Spain but led to an endless succession of uprisings and suppressions, expulsions and defeats, and through it all the threat of famine and constant poverty. Naples finally fell to the Austrians in 1707 and then to the Bourbons in 1732.

It was under the French that Naples began to gain its reputation as the most cosmopolitan and luxurious city in southern Europe. Court life revolved around magnificent parties and banquets, and the opera rivaled Milan's La Scala. The city became a mecca for the cultured and the well-to-do. Palaces equipped with servants and gilded furniture could be rented as well as owned, and the reigning evening's entertainment was an invitation to accompany the king as he circled the Bay of Naples in his royal barge, serenaded by a string orchestra that followed close behind in a separate barge.

There was political disruption when Napoléon's army approached in 1799, and Ferdinand IV and his entire court were forced to flee to Palermo. But in 1815, with Napoléon defeated, Ferdinand signed a treaty

with Austria, regained Naples, and gave a reunited Sicily and Naples that almost fairy-tale name—the Kingdom of the Two Sicilies. He even declared himself Ferdinand I, King of the Two Sicilies. But his dynasty was short-lived, for in 1860 Garibaldi and his thousand men, backed by Victor Emmanuel of Savoy, King of Sardinia, landed at Marsala and declared the existence of modern Italy.

Still the French influence prevailed. The aristocracy of southern Italy was enamored of everything French—court banquets abounded in French dishes, were served on French china, and it became the rage to import one's chef from Paris. Since experienced chefs willing to leave France were a scarce commodity, it soon became necessary to send Sicilian and Neapolitan chefs to France to serve an apprenticeship there. Upon their return these chefs were known as *monzùs*, a corruption of the French word *monsieur* that quickly became a much coveted title. Having a *monzù* was a sign of great distinction and a cause for considerable envy. The *monzùs* introduced many French dishes and sauces into the culinary repertoire, at least at one level of society—the grandest families of southern Italy, who, for the most part, jealously guarded those elaborate recipes that were the *pièces de résistance* of their receptions and buffets.

Today there are very few *monzùs* left, and almost none of them still prepare those legendary banquets that gave Palermo its reputation as one of the most opulent social capitals of Europe. Giuseppe di Lampedusa describes one such banquet:

> *Beneath the candelabra, beneath the five tiers bearing toward the distant ceiling pyramids of homemade cakes that were never touched, spread the monotonous opulence of buffets at big balls: coralline lobsters boiled alive, waxy chaud-froids of veal, steely-tinted fish immersed in sauce, turkeys gilded by the oven's heat, rosy foie gras under gelatin armor, boned woodcock reclining on amber toast decorated with their own chopped insides and a dozen other cruel colored delights. At the end of the table two monumental silver tureens held clear soup the color of burnt amber.*

The *monzù* symbolized an age of extravagance and luxury on a scale that has virtually disappeared. Gone are the days when a *monzù* such as the late Giovanni Messina could proudly claim in a newspaper article that he needed 22 pounds of liver to produce a pound of his own special pâté. But the *monzù* legacy lives on in such culinary inventions as *pasticci*, those elaborately filled savory pies intended as the centerpiece of an elaborate dinner that can still be found in the South. Baked in a crust, sometimes filled with pasta and sometimes with a rich mélange of meats, mushrooms, cheeses, and vegetables, *pasticcio* remains one of the delights of southern Italy.

Naples and Palermo, the twin capitals of the old Kingdom of the Two Sicilies, are still the most important focal points of the South. The two cities are similar in some ways: both abound in ice cream shops and outdoor restaurants; both excel in noise and traffic; both are bustling, confused, and overpopulated. They are also very different from each other. Life in Naples seethes with turmoil and excitement. Its sounds and smells are sometimes suffocating but have an undeniable appeal. Even today housewives hang out limp strands of newly made pasta to dry on the overhanging balconies that line the back streets and narrow alleyways. Flower sellers set up shop on almost every street corner, and there are children everywhere. Naples is a city where exaggerated gestures and expressive shrugs have become almost a new art form.

Palermo, on the other hand, is a city of extremes, a mixture of panache and poverty. Even the people are a study in contrasts—reserved yet courteous, resigned but nonetheless nearly always cheerful, initially suspicious of strangers but incredibly hospitable once you have become their friend. Almost every building in Palermo reveals the influence of more than one of its past civilizations, and everywhere there are hints and signs of the powerful Arab influence. There is always that languid air of Eastern mystery and sensuality.

Between these two cities lies a marvelous variety of culture and geography: the mountainous ridges of Calabria; the luxurious coastline and rich plains of Campania; the high altitudes and coastal plateaus in Puglia; the

wild, spectacular mountains of Abruzzi; the meandering coastline and abundant fruit trees and olive groves of Sicily. And each one of these areas has its own culinary traditions and specialties. Out of this varied terrain, marked by its turbulent history, have come dishes as distinctive as its towns and dialects, their differences reflecting the influence of the many cultures that have left their varied imprints. Then, threading its way through these different traditions is the undeniable influence of the Church.

During the Middle Ages the convents and monasteries in Italy became enormously wealthy, and one of their main functions was to provide a luxurious life for the younger children of the aristocracy. This practice continued until the late 18th century, and contemporary accounts present fascinating glimpses of such extravagant monastic pleasures as dinners with 24 main dishes and 64 secondary dishes, not including desserts and ices.

While the monks seem to have focused their energies on eating and entertaining and lives of exuberant self-indulgence, their convent sisters were busy sublimating their desires into perfecting their pastry-making skills. Far more of their time, it appears, was spent in the kitchen than in church, and there was often fierce competition over who could produce the most elaborate sweet or dessert. At first these pastries were destined exclusively for the convent table or presented to confessors and spiritual directors. By the 19th century, however, most Church property had been confiscated by the state, and many religious orders had closed. Those that survived, greatly impoverished, did so by selling their sweets and pastries commercially. By the end of the 19th century many of the larger convents had become regular purveyors of sweets to the aristocracy.

The dessert table at one great house, undoubtedly prepared by the local convent, is eloquently described by Giuseppe di Lampedusa:

> *Scorning the table of drinks, glittering with crystal and silver on the right, he moved left towards that of the sweetmeats. Huge sorrel babas, Mont Blancs snowy with whipped cream, cakes speckled with white*

almonds and green pistachio nuts, hillocks of chocolate covered pastry, brown and rich as the topsoil of the Catanian plain from which, in fact, through many a twist and turn they had come, pink ices, champagne ices, coffee ices, all parfaits, which fell apart with a squelch when the knife cleft them, melody in major of crystallized cherries, acid notes of yellow pineapple and those cakes called a "triumph of gluttony" of green pistachio paste, shameless virgin's cakes shaped like breasts. Don Fabrizio asked for some of these and, as he held them in his plate, looked like a profane caricature of St. Agatha . . . why ever didn't the Holy Office forbid these cakes when it had the chance? St. Agatha's slice of breasts sold by convents, devoured at dances! Well, well!

The Leopard,
trans. ARCHIBALD COLQUHOUN

Today there are a few Sicilian convents that prepare and sell their specialties. For instance, in Palermo a Benedictine convent still makes legendary *cannoli* and "Triumphs of Gluttony," and the Badia del Santo Spirito in Agrigento is famous for its sweet couscous made with chopped pistachios.

The southern Italian menu rarely has any set rules; often a variety of dishes arrive together or follow in rapid succession. In Palermo you might well begin a meal with a *pasta con le sarde*, that magical Sicilian dish made from fresh sardines, fennel, raisins, pine nuts, and saffron tossed with *penne*, and follow it with the sophisticated, sweet-sour mélange of whatever vegetables are in season known as *caponata*. Next might come a simple grilled fish or *involtini di pescespada*—thin slices of swordfish wrapped around a succulent stuffing of cheese, basil, and bread crumbs and neatly parceled into little rolls. Then a tart lemon salad to cleanse the palate, before going on to a dessert such as *cannoli*—deep-fried pastry tubes stuffed to overflowing with an intriguingly sweet mixture of *ricotta* cheese, chocolate, candied orange peel, and pistachio nuts.

On the mainland a meal might also begin with the *caponata* but served in a pastry crust. The pasta could well be a *puttanesca*, tossed with olives,

capers, anchovies, and tomatoes, then perhaps a hearty casserole of lamb, cooked with lashings of garlic and hot pepper and served with a sauce of anchovies and vinegar. The perfect accompaniment could be *patate Abruzzesi*, the traditional Abruzzi potato dish—tasty new potatoes steeped in garlic and rosemary. Such a meal would almost certainly conclude with an irresistibly creamy ice (Neapolitan and Sicilian ice creams are both, with good reason, considered the best in the world). A possible alternative, if appetites are beginning to flag, would be the thinnest slice of a smooth and creamy *ricotta* cake.

But these are only a few of the many, many recipes that follow. Most come from local families, having been treasured and passed down from one generation to the next. Many are largely unknown outside the family, but each testifies to a lively tradition of resourceful and imaginative cooking and to a rich cultural inheritance.

JANE GARMEY

A NOTE
ON COLLECTING
THE RECIPES

In my cooking school in Rome, Lo Scaldavivande (The Covered Dish), I teach Italian cooking to Italians, who don't seem to mind at all that their teacher is an American who had her first taste of garlic at the age of 20 in New York City. I didn't learn to cook at my mother's knee or my grandmother's knee; in fact it was my husband, Angelo, who taught me. His family has been selling wines since the 16th century in Italy and running hotels since 1875, so I had a wonderfully knowledgeable teacher. Angelo buys the wine and thunders approval and disapproval in the restaurants, having inherited the family palate.

But I grew up in the American South, in Georgia, where good food is also much appreciated. There a meal is considered an important part of the

A
Note
o n
Collecting
t h e
Recipes

day, and everyone sits down to eat, a thing I still consider important. When I first traveled to southern Italy, where my husband has extended family, I had an immediate sense of recognition for both the people and the food. I have a theory that all southerners, whatever their country, have certain things in common . . . usually they're poorer than their northern cousins but have the better climate and more fun. The atmosphere is usually much more relaxed and easygoing. Family is deeply important— and this is particularly true in southern Italy. The central events are celebrations, religious holidays, family gatherings. The list goes on and on: first Communions, christenings, marriages, funerals, saint's days, anniversaries, engagements, carnival . . . I think they just like parties, as all true southerners do. And as the Italians say, *"Tutte le feste finiscono a tavola"*—all the holidays end at the table.

On my trips South in this culinary adventure I had wonderfully imaginative meals, almost always in private homes. The people are as hospitable as American southerners, a tradition that surely comes from their history (as in the American South) as a predominantly agricultural society. Distances were great, so guests were invited to spend the night, week, or month. The distances also meant that food had to be raised or grown on one's own property. Many varieties of vegetables were prepared in hundreds of ways; in fact I encountered so many spectacular eggplant recipes that I briefly considered making an entire chapter of eggplant, including the somewhat startling recipe for chocolate eggplant. Sheep were raised for wool and cheese but eaten rarely, since the milk and cheese were more appreciated. Very little beef appeared on the table because the animals, scarce at best, were needed in the fields. Gelatins, ices, sherbets, and all kinds of cooling desserts have always been the joy of warm climates and have their motherland in southern Italy.

With one exception all the recipes in this book were given to me by the generous southerners—sometimes after they had extracted a solemn promise that I would never publish the recipe in Italy. Virtually all of these recipes are in the category of family treasure, some of them generations old and not previously revealed to outsiders. I was passed along from friend to friend once the southerners had decided my heart was in the right place, and almost always they would prepare the food for me—though I was never invited into the kitchen. The entire family would assemble for these occasions—cousins, in-laws, aunts, and uncles. I found only one person who did not give me recipes (but her cousin did), and that refusal was generally condemned by everyone else.

One of the best cooks, Rosa Parisi Bruna, might have been flattered by my asking for recipes, but she certainly never lost her composure or showed signs of being impressed. She sat calmly for about three hours in one of the d'Alì drawing rooms and explained her recipes, specifying weights, times, even kinds of pots. This was unusual; most of the cooks were vague about the details. Of course she spoke in Sicilian dialect and I could hardly understand a word, but the baron patiently translated, enjoying himself and explaining why the poem to cure the eyes was said over a certain sweet. In fact Rosa prayed over almost everything, or at least made the sign of the cross, particularly when she tucked something into the oven or had completed a dish and was setting it aside to "rest." Such cautions are typically southern, but they're also very Italian. Even up north in Parma, when the milk is set for Parmigiano, the sign of the cross is cut into it.

Another cook, in Naples, bought the Christmas eel early to fatten it for the feast. She put it into her bathtub to keep until Christmas and fed it *spaghetti*—but she became quite fond of the eel and in the end refused to cook it.

Generous as the cooks were, testing their recipes was difficult because people forget things when they give you recipes and family cooks are often instinctively protective. Traditionally *monzùs* never gave out their recipes; they were, after all, their fortune. I was lucky to meet a *monzù* at all, and particularly lucky to be given his recipes. For some recipes I waited literally years, but other times I had help from good friends who even managed to get convent recipes for me. In all of this I had an extraordinary advantage: I had tasted the food as it should be prepared.

A
Note
on
Collecting
the
Recipes

Sometimes the recipes look a little complicated, and a few of them are—I tell you frankly in the introductions to the recipes if they are—but in most cases they only *look* complicated. Although the flavors are complex and intriguing, this food is actually quite simple. And it is simply extraordinary; my passion for it has been vindicated for me by the fact that my Italian students at the cooking school, who think there's no food like Roman food (and have a traditionally snobbish attitude toward southern food), have actually asked me to put together a course of southern Italian cooking. I can imagine no higher compliment for a regional Italian cuisine.

J.B.

WINE NOTE

Not all the wines listed are available in the United States at this time, but that situation is changing rapidly, so it seems best to list the optimum wines for these dishes. Very often it's suggested that a wine be served at cold room temperature, chilled, very chilled, or cold; although it may seem that these are extremely subtle distinctions, if you follow the advice, you'll be rewarded with a wine that's served at its very best.

Piccolo Buffet di Francesca di Carpinello

FRANCESCA DI CARPINELLO'S SMALL BUFFET

Pasta al Forno alla Siciliana
BAKED SICILIAN PASTA

Carciofi all'Arancia
ARTICHOKES WITH ORANGE JUICE

Salsicce con Ragù
SAUSAGE RAGOUT

Involtini con Foglie d'Alloro
VEAL ROLLS WITH BAY LEAVES

Insalata di Arancie e Lattuga
ORANGE AND LETTUCE SALAD

Crema di Gianduia con Panna Montata
CHOCOLATE HAZELNUT CREAM

Gelatina di Limone di Campofelice
LEMON GELATIN FROM CAMPOFELICE

WINES
White: Rocche di Rao (Corleone); serve cold
Rosé: Pignatello (Trapani); serve chilled
Red: Ciclopi (Etna); serve cool
Dessert: Pollio (Avola); serve cool

This menu comes from Francesca di Carpinello, a Sicilian painter living in Palermo. Two of the recipes—*Carciofi all'Arancia* and *Gelatina di Limone di Campofelice*—were given to her by her great uncle Nicolino, who over the years assembled a collection of family recipes and wrote them down by hand in a child's copybook. This well-thumbed and now somewhat tattered volume is a much treasured family possession.

The Carpinellos are one of the few lucky families in Palermo to still have their own *monzù*. The word *monzù* is a corruption of *monsieur* and dates back to the late 18th century, when it was fashionable for Sicilian aristocrats to import their chefs from Paris. The title was originally given to those Frenchmen, but later to Sicilians or Neapolitans who had served a culinary apprenticeship in Paris and were judged to have reached a very high level of expertise. The appellation was not given lightly, and employing a *monzù* was a sign of great distinction and cause for much envy from one's friends. Nevertheless, having a *monzù* was often a prohibitively costly privilege. The story is told of one Sicilian aristocrat who was given a *monzù* as a wedding present but returned him after being presented with the first month's grocery bills.

Today a *monzù* is a scarce and much treasured person. When he grows too old to cook, he expects to live with and be looked after by the family he has served, for the rest of his life. The Carpinellos' *monzù*, a man well into his sixties, seemed much amused by the idea that anyone would want to write down the recipes for such typically Sicilian dishes. In spite of his skepticism, he was extremely courteous and painstakingly careful in setting down each recipe and checking the exact amount of each ingredient. He cooked the entire dinner and served it with great dignity in a dining room whose walls were covered with a collection of 200 18th-century handpainted dessert plates.

Pasta al Forno alla Siciliana
BAKED SICILIAN PASTA

A pasta perfumed with nuts and spices is typically Sicilian and would be unheard of in the north of Italy. It is fragrant evidence of the omnipresent Arab influence in Sicilian cooking. Baked pasta dishes are very common to Sicily and southern Italy, and you will find them served everywhere.

SERVES 6

10¹/₂-inch cheesecake pan
with 2-inch sides (27 by
5 cm), preferably nonstick

3/4	pound ground beef (330 grams)
1	cup dry red wine (250 ml)
4	cloves
1	large bay leaf or 2 small bay leaves
5	tablespoons olive oil plus olive oil for frying the eggplant
1	eggplant, about 10 ounces, peeled and cut into 1/2-inch dice (280 grams), plus an eggplant for garnish, peeled and diced (optional) salt to taste
1	medium onion, finely chopped
3	tablespoons finely chopped parsley
1/4	teaspoon ground cinnamon
1	1-pound can Italian plum tomatoes, chopped, with juice (450 grams)
1/2	cup chopped shelled walnuts (60 grams) freshly ground pepper to taste unsalted butter for the pan
3	tablespoons fine dry bread crumbs
1	pound small pasta such as *fusilli, bucatini, or pennette* (450 grams)
3/4	cup freshly grated *pecorino* cheese (100 grams)
2	ounces *caciocavallo* cheese, cut into tiny dice (1/2 cup) (60 grams)

Put the ground beef in a bowl and pour the wine over it. Break up the meat with a fork and add the cloves and bay leaf. Marinate at cool room temperature or in the refrigerator for at least 2 hours.

Put enough oil in a frying pan to generously cover the bottom, add the eggplant, and fry over low heat until browned. Drain the eggplant on paper towels and salt it lightly. If you're using eggplant for garnish, fry that too.

Drain the meat, reserving the marinade, and discard the cloves and bay leaf. Heat the 5 tablespoons oil in a saucepan and add the onion and parsley. Cook over low heat until the onion is transparent, about 20 minutes. Add the meat and brown it. Add the marinade and allow it to evaporate partially. Add the cinnamon, tomatoes, and walnuts and cook, covered, over low heat for about 20 minutes. Do not allow the sauce to dry out too much. Season with salt and pepper. When the mixture is slightly cooled, add the eggplant prepared for the sauce and reserve.

Butter the cheesecake pan heavily and coat the inside liberally with bread crumbs. Set aside. Preheat the oven to 375° (190) .

Cook the pasta in boiling salted water until *al dente*. (If you're using *bucatini*, break it into 2-1/2-inch pieces.) Drain and dress with the *pecorino*. Put the *caciocavallo* in the sauce and dress the pasta with the sauce. Pour the pasta into the prepared pan and bake for 30 minutes. Allow to rest at least 15 minutes before turning out. Turn out on a round plate and garnish with the extra eggplant.

Carciofi all'Arancia
ARTICHOKES WITH ORANGE JUICE

Citrus fruits, first brought to Sicily by the Arabs, grow in profusion throughout the island, and you can feel their perfume in the air. The best oranges and lemons are thought to be grown in the province of Catania. Oranges come in an almost overwhelming variety. There are the blood oranges, which account for 77 percent of the orange crop; the *Tarocco*, grown throughout Sicily, is the first blood orange of the year. Next to arrive are the oblong-shaped *Sanguinello*, from Paternò, Santa Maria di Locodia, Palagonia, Scordia, and Francofonte; the *Moro*, with its dark purplish flesh; and the *Sanguigno Commune*, which is grown all over Sicily. Of the blond oranges the *Washington Navel* and the *Ovale* are the most popular. There is also an unlimited supply of tangerines. They include the *Avana*, *Avana di Palermo,* and *Avana di Paternò*. Bitter or sweet, with or without seeds, soft or leathery-skinned, all are indigenous and plentiful. Not surprisingly, Sicilians love to use oranges and lemons in their cooking.

This old Palermo recipe can be prepared well in advance as it is served cold; in fact it tastes better when eaten the next day. The artichokes are pan-fried in a combination of citrus juices, wine, oil, and anchovy paste, giving them a judicious bite and the kind of taste you would never find in the North. This is a good party recipe; you can double the quantities with no problem. For an elegant effect, serve the artichokes in a glass bowl, sprinkled with capers.

SERVES 6 TO 8

13-inch (33 cm) frying pan
with a lid

    10 artichokes, cleaned (see page 420) and cut in half
1/4 cup freshly squeezed lemon juice (60 ml)

<pre>
1/4   cup freshly squeezed orange juice (60 ml)
1/2   cup extra-virgin olive oil (125 ml)
  1   scant cup dry white wine (200 ml)
  1   tablespoon anchovy paste dissolved in 1/4 cup
       white wine vinegar (60 ml)
       pinch of salt
  2   teaspoons flour
1/4   cup sugar (55 grams)
       capers for garnish
</pre>

Put all the ingredients except the flour, sugar, and capers in a large frying pan with a lid. Cook, covered, over low heat for 30 minutes or until the artichokes are tender but *al dente*. Remove the artichokes to a serving platter and cool the sauce completely.

Put the flour in a small cup and add 2 or 3 tablespoons of the cold sauce, stirring to dissolve the flour. Pass this through a sieve into the rest of the sauce. Add the sugar. Bring to a low boil and cook, stirring, for 3 or 4 minutes or until thickened slightly. Pour the sauce over the artichokes. Serve cold, sprinkled with capers.

*Francesca
di
Carpinello's
Small
Buffet*

Salsicce con Ragù
SAUSAGE RAGOUT

In Sicily each family tends to have its own favorite recipe for *ragù*. The differences among the many versions served often come down to economics—that is, the amount of meat used.

There is nothing to compare with a steaming *ragù* that has been simmering gently for several hours. It is hearty and filling, definitely a dish for a winter night. This particular recipe would be considered a rather simple *ragù*, since it uses only sausages. Sicilian sausages, made of pork and flavored with fennel, are quite deliciously spicy, so you should use a hot variety of Italian sausage when making this dish. If the hot sausage doesn't include fennel, add a few sweet sausages.

SERVES 6

14	fresh Italian sausages (see above), about 2 pounds (900 grams)
2	tablespoons olive oil
1	medium onion, finely chopped
3	tablespoons finely chopped parsley
	salt
	a piece of shinbone, with marrow if available
3	bay leaves
1	tablespoon tomato paste
1/3	cup dry red wine (80 ml)
1-1/3	pounds fresh tomatoes, peeled and seeded (600 grams), *or* 1 1-pound can Italian plum tomatoes, drained slightly (450 grams)
1	teaspoon (or more to taste) sugar

Prick 12 of the sausages (1-2/3 pounds/750 grams) with a fork and cook over medium heat in a pan with water that comes halfway up the sausages. Turn occasionally. When the water has cooked away, continue turning the sausages to brown them. Reserve.

Put the oil in a saucepan, preferably terra-cotta, and add the onion and parsley. Salt lightly. Cook over medium heat for 10 minutes, adding a few tablespoons of water to avoid browning the onion.

Remove the casing from the remaining sausages and cut them into small pieces. Add the pieces to the onion and cook until the meat is no longer pink. Add the bone, bay leaves, tomato paste dissolved in the red wine, tomatoes cut into pieces, and sugar. Mix well and cook over medium-low heat, half covered, for 15 minutes. Add the browned sausages and enough water to almost cover them. Simmer, covered, for 2 hours, stirring occasionally. Discard the bay leaves. Serve the sausages separately and save the sauce to dress pasta, with grated *pecorino* sprinkled on top, another night.

*Francesca
di
Carpinello's
Small
Buffet*

Involtini con Foglie d'Alloro
VEAL ROLLS WITH
BAY LEAVES

Involtini—slices of meat, fish, or even eggplant wrapped around bread crumbs seasoned with spices, pine nuts, and raisins—is a popular Sicilian specialty that can be found on the menu of almost every restaurant in the region. Bread crumbs are a common ingredient in Sicily, a sign of frugality in a country that has never been rich.

Sicilians treat bread with the greatest respect. They even have a tradition, stemming from its use in the Mass, of not cutting into a loaf of bread without first making the sign of the cross over it. Sicilian children used to be taught that if they let a bread crumb fall on the floor and did not pick it up right away, it would be waiting for them when they died and they would have to pick it up with their eyelashes before they could get to heaven!

SERVES 6 (ABOUT 12 ROLLS)

About 4 10-inch wooden
skewers, soaked in cold water
for 30 minutes and drained

3/4	cup fine dry bread crumbs
7	tablespoons olive oil (110 ml)
3/4	cup freshly grated *pecorino* cheese (105 grams)
1/2	cup plus 1 tablespoon pine nuts, chopped (90 grams)
1/3	cup raisins, chopped (60 grams)
1	garlic clove, finely chopped
5	tablespoons finely chopped parsley
1-1/3	pounds veal *scaloppine* (600 grams)
2	ounces *caciocavallo* cheese, julienned (1/2 cup) (60 grams)

**16 bay leaves, approximately, plus extra leaves for
garnish
salt and freshly ground black pepper to taste**

Toast the bread crumbs with 1 tablespoon oil in a skillet, preferably iron, over medium heat, stirring constantly. When the crumbs are a light brown, remove from the heat and cool.

In a small bowl, mix together the bread crumbs, *pecorino,* pine nuts, raisins, garlic, and parsley. Preheat the oven to 375° (190).

Prepare the *scaloppine.* Cut away any fat and any sinews or nerves and pound the meat until thin. If the *scaloppine* are very large, cut the slices in half. Lay the meat flat on a work surface. Put the remaining oil in a bowl and with a brush paint one side of the meat liberally with some of the oil. Divide the stuffing mixture among the meat slices, spreading it all over the oiled side of the meat. Put 3 or more pieces of *caciocavallo* at one edge of the meat and roll up, making little sausages. Alternately thread bay leaves and veal rolls crosswise on wooden skewers, about 3 rolls to a skewer, depending on the size of the rolls.

Oil the bottom of an ovenproof dish and place the skewered rolls in it. Paint the tops generously with oil, reserving 1-1/2 tablespoons to paint the rolls after they are turned. Season with salt and pepper.

Bake for 15 minutes. Turn the rolls and paint with the reserved oil. Cook for 15 minutes more. Serve hot, garnished with the extra bay leaves.

NOTE: Watch the baking time. It is impossible to give an exact time; it all depends on the meat.

Insalata di Arancie e Lattuga
ORANGE AND LETTUCE SALAD

*Francesca
di
Carpinello's
Small
Buffet*

The contrasts—in color, flavor, and texture—between the lettuce and the oranges make this a ravishingly attractive dish. For high drama, use blood oranges.

SERVES 6

> **2 small heads of lettuce, Boston or Bibb if possible**
> **3 large oranges**
> **extra-virgin olive oil**
> **salt and freshly ground black pepper to taste**
> **black Gaeta olives, pitted, for garnish (optional)**

Wash and dry the lettuce. Shred it into 3/4-inch-wide pieces.

Peel the oranges, carefully removing the white pith. Cut the oranges into sections into a colander set in a bowl to catch the juice. Toss the oranges with the lettuce when you're ready to serve and dress with olive oil and some of the orange juice. Season with salt and pepper. Serve in a glass bowl, garnished with black olives if desired.

Crema di Gianduia con Panna Montata
CHOCOLATE HAZELNUT CREAM

This chocolate dessert is believed to have been brought to Sicily by Garibaldi. *Gianduia* is a soft chocolate flavored with ground hazelnuts; it comes from Turin, in Savoia territory. Any good-quality, semisweet chocolate can be substituted.

SERVES 6

1/2	**pound good-quality semisweet chocolate (225 grams)**
2-1/2	**cups milk (350 ml)**
6	**egg yolks**
1/3	**cup sugar (75 grams)**
2	**tablespoons flour (20 grams)**
2	**tablespoons dark rum *or* cognac to taste**
2/3	**cup finely chopped toasted hazelnuts (110 grams) plus extra hazelnuts, toasted and chopped, for garnish**
	softly whipped cream for serving

Melt the chocolate in a double boiler over simmering water. Whisk in the milk.

Using an electric mixer, beat the egg yolks with the sugar until lemon-colored. Add the flour, beating well. Add this mixture to the milk and chocolate in the double boiler, whisking, and bring almost to the boil but *do not boil*. Remove from the heat and stir in the rum and finely chopped hazelnuts. Cool and pour into a serving bowl. Refrigerate until serving time, garnish with chopped hazelnuts, and pass the whipped cream at the table.

Gelatina di Limone di Campofelice
LEMON GELATIN FROM CAMPOFELICE

Here is another of Great Uncle Nicolino's recipes. Campofelice is the name of the Carpinellos' property near Palermo, where innumerable kinds of lemons grow in great abundance as far as the eye can see. This very old Sicilian dish—a simple but refreshing lemon jelly—was originally served between two rich courses to cleanse the palate and act as a digestive. The Carpinellos' *monzù* made it in a ring mold and presented it surrounded by lemon leaves with two small green lemons at the center of the mold. The effect was simple but quite stunning. Remember to prepare this dessert a day ahead.

SERVES 8

5-cup ring mold

> 2 1/4-ounce envelopes plus 1 teaspoon unflavored gelatin
> 2-1/2 cups plus 2 tablespoons cold water (650 ml)
> 2 scant cups sugar (400 grams)
> 1 cup plus scant 1/2 cup freshly squeezed, strained lemon juice (350 ml), about 7 lemons
> almond or vegetable oil for the mold
> lemon leaves and small lemons or chocolate "lemon leaves" for garnish

Put the gelatin and 1/2 cup plus 2 tablespoons cold water in a small bowl to soften the gelatin, about 5 minutes.

Put the sugar and the rest of the water in a saucepan and bring to a simmer over medium heat, stirring constantly. Add the softened gelatin and stir until completely dissolved. Set the pan in a sink of cold water to cool.

When the gelatin mixture has cooled, add the lemon juice. Oil the mold with almond or vegetable oil. Pour in the gelatin mixture and refrigerate for a day.

Turn the gelatin out on a round platter and garnish with lemon leaves and small lemons in the center or with chocolate "lemon leaves" at the base and in the center.

*Una Passeggiata dopo Colazione
nel Giardino Savona*

A WALK AFTER LUNCH IN THE SAVONAS' ORANGE AND LEMON GARDEN

*A Walk
After Lunch
in the
Savonas'
Orange
and Lemon
Garden*

Brioscia Anzon
ANZON BRIOCHE

Pescespada al Latte
SWORDFISH MARINATED IN MILK

Caponata di Carciofi
SWEET-SOUR ARTICHOKES

Arancie Condite
ORANGES IN ORANGE LIQUEUR

WINE
White: Mamertino Bianco Secco (Messina); serve very cold

Signora Savona lives near Cefalù in a villa surrounded by an enormous garden of lemons and oranges overlooking the sea. (In Sicily fruits are said to grow in gardens, and the word *grove* is used only for olives.) This particular garden has a magic all its own. Heavy with citrus perfume, it boasts a number of rare botanical specimens and hedges of laurel stretching down to a deserted beach. The 18th-century villa is covered with wisteria vines and filled with unusual Empire furniture. It is still a working farm, and the Savona family has lived here for many generations.

Brioscia Anzon
ANZON BRIOCHE

This is an old family recipe given to Signora Savona by Signorina Anzon. Signorina Anzon could remember a very hot day one summer when she was a child and her entire family—there were 36 of them—was assembled for an important family celebration. First they attended Mass in their own chapel; then came a big family lunch, where a number of these savory brioches were to be the main dish. It was so hot, however, that many of the brioches failed to rise. Signorina Anzon never forgot the embarrassment of the occasion—both she and her sister were so upset they cried bitterly all afternoon!

SERVES 8 TO 10

10½-inch round pan with
3-inch sides (26 by 8 cm),
buttered

FOR THE FILLING:
- **1 cup milk (250 ml)**
- **1/4 cup flour (40 grams)**
  salt and freshly ground pepper to taste
  freshly grated nutmeg to taste
- **3 tablespoons unsalted butter (45 grams)**
- **1 cup heavy cream (250 ml)**
- **1/2 cup freshly grated Parmesan cheese (65 grams)**
- **2 ounces *caciocavallo* cheese, coarsely grated (1/2 cup) (60 grams)**
- **10 ounces *mozzarella* cheese, coarsely grated (2-1/3 cups) (280 grams)**
- **1/3 pound boiled ham, chopped (1-1/4 cups) (150 grams)**

continued

*A Walk
After Lunch
in the
Savonas'
Orange
and Lemon
Garden*

FOR THE *BRIOSCIA* (BRIOCHE):

  2 1/4-ounce envelopes active dry yeast
1/2 cup warm milk (125 ml)
  4 cups flour (450 grams)
  **1 cup (1/2 pound) unsalted butter at room
   temperature, cut into pieces (225 grams)**
  5 medium eggs at room temperature
  1 teaspoon salt
  2 tablespoons sugar (30 grams)

Make the béchamel. Put the milk, flour, salt, pepper, and nutmeg in a blender and blend for 30 seconds. Melt the butter in a saucepan and add the milk and cream. Bring to a simmer over low heat, stirring, and simmer for 5 minutes, stirring constantly. Remove the saucepan from the heat and add the Parmesan.

Place plastic wrap directly on the surface of the sauce and set it aside to cool. When it has cooled, add the *caciocavallo, mozzarella,* and ham. Refrigerate until needed. Bring the béchamel to room temperature before using it.

Make the brioche. Dissolve the yeast in the warm milk. Put the flour, butter, eggs, salt, and sugar in the large bowl of an electric mixer. Pour the yeast and warm milk into the bowl a little at a time, mixing with the paddle attachment. Beat the brioche for 10 minutes or until the mixture comes away from the sides of the bowl and is elastic.

Put half the dough in the prepared pan, spreading it over the bottom evenly with your hands. Spoon the filling over the dough, leaving a 1/2-inch border around the sides to permit sealing. Put the rest of the dough over the filling, smoothing and sealing the edges. If necessary, oil your hands. Set the brioche aside in a draft-free place, covered, and allow to rise for about 2 hours or until the dough doubles and reaches the top of the pan.

Fifteen minutes before baking the brioche, preheat the oven to 350° (180). Bake for 45 minutes. After 30 minutes, check the brioche; if it is browning too rapidly, cover it loosely with foil. Allow the brioche to rest for 15 minutes before serving. Turn it out on a round platter with a little rim and serve with a knife to cut the brioche and a spoon for the béchamel.

VARIATIONS: The filling may be varied, as it often is in Sicily. Some possibilities are chicken giblets or livers alone, cooked in wine and cut into pieces, small bits of leftover chicken, peas cooked with onion, and other cheeses to taste.

NOTE: Wrap leftover brioche tightly in foil and heat for 15 minutes in a 375° (190) oven. (Or the whole brioche can be prepared in advance and reheated.)

SWORDFISH MARINATED IN MILK

Swordfish is considered the prince of Sicilian fish and a chief pride of the kitchen. At one time the Strait of Messina was the only place in Europe that swordfish could be found. Many 18th- and 19th-century English travelers on their Grand Tour wrote about this wondrous new fish with great delight. Even then the swordfish season was short and the method of fishing both arduous and slow, making swordfish an expensive delicacy eaten only by the well-to-do.

The traditional method of catching swordfish is very similar to whaling. In a long, narrow, lightweight boat manned by 10 oarsmen, one man would crouch on top of a very tall center mast. He served as lookout, and when he saw a swordfish jump he would sing out for the boat to follow it. Another man, standing on a long gangplank stretching off the prow, would then harpoon the fish, often from a considerable distance. If no other fish were in sight, he would fight it until it got tired and he could bring it in. If there were other fish nearby, he would be put out in a wooden tublike small boat and left to stay with the fish until it was exhausted. In due course he would be fetched by the main boat, which in the meantime had gone in pursuit of additional prey. In some parts of Sicily swordfish are still fished this way, using harpoons, but most of the oarsmen have been replaced by engines.

Sicilians cook swordfish in a number of ways—stewing, grilling, frying, baking, and roasting are all acceptable methods. In this recipe the fish is first marinated in milk and then baked in the oven. In this way it loses none of its sweet natural flavor; any trace of fishiness disappears.

    4 swordfish steaks with the skin removed, about
       2 pounds altogether (900 grams)
       milk, about 1 quart (1 liter)
       fine dry bread crumbs, about 1 heaped cup
       olive oil, about 1/4 cup (60 ml)
       salt and freshly ground pepper to taste
    6 medium-size ripe tomatoes, peeled if skins are
       thick

Put the slices of fish in a dish and cover with milk. Leave for an hour. Drain the fish and pat dry. Put the bread crumbs in a dish and bread the slices of fish thoroughly. Preheat the oven to 350° (180).

Oil an ovenproof dish large enough to hold the swordfish in one layer. Place the fish in the dish and season with salt and pepper. Slice the tomatoes thinly and layer them over the fish slices. Trickle olive oil over the tomatoes and add salt and pepper again.

Bake for 30 minutes. Serve hot.

Caponata di Carciofi
SWEET-SOUR ARTICHOKES

*A Walk
After Lunch
in the
Savonas'
Orange
and Lemon
Garden*

The origin of the word *caponata* is unknown, but it is a true Sicilian specialty, thought to have originated as ship food since, thanks to the vinegar, it keeps well. A *caponata* can be a very simple one-vegetable dish, as in this recipe, or an extremely elaborate affair with lobster tails, shrimp, and asparagus. In 1853 Vincenzo Mortillaro wrote in his *Dizionario Siciliano-Italiano* that a *caponata* should be eaten cold between courses or after the first hot dishes.

Today every Sicilian town and village boasts its own *caponata* recipe. This particular one is very simple but unusual—the capers, vinegar, and sugar give the artichokes an interesting edge. Sicilian artichokes, often called *spinelli* (spiny), are small with spiny points. They are remarkably succulent, renowned throughout Italy for their delicate flavor.

SERVES 4 TO 6

6	artichokes
1	lemon, cut in half
3	tablespoons olive oil
1	medium onion, thinly sliced
	salt to taste
2	inner celery stalks, cut into 2-inch julienne (1/2 cup)
1/2	cup water (125 ml)
2	tablespoons capers, rinsed and dried
	heaped 1/2 cup green Sicilian olives, pitted and halved (100 grams)
1	tablespoon sugar
1/4	cup white wine vinegar (60 ml)
	freshly ground pepper to taste

Clean the artichokes (see page 420) and rub with lemon. Soak in cold water with the lemon halves until needed.

In a skillet, heat the olive oil and in it sauté the onion with salt, adding water by the tablespoon as necessary to prevent browning—about 8 minutes over low heat. Cut the artichokes into 4 pieces (6 if you're using globe artichokes) and add them to the onion. Add the celery and 1/2 cup water, cover, bring to a boil, and cook for 10 minutes over medium-low heat.

Add the capers, olives, sugar, vinegar, and salt and pepper to taste. Simmer, uncovered, for 5 minutes or until the vinegar has evaporated. Serve at room temperature.

A Walk
After Lunch
in the
Savonas'
Orange
and Lemon
Garden

Arancie Condite

ORANGES IN ORANGE LIQUEUR

This is the simplest of desserts and typically Sicilian in its choice of ingredients. Sicilian oranges are so delicious that it's easy to believe the old Sicilian story that the Norman conquest of southern Italy and Sicily was the result of a gift of oranges sent to the duke of Normandy by a prince from Salerno in the 11th century. The duke apparently was so delighted with his present that he immediately decided he must have the country that produced these delicacies.

SERVES 6

> 8 oranges, about 4 pounds (1.800 grams)
> 5 tablespoons orange liqueur (75 ml)
> 3 tablespoons dried currants *or* sultanas (30 grams) (optional)
> 1/3 cup coarsely chopped lightly toasted almonds (60 grams)

Using a sharp paring knife, peel the oranges, removing all the white pith. Over a colander with a glass serving bowl underneath to catch only the juice from the sections (don't squeeze the skin), cut away each section, removing all the skin with care. Place the sections in the glass bowl with the orange liqueur and currants. Macerate for 2 or 3 hours. Just before serving, add the almonds, leaving a few to decorate the top.

Cena sulla Spiaggia da Zia Irene

ZIA IRENE'S PICNIC ON THE BEACH

Timballo di Riso con Salsa di Pomodoro
RICE IN A MOLD WITH TOMATO SAUCE

Dentice alla Griglia con Salsa Salmoriglio
GRILLED RED SNAPPER WITH SALMORIGLIO SAUCE

Insalata di Limoni
LEMON SALAD

Fichi
FIGS

Liquore di Limone
LEMON CORDIAL

WINE
White: Carizzi Bianco (Messina); serve cool

Zia (Aunt) Irene, my husband Angelo's aunt, was married to a Sicilian from Messina and spent her summers in Rodia near Messina. Every Christmas she would send her friends and relatives in Rome baskets of oranges, lemons, and tangerines—the sweetest and most aromatic fruit imaginable. Zia Irene was a marvelous cook (60 years ago she had attended classes at the then-fashionable Ada Boni's cooking school in Rome). She loved to share her recipes, and the next two menus are for meals that she served one summer at her house in Sicily. The first was a simple picnic supper, served under the stars on the beach, and the other a more formal dinner in her garden.

Timballo di Riso con Salsa di Pomodoro
RICE IN A MOLD WITH TOMATO SAUCE

Zia Irene was particularly fond of this recipe—one of those infinite variations of eggplant and rice with a tomato sauce that are so popular in the South. It's essentially a very simple dish but dressy enough to use for company, and it can be made well in advance. At Zia Irene's picnic it was served as a first course before grilled fish.

SERVES 8

10-inch (25 cm) ring mold,
2½-quart capacity, buttered

1-2/3	pounds eggplant, peeled and sliced lengthwise a generous 1/4 inch thick (750 grams)
	salt
	olive oil for frying
1/2	cup (1/4 pound) unsalted butter (110 grams)
1	small onion, finely chopped
2	cups Arborio rice (400 grams)
2	beef or chicken bouillon cubes dissolved in 1 quart boiling water (1 liter)
3/4	cup freshly grated Parmesan cheese (105 grams)
3	tablespoons fine dry bread crumbs, approximately
9	ounces *mozzarella* cheese, coarsely grated (2 cups) (250 grams)
	freshly ground pepper to taste
	Salsa di Pomodoro (recipe follows)
4	or 5 fresh basil sprigs for garnish

continued

Layer the eggplant slices in a colander, salting each layer. Put a weighted plate on top and leave for an hour. Rinse and pat dry. Heat 1 inch of oil in a large skillet and fry the eggplant in batches over medium-high heat until lightly browned. Drain on paper towels in a colander.

In a medium-size skillet, heat 1-1/2 tablespoons butter and in it sauté the onion over medium-low heat until transparent, adding a few tablespoons water to prevent browning. Add the rice and stir until the grains are shiny, about 2 minutes. Pour the boiling broth over the rice, cover, and cook over the lowest heat for 16 minutes.

Drain the rice and quickly dress it with the remaining butter and the Parmesan. Turn it out onto a large plate and spread the rice to cool. (This is important; otherwise the rice will be overcooked.)

Dust the buttered mold with bread crumbs. When the rice is cold, put one third on the bottom of the mold, pressing with the back of a spoon. Put half the eggplant slices on top and cover with half the *mozzarella*. Salt lightly and grind black pepper over. Put another third of the rice in the mold, add the rest of the eggplant slices and *mozzarella,* and grind more pepper over. Cover with the remaining rice. Cover and refrigerate until ready to serve.

To serve the *timballo,* remove it from the refrigerator an hour before baking. Preheat the oven to 375° (190). Bake for 45 minutes or until the surface is lightly browned. Allow it to rest 10 minutes before turning it out onto a platter. Fill the center with fresh basil and serve the hot tomato sauce separately.

Salsa di Pomodoro
TOMATO SAUCE

- 1 tablespoon unsalted butter (15 grams)
- 2 tablespoons olive oil
- 1 small onion, finely chopped
- 1 2-pound can Italian plum tomatoes, drained (900 grams), *or* 3 pounds fresh ripe tomatoes, peeled and seeded (1.350 grams)
- 20 fresh basil leaves
   salt and freshly ground pepper to taste
   pinch of sugar
- 1/4 cup heavy cream (60 ml) (optional)

Heat the butter and oil in a skillet and in it sauté the onion over low heat until transparent. Add the tomatoes, mashing them with a wooden spoon. Add the basil, salt and pepper, and sugar. Cook, uncovered, over medium-high heat for 20 minutes or until thickened. Add the cream if desired. Discard the basil before serving the sauce.

Dentice alla Griglia con Salsa Salmoriglio
GRILLED RED SNAPPER WITH SALMORIGLIO SAUCE

SERVES 8 TO 10

1   red snapper, about 8 pounds before cleaning
(3.600 grams) or 7-1/3 pounds after cleaning,
approximately 5-1/2 pounds fish (without the
head) for the table (2.550 grams)
salt and freshly ground pepper to taste
1   tablespoon dried oregano
1/4   teaspoon fennel seeds, pulverized
1   large lemon, peeled, all white pith removed,
sliced
4   garlic cloves
2   tablespoons extra-virgin olive oil
parsley sprigs for garnish
Salsa Salmoriglio (recipe follows)

Wash and dry the fish. Rub the fish inside and out with salt, pepper, oregano, and fennel seeds. Place one third of the lemon slices inside the fish and place the remaining slices over the top of the fish. Put the garlic inside.

Lay 3 thicknesses of aluminum foil 6 inches longer than the fish on a flat surface. Lay the fish on the foil, the side with the lemon slices on top. Trickle the olive oil over the fish. Lay another length of foil (only one thickness) on top of the fish and roll the foil up together with the bottom thicknesses of foil to enclose the fish in a papillote. Make 5 or 6 holes with a kitchen needle in the top of the foil.

Lay the fish on a preheated grill, the part with the 3 thicknesses of foil on the bottom, toward the heat, and cook the fish, without turning it, for 45 to 50 minutes. To assure that the fish is done, insert a skewer in the flesh just below the head. If the fish is done, the skewer will enter the flesh easily and the tip of the skewer will be hot when laid on your wrist.

Place the fish, with the foil opened, on a large platter, surrounded by parsley. Discard the garlic when you slice the fish. Pass the hot sauce separately.

Salsa Salmoriglio
SALMORIGLIO SAUCE

SERVES 8 TO 10

> 3/4 cup extra-virgin olive oil (185 ml)
> 1/3 cup plus 1 tablespoon hot water (90 ml)
> 3/4 cup freshly squeezed lemon juice (185 ml)
> 3 garlic cloves, crushed
> salt and freshly ground pepper to taste
> 1-1/2 tablespoons dried oregano
> 6 tablespoons finely chopped parsley

Whisk together the oil and hot water. Add the lemon juice, whisking constantly as though for mayonnaise. Add all the other ingredients, and when the sauce is whipped, cook it in a double boiler over simmering water for 5 minutes, whisking. Serve hot in a sauceboat.

Z i a I r e n e ' s
P i c n i c
o n t h e
B e a c h

Insalata di Limoni
LEMON SALAD

Zia Irene's gardens were full not only of fig but lemon trees. What could be more natural than a lemon salad in a country where they don't grow just lemons but *Femminellos, Monachellos, Verdellos,* and *Interdonatos?* In Sicily a workman's midday meal often consists of a lemon with its pulp scooped out and mixed with olives, olive oil, and salt. Sicilians love to pick lemons off the tree, peeling and eating them there and then with a pinch of salt. Granted, their lemons are a bit sweeter than ours—if you can find Meyer lemons, they'll work well in this recipe. Prepare this salad at the last minute—it will not wait.

SERVES 8

> 8 small lemons, peeled
>   coarsely chopped parsley to taste
>   extra-virgin olive oil to taste
>   salt and freshly ground pepper to taste
>   black Gaeta or spicy olives, pitted (optional)

Remove as much white pith as possible from the lemons. Slice thinly, removing the seeds as you slice them. Sprinkle the parsley over the lemon slices and dress with the olive oil. Add salt and pepper and olives if desired. Serve at once.

Fichi
FIGS

To eat figs off the tree in the very early morning, when they have been barely touched by the sun, is one of the exquisite pleasures of the Mediterranean.

ELIZABETH DAVID

Sicilians adore figs and like nothing better than to serve them at the end of a meal, unadorned and unembellished. The most attractive way to serve figs is to peel them but not to remove the skins. Fold the skins back and present the figs sitting on their leaves as though they were flowers. Figs should be served chilled but not refrigerator-cold.

Z i a   I r e n e ' s
P i c n i c
o n   t h e
B e a c h

Liquore di Limone
LEMON CORDIAL

In both Sicily and southern Italy it is common practice to serve a lemon cordial as a digestive in place of an after-dinner liqueur. Nothing could be simpler to prepare than this cordial, and it will keep indefinitely. All you need is a little patience—80 days for the liqueur to ripen. A fat, round bottle makes the best container—large pretty sugar crystals will form on the sides.

MAKES ABOUT 1 QUART

> 2   large or 3 small lemons with aromatic peel
> 2-1/2   cups alcohol for cordials (625 ml) *or* vodka
> 2   cups sugar (450 grams)
> 1   cup water (250 ml)

Carefully cut away the colored zest from the lemons; there must be no white pith. Put the zest into a jar with a lid with 1/2 cup alcohol (125 ml). Close tightly and place in a cool, dark place for 40 days.

Prepare a sugar syrup. In a saucepan, bring the sugar and water to a boil, stirring. Simmer for 5 minutes, undisturbed. Cool completely.

Add the lemon essence to the syrup and remaining alcohol, stirring to mix well. Strain the liqueur into a bottle. Close tightly and place in a cool, dark place for 40 days before using. Serve as a digestive after dinner.

SICILY

Cena in Giardino "Sufficenza di Pescespada"

"SURFEIT OF SWORDFISH" DINNER IN THE GARDEN

Pasta con i Peperoni
PASTA WITH PEPPERS

Involtini di Pescespada
SWORDFISH ROLLS

Insalata di Zucchine Crude con Olio, Limone, e Menta
RAW ZUCCHINI SALAD WITH OIL, LEMON,
AND MINT

Semifreddo con Frutta e Croccante
FROZEN CREAM WITH FRUIT AND PRALINE

WINES
White: Barcellona (Messina); serve cold
Dessert: Malvasia delle Lipari DOC; serve chilled

Until recently, swordfish was available only in season, May to August, when the swordfish came nearer the coasts. There was so much swordfish served in this brief season that unusual preparations were devised—this menu features one of them, delicious even when swordfish is available year-round, as it is now.

Pasta con i Peperoni
PASTA WITH PEPPERS

This simple recipe always looks particularly appetizing. Most Italian families roast their own peppers and preserve them in olive oil, seasoned with herbs (see page 421).

SERVES 6 TO 8

6	**large bell peppers, a mixture of red and yellow**
1-1/3	**pounds *spaghetti or bucatini* (600 grams)**
	salt to taste
1/2	**cup (1/4 pound) unsalted butter (110 grams)**
2	**tablespoons olive oil**
1/2	**cup hot pasta water (125 ml)**
1	**cup freshly grated Parmesan cheese (135 grams)**
	freshly ground pepper

Roast the peppers in a preheated 400° (200) oven for about 40 minutes or until the skins are blistered and blackish, turning them as needed. Wrap each pepper in foil and allow to cool. When cooled, remove the stems, skins, and seeds and cut 4 strips to garnish the pasta. Reserve the strips and cut the rest of the peppers into pieces. The peppers can be prepared up to 2 days in advance and refrigerated, covered.

Cook the pasta until *al dente* in boiling salted water. While the pasta is cooking, puree the peppers in a blender or food processor. When the pasta is done, drain it, reserving 1/2 cup of the cooking water. In a medium saucepan, heat 2 tablespoons of the butter with the oil and add the pureed peppers, salt to taste, and the pasta water. Bring to a simmer.

Cut up the rest of the butter into a warm serving dish and mix the drained pasta with the butter. Add the Parmesan, mixing. Add half the sauce, mix well, and pour the rest of the sauce on top. Garnish with the reserved pepper strips and pass the pepper mill.

Involtini di Pescespada
SWORDFISH ROLLS

Thin slices of swordfish rolled around an herb stuffing are a Sicilian specialty and the glory of Messina. Zia Irene had three different recipes for this dish—this one is the simplest and the best.

"Surfeit of Swordfish" Dinner in the Garden

SERVES 6

Toothpicks or kitchen string

10	very thin slices (about 5/16 inch/1 cm) of swordfish, about 2-1/4 pounds (1 kilogram)
2	ounces *caciocavallo* cheese, grated (1/2 cup) (60 grams)
	a handful of fresh basil leaves, chopped
	a handful of parsley leaves, chopped
2	tablespoons fine dry bread crumbs
	salt and freshly ground pepper to taste
5	tablespoons olive oil (75 ml)

FOR THE SAUCE:

1	small onion, finely chopped
	salt to taste
8 or 9	fresh plum tomatoes, peeled and seeded, *or* drained canned Italian plum tomatoes
1/4	pound (about 1/2 cup) black Gaeta olives, pitted and halved (110 grams)
2	tablespoons capers, rinsed and dried
1	small celery stalk, sliced and blanched for 2 minutes in boiling salted water

Trim and discard the swordfish skin. Cut the fish slices into shapes as close to rectangles as possible, reserving the trimmings. Flatten slightly with a meat pounder, being careful not to tear the fish.

Mix together the *caciocavallo,* basil, parsley, bread crumbs, fish trimmings, salt, pepper, and oil. Lay out the fish slices on a work surface and divide the mixture among them. Roll up and close with toothpicks or tie with string.

Make the sauce. In a skillet, simmer the onion over medium heat, uncovered, with a few tablespoons water and salt. When the onion is transparent, add the tomatoes, olives, capers, and celery. Cook over medium-low heat for 15 minutes.

Put the rolls in the sauce and cook, covered, for 10 minutes. Remove the lid, turn the rolls, and cook, uncovered, for 10 to 12 minutes more, until the flesh is opaque and firm to the touch. Serve hot or cold.

Insalata di Zucchine Crude con Olio, Limone, e Menta

RAW ZUCCHINI SALAD WITH OIL, LEMON, AND MINT

Zucchini is a staple of Italian cuisine. In Sicily it is frequently served raw, and in this salad it is chilled and then dressed.

SERVES 6

> 1-1/2 **pounds zucchini (675 grams)**
> 4-1/2 **tablespoons olive oil (65 ml)**
> 1-1/2 **tablespoons (or to taste) freshly squeezed**
> **lemon juice**
> **salt to taste**
> **small fresh mint leaves plus extra mint for garnish**

Wash and dry the zucchini. Slice very thin, using a mandoline if available. Put the slices in a serving bowl and refrigerate until serving time.

When you're ready to serve the zucchini, mix together the oil and lemon juice and toss the zucchini with it. Add salt and the mint, tossing to mix. Garnish with extra mint and serve at once.

Semifreddo con Frutta e Croccante
FROZEN CREAM WITH FRUIT AND PRALINE

In this summer dessert the crunchiness of the almond praline provides just the right contrast to the smoothness of the cream. Throughout southern Italy the word *semifreddo* is used to describe almost any kind of frozen dessert made from a rich concoction of eggs and cream. In Naples the same dish is called a *coviglia*. Traditionally reserved for the rich man's table, it can be flavored with chocolate, nuts, or fresh fruit. A *semifreddo* is deceptively simple to prepare and never fails to make what the Italians call a *bella figura,* or handsome showpiece.

SERVES 6 TO 8

10¹/₂- by 4- by 3-inch (27 by
10 by 8 cm) loaf pan lined
with plastic wrap

FOR THE *CROCCANTE* (PRALINE):

  vegetable oil
1 lemon *or* orange
1/2 cup sugar (110 grams)
2/3 cup lightly toasted peeled almonds (110 grams)

FOR THE CREAM:

4 egg yolks
1/2 cup sugar (110 grams)
1-1/2 pounds ripe fruit, such as peaches *or* apricots, peeled and pitted (675 grams), plus 1/2 pound of the same fruit for garnish, sliced (225 grams)
1 tablespoon freshly squeezed lemon juice
2 tablespoons white rum
2 egg whites
  pinch of salt
1-2/3 cups heavy cream (400 ml)

continued

Prepare the praline. Lightly oil a marble surface or a large platter. Place the lemon nearby. Cook the sugar in a small, heavy saucepan over medium-high heat until it turns a caramel color. Add the almonds and cook for 1 minute, stirring. Turn the mixture out onto the oiled surface and press with the lemon to flatten. Leave to harden, then chop coarsely.

Beat the yolks with 1/4 cup sugar until thick and lemon-colored. In a blender or food processor fitted with the steel blade, puree the 1-1/2 pounds fruit with the lemon juice and add the rum. Fold the puree into the yolks.

Beat the egg whites with a pinch of salt until frothy and gradually add the 4 tablespoons sugar, beating until stiff but not dry. Whip the cream until stiff but not dry.

Fold the egg whites into the fruit puree. Add half the praline and fold in the whipped cream. Spoon the mixture—do not pour it—into the prepared pan. Cover and place in the freezer overnight.

When you're ready to serve, turn the *semifreddo* out onto a platter, tugging gently on the wrap to unmold it. Garnish with the sliced fruit and sprinkle the remaining praline over it. Let it soften for 30 minutes before serving.

Colazione in Campagna dai Ravidà

LUNCH IN THE
COUNTRY
AT THE RAVIDÀS'

*Lunch
in the
Country
at the
Ravidàs'*

Pasta con Ragù di Maiale Ravidà
PASTA WITH PORK RAGOUT RAVIDÀ

Polpettone con Ricotta
MEAT LOAF WITH RICOTTA

Insalata di Arancie, Finocchi, ed Olive Nere
ORANGE, FENNEL, AND BLACK OLIVE SALAD

Gelatina di Mandarini Ravidà
TANGERINE GELATIN RAVIDÀ

WINE
Red: Menfi (Menfi-Sciacca); serve cool

Natalia Ravidà's family has lived on the same farm in Menfi since 1773. The farmhouse is typically Sicilian, built of stone and facing into a courtyard. For this menu Natalia opened up her "secret book" and shared her old family recipes.

Pasta con Ragù di Maiale Ravidà

PASTA WITH
PORK RAGOUT RAVIDÀ

This pork *ragù* is a typical winter meal for the Ravidà household. In Sicily it is also traditional to serve *ragù* on Shrove Tuesday, which even today is one of the most important culinary occasions of the year. In the past the rigors of the Lenten fast—not only a strict observance of faith but often a necessity of poverty and the lack of fresh food available during the winter months—made the feasting and indulgence of the February Carnival holiday all the more significant. Carnival was also the time to use up the meat and eggs that could not be eaten during Lent. While the English have always made pancakes to use up their butter and eggs, those Sicilians lucky enough to have chickens (something of a luxury) made egg noodles. However, even if you couldn't afford a chicken, you were likely to own at least one hog, and this would be slaughtered shortly before Carnival time. Nothing from the animal was wasted—the fat was rendered into lard, the blood and innards used to make sausages, and what could be salted and cured was set aside until after Easter. The remaining meat went into the Shrove Tuesday *ragù* pot, and the richer the family, the more meat there would be.

SERVES 8

FOR THE *RAGÙ*:
- 2-1/2 pounds boneless pork roast, not too lean (1.100 grams)
- 3 tablespoons olive oil
- 3/4 cup dry red wine (185 ml)
- 1/4 pound *pancetta,* finely chopped (about 1 cup) (110 grams)
- 1 pig's ear, 1 pig's tail, and pork rib bones (from 1 side or all the ribs), if available

continued

> 1 6-ounce can tomato paste (170 grams)
> 1/4 cup hot water
> 1 28-ounce can Italian plum tomatoes with juice (800 grams)
> 1 medium onion, finely chopped
> 20 fresh sage leaves, finely chopped
> 4 bay leaves
> 1 tablespoon fennel seeds, pulverized in a blender or spice grinder
> salt and freshly ground pepper to taste

FOR THE PASTA:
> 1/2 pound *ricotta* cheese (225 grams)
> 1-1/2 pounds *rigatoni or* other short pasta (675 grams)
> freshly grated *caciocavallo* cheese, if available, *or* freshly grated *pecorino* cheese for serving
> freshly ground pepper

Brown the pork in 2 tablespoons of the oil in a skillet over high heat, turning it to brown it evenly. Pour 1/2 cup of the red wine over the meat and allow to evaporate.

Heat the remaining oil in a deep flameproof casserole, preferably terracotta, and add the *pancetta,* ear, tail, and bones. Cook over medium-high heat until the *pancetta* has browned slightly. Add the remaining wine and allow to evaporate.

Add the roast with its pan juices, the tomato paste diluted in the hot water, the tomatoes, onion, sage, bay leaves, and pulverized fennel seeds. Add enough water to come two thirds of the way up the meat and turn up the heat to high (the Ravidàs' recipe says to add wood to the fire). When it starts to boil, lower the heat and simmer the *ragù* for 3 hours, partially covered. (The recipe then says it should simmer all night long with the heat from the added wood to "raise the boil.") This dish cannot be abandoned, since the meat must be turned occasionally and water added a little at a time if necessary. After 3 hours, remove the ear, tail, and bones.

If necessary, cook, uncovered, to reduce the sauce; it should be a little thick. Season with salt and pepper. If possible, allow the *ragù* to rest a day before serving it.

When you're ready to serve the dish, remove the roast, slice it, put it on a platter, and serve separately. Or part of the roast may be chopped and added to the sauce. Put half the *ricotta* in a pasta serving dish. Heat the *ragù* and mix with the *ricotta* in the dish. Cook the pasta until *al dente* in boiling salted water and mix with the sauce. Serve with the rest of the *ricotta* spooned on top and the grated cheese passed separately together with a pepper mill.

Polpettone con Ricotta
MEAT LOAF WITH RICOTTA

*Lunch
in the
Country
at the
Ravidàs'*

Meat loaf seems like a quintessential American dish, but it's also Sicilian. This stovetop version, using a combination of turkey breast and *ricotta* elegantly wrapped in *prosciutto,* is delicate and light—excellent served cold on a hot summer day.

SERVES 8

Kitchen string

- 1 **pound boneless turkey breast, ground twice (450 grams)**
- 1/2 **pound *ricotta* cheese (225 grams)**
- 1 **egg**
- 2 **egg yolks**
- 1/4 **cup freshly grated Parmesan cheese (35 grams) freshly grated nutmeg to taste**
- 1 **teaspoon salt**
- 1/4 **teaspoon freshly ground black pepper**
- 1/4 **cup chopped parsley flour**
- 1/4 **pound *prosciutto*, thinly sliced (110 grams)**
- 2 **tablespoons unsalted butter (30 grams)**
- 1 **tablespoon olive oil**
- 1/4 **cup dry white wine (60 ml) parsley sprigs for garnish**

Mix together the turkey, *ricotta,* egg, egg yolks, Parmesan, nutmeg, salt, pepper, and parsley. Wet your hands with cold water and form the mixture into a loaf.

Sift a film of flour over a work surface and roll the loaf in the flour. Lay out the slices of *prosciutto,* overlapping, on a clean surface and place the loaf on the *prosciutto.* Roll up the loaf in the *prosciutto* slices, completely covering the loaf. Tie it loosely with string.

Heat the butter and oil in a heavy oval pan, with a tight-fitting lid, in which the loaf will fit snugly and brown the loaf all over, about 10 minutes over medium-high heat, turning it carefully with the aid of 2 spatulas. Lower the heat to a simmer, cover, and cook for 45 minutes to 1 hour, until the loaf is firm to the touch, turning it every 15 minutes.

Remove the meat to a platter and cool. Pour off the fat and add the white wine to the pan. Over medium-high heat, scrape the bottom of the pan with a wooden spoon to loosen the meat particles. Cook for about 1 minute. Remove the string from the loaf and slice. Pour the hot pan juices over it and garnish with parsley.

Insalata di Arancie, Finocchi, ed Olive Nere

ORANGE, FENNEL, AND BLACK OLIVE SALAD

On most Sicilian farms there's an abundance of both oranges and olives. Fennel, wild or cultivated, is also likely to be growing, and together the three ingredients make a refreshing salad.

SERVES 8

  4 small fennel bulbs, washed and dried
  6 oranges, peel and white pith removed
      chopped parsley to taste
      salt and freshly ground black pepper to taste
  1/2 cup black Gaeta olives, pitted (100 grams)
      extra-virgin olive oil

Slice the fennel thinly. Slice the oranges thinly and remove any seeds. When you're ready to serve, mix together the fennel, oranges, parsley, salt, pepper, and olives. Dress with a trickle of olive oil and serve at once.

Gelatina di Mandarini Ravidà

TANGERINE GELATIN RAVIDÀ

Simple jellies are a popular dessert year-round in Sicily, and tangerines with lots of flavor are the secret of this recipe. In a pinch, you could use reconstituted frozen tangerine juice concentrate.

SERVES 8

1-quart ring mold

> 3   cups freshly squeezed, strained tangerine juice (750 ml)
> 1/3   cup freshly squeezed lemon juice (80 ml)
> 2   1/4-ounce envelopes unflavored gelatin (15 grams)
> 1/3   cup cold water (80 ml)
> 2/3   cup sugar (150 grams)
>   almond or vegetable oil for the mold
>   very thin peeled and seeded tangerine slices for garnish

Strain the tangerine and lemon juices into a pitcher.

Sprinkle the gelatin over the cold water in a small saucepan and leave for 5 minutes to soften. Place over low heat and stir until the gelatin dissolves. Add 1/2 cup of the juice and the sugar and stir over low heat until the sugar dissolves. Add this mixture to the remaining tangerine juice.

Oil the mold with almond or vegetable oil. Pour the tangerine mixture into the mold and refrigerate overnight. Turn it out onto a platter and garnish with the tangerine slices, placed at the base of the dessert.

Colazione in Palermo nell'Appartamento di Toti

LUNCH IN
TOTI'S APARTMENT
IN PALERMO

Pasta al Limone
LEMON PASTA

Pescespada al Piatto
SWORDFISH IN A PLATE

Caponata Barocca
BAROQUE CAPONATA

Gelato di Melone
WATERMELON SHERBET

Gelo di Melone
WATERMELON CREAM

WINE
White: Fontanamurata (Palermo); serve very cold

Tall, handsome, and charming, Salvatore (Toti) Corleone manages a bank in Palermo and lives on the next-to-top floor of a modern apartment building at the center of the city, built on the site of what was once his family's villa. The loss of the house does not upset Toti in the least, since his most vivid memory of childhood in that house was the terrible cold in winter. He is not about to forget having done his homework fully dressed and huddled in bed, trying to keep warm. (Old Sicilian houses can be notoriously cold and drafty in the winter as their owners, convinced that warm weather will arrive at any moment, pay very little attention to insulation or heating.)

Toti lives within walking distance of Vucciria, Palermo's extraordinary open-air market in the heart of old Palermo. Its name is strange: literally it means "voices." (Does it have something to do with the noise and bustle of sellers and buyers magnified by the narrowness of the winding streets?) Vucciria is one of the great food markets of southern Europe, and Paula Wolfert gives a marvelous description of her first impressions:

> *Piles of fennel both wild and sweet. Sturdy, thick cardoons. Eggplants in all sizes and hues, from whitish-pink to black. Bronze lobsters, blue mackerel, silver fish flashing in the sun. Pyramids of olives. Strings of garlic. Meats, sausages, and hams hanging from hooks. There are hordes of people, sellers calling out the quality of their produce, buyers haggling over price. Firm cheeses bound with rope, soft cheeses oozing onto plates. It is a magnificent scene, and it all comes triumphantly together in the square called Piazza Garraffello.*
>
> PAULA WOLFERT'S *World of Food*

Toti's dessert is a gorgeous watermelon sherbet. I've also given an alternative, the famous Palermo classic called *gelo di melone* (watermelon cream).

Pasta al Limone
LEMON PASTA

Toti is an excellent cook who loves to entertain his friends, but he is also a great pragmatist who believes in making things simple for himself. For this reason he particularly likes easy recipes that can be made ahead of time. This pasta, which he serves as a first course, is an excellent example; the pasta is cooked at the last minute, but everything else is prepared earlier in the day.

Lunch

in

Toti's

Apartment

in

Palermo

SERVES 6 AS A FIRST COURSE

> 1-1/2 cups heavy cream (375 ml)
> 6 lemons
> 1/2 cup (1/4 pound) unsalted butter (110 grams)
> 1 pound *spaghetti or linguine* (450 grams)
> 2 tablespoons freshly squeezed lemon juice
> 1 cup freshly grated Parmesan cheese (135 grams)
> freshly ground pepper
> thin lemon slices for garnish

Put the cream in a small saucepan and simmer for 10 minutes or until thickened. Wash the lemons with kitchen soap and rinse thoroughly. Grate the colored zests into another small saucepan, add the butter, and melt over the lowest heat; do not brown. Set aside both saucepans. These steps may be done up to 1 hour in advance; set aside in a cool place (do not refrigerate).

Cook the pasta until *al dente* in boiling salted water. Drain, return the pasta to the pot, and toss with the lemon juice and Parmesan. Add the butter and then the cream. Mix thoroughly over low heat. Serve hot and pass the pepper mill. Garnish with thin lemon slices.

Pescespada al Piatto
SWORDFISH IN A PLATE

At Vucciria, where Toti buys his swordfish, it is displayed *in situ,* with the sword still attached to its head; elsewhere the fishmonger usually keeps the sword and sells the fish cut crosswise into wheels. Toti prepares it very simply and in a way—steamed between two plates—that retains all its natural flavor. Be sure to use plates that fit into a steamer.

SERVES 6

2 plates that fit tightly into a
steamer or pan

2	large swordfish steaks, about 2-1/4 pounds (1 kilogram)
3	tablespoons extra-virgin olive oil
1-1/2	tablespoons freshly squeezed lemon juice
	salt and freshly ground black pepper to taste
3	tablespoons finely chopped parsley
3	tablespoons finely chopped fresh basil
1	teaspoon dried oregano
	fresh basil leaves for garnish

Place one of the slices of swordfish on a heavy porcelain plate. Pour over it half the oil and half the lemon juice and sprinkle with salt and pepper. Add half the parsley and half the basil and oregano. Cover with the other slice of swordfish and sprinkle with the rest of the ingredients.

Heat a pan of water or a steamer into which the plate fits tightly. Cover the prepared fish with another plate or cover tightly with foil. Cook over boiling water for 30 to 40 minutes. The fish is ready when it is white and firm to the touch. Serve at once, garnished with basil. Cut like a pie.

Caponata Barocca
BAROQUE CAPONATA

Lunch
in
Toti's
Apartment
in
Palermo

There are two secrets to a true Sicilian *caponata:* first the vinegar, which gives the vegetables a sweetish sour taste; second, when more than one vegetable is used in a *caponata* each one is cooked separately and seasoned with its own herbs and spices, so they retain their own distinct flavors and the vegetables are mixed together only after all the cooking has been done. This is what distinguishes a *caponata* from a *ratatouille*—for *ratatouille*, the vegetables are usually sautéed separately but then are stewed together so that the juices take on a blended flavor. When preparing his *caponata*, Toti likes to follow the Palermo custom of serving hot fried octopus on top.

SERVES 6 TO 8

2-1/2	pounds eggplant (1.100 grams)
	salt to taste
	olive oil for frying, about 1-1/2 cups (375 ml),
	plus 3 tablespoons extra-virgin olive oil
3/4	cup diced celery heart
1	medium-large onion, finely chopped
6	tablespoons white wine vinegar (100 ml)
1-1/2	tablespoons sugar
3/4	cup pureed tomatoes, fresh if possible (185 grams)
2-1/2	tablespoons capers, rinsed and dried
1	scant cup green Sicilian olives, pitted (150 grams)
1/4	pound *bottarga* (smoked tuna roe), thinly sliced (110 grams)
2	tablespoons chopped parsley *or* fresh basil
	freshly ground pepper to taste
1	pound baby octopus, cleaned (see page 419) (450 grams)
	flour for dredging

Peel the eggplant if the skin is not shiny. Cut the flesh into 1-inch dice and layer it in a colander, salting each layer. Put a weighted plate on top and leave for at least an hour to drain.

Rinse the eggplant and pat it dry. Heat about 1/2 cup of the olive oil in a skillet and in it fry the eggplant over medium-high heat until golden brown. Drain on paper towels. Reduce the heat to low and fry the celery in the same oil until barely colored. Drain on paper towels.

Heat the 3 tablespoons oil in another skillet and cook the onion with salt and a little water over low heat until transparent. Add the vinegar, sugar, and tomato puree. Cook over low heat for 15 minutes and add the capers, olives, *bottarga,* and parsley, mixing. Taste for seasoning and add salt and pepper to taste. Add the eggplant and celery, mixing gently. Remove from the heat and allow to cool completely.

When you're ready to serve the *caponata,* rinse and dry the octopus. Flour the octopus lightly and fry in about a cup of hot olive oil (oil should be about 1/2 inch deep) in a skillet until crisp and a light nut brown.

Serve the *caponata* at room temperature with the hot octopus on top. This dish may be prepared ahead of time except for the octopus, which should always be added at the last moment. Refrigerate the *caponata* or set it aside in a cool place and then let it come to room temperature before serving.

Gelato di Melone

WATERMELON SHERBET

Lunch
in
Toti's
Apartment
in
Palermo

During the summer months watermelons are sold all over Italy from the back of pickup trucks, and often you will see men of all ages, obviously dispatched by their wives or mothers, struggling home under the weight of these gigantic fruits. You know this dish is Sicilian because there watermelon is called *melone*—elsewhere in Italy it's *cocomero*. It's also a sherbet, not a true *gelato*.

You'll need a whole 14-pound watermelon to produce enough juice for this recipe as well as the next.

SERVES 6 TO 8

6-cup (1½ liters) domed or
melon mold, dampened and
lined with plastic wrap

1/2	**14-pound watermelon (see above)**
2	**tablespoons jasmine water (see below; optional)**
1	**cup plus 2 tablespoons sugar (250 grams)**
2	**ounces semisweet chocolate, cut into small dice (60 grams)**
2	**ounces candied citron, cut into small dice (60 grams)**
1-1/2	**tablespoons shelled unsalted pistachios, blanched and skins removed**
	ground cinnamon (optional)
	shelled unsalted pistachios *or* jasmine flowers for garnish (optional)

Grate the watermelon a little at a time into a bowl. Place a strainer over a large pitcher and strain the juice. You'll need 1 quart. Pour this juice into a stainless-steel saucepan and add the jasmine water and sugar. Heat, stirring constantly, just until the sugar melts. Do not boil. Cool.

Process in an ice cream machine following the manufacturer's instructions. Place the empty mold in the freezer.

After the sherbet is prepared but before putting it into the mold, add the chocolate, citron, and pistachios. Mix well, spoon it into the cold mold, and cover tightly. Freeze overnight or for several hours.

When you're ready to serve the sherbet, turn it out onto a round platter, tugging gently on the plastic wrap. If desired, sprinkle cinnamon on top. Garnish with pistachios at the base or with jasmine flowers, if available.

HOW TO MAKE JASMINE WATER: Simply put 4 or 5 white jasmine flowers in a little cold water in the refrigerator for 2 or 3 days, changing the flowers each day.

Gelo di Melone

WATERMELON CREAM

Both thirst-quenching and pretty, watermelon makes the perfect summer dessert—this exotic version is one of Palermo's best-loved recipes.

SERVES 6 TO 8

6-cup mold or platter with rim

1 quart watermelon juice, strained (see preceding recipe) (1 liter)
2 tablespoons jasmine water, if available (see preceding recipe)
1 scant cup sugar (200 grams)
1 tablespoon freshly squeezed lemon juice
1 cinnamon stick
10 tablespoons wheat starch *or* cornstarch (70 grams)
 semisweet chocolate, coarsely chopped, for garnish
 shelled unsalted pistachios, coarsely chopped, *or* jasmine flowers for garnish

Put the watermelon juice, reserving 1/2 cup, in a stainless-steel saucepan. Add the jasmine water, sugar, lemon juice, and cinnamon stick. Mix the wheat starch or cornstarch with the reserved juice, stirring until dissolved. Strain this mixture into the juice. Put the pan over low heat and bring to a simmer, stirring constantly. Simmer for 2 minutes. Remove from the heat. Rinse out the mold or platter with cold water and pour in the *gelo,* removing and discarding the cinnamon stick. Cool and refrigerate until set.

To serve, turn it out at the last minute. Sprinkle the chocolate over it and decorate the base with pistachios or surround the base with jasmine flowers and leaves.

SICILY

Cena sulla Terrazza di Toti

DINNER ON TOTI'S TERRACE

*Dinner
on
Toti's
Terrace*

Pasticcio di San Giuseppe
SAINT JOSEPH'S PIE

Falsomagro
FALSELY THIN

Involtini di Melanzane Anzon
EGGPLANT ROLLS ANZON

Gelo di Caffè di Toti
TOTI'S COFFEE CREAM

WINE
White: Donnafugata (Trapani); serve cold

Toti's apartment is surrounded by a terrace filled with olive trees, white roses, and trailing perfumed jasmine—the perfect setting for a dinner party. Toti also has an impressive collection of Sicilian ceramic pots on his terrace. On one occasion a tornadolike wind blew one of the pots off the terrace, and it landed on the hood of a moving car eight stories below. The driver stopped, looked up, shrugged his shoulders, and then proceeded to drive on with the pot still balanced on the hood of his car.

A small wrought-iron gate and staircase connect Toti's terrace to another terrace belonging to his parents, who live above him—when Toti gives a party, his guests can use both terraces. The view is spectacular—on one side is the sea, on the other Monte Pellegrino (the Pilgrim's Hill and resting place of Saint Rosalia, patron saint of Palermo).

The following menu was planned by Toti for a dinner party he gave on the feast of Saint Joseph, celebrated all over Italy on the 19th of March, roughly coinciding with the spring equinox. It replaced the ancient festival of Demeter, celebrating the arrival of Sicily's early spring, and in Sicily it is one of the most important festivals of the year.

Devotion to Saint Joseph, considered the defender of the weak and the saint who can turn divine laws inside out, dates back to the Middle Ages. One legend tells of an argument between God and Saint Joseph over an obviously repentant thief languishing in hell. God was obliged to give way when Saint Joseph threatened to abandon heaven and take Mary with him if the thief were not admitted to heaven.

Devotion to Saint Joseph is so strong that there is hardly a town in Italy without its own special sweet fried pastry to be eaten on his feast day. In fact throughout southern Italy Saint Joseph is known as San Giuseppe Frittellaro—Saint Joseph who fries.

One Saint Joseph's Day custom that dates back to the Middle Ages is the holding of a public auction where different foods are sold to the highest bidder and the proceeds given to the poor. Another custom still followed in many villages is known as giving a dinner for Saint Joseph. Someone (usually a woman) who has received a particular blessing or has recovered from a serious illness will prepare a thanksgiving dinner for the saint.

The preparations for such a meal are highly ritualistic and begin on the first Friday in March. Kernels of wheat are planted in vases, kept in the dark, and watered frequently. A week before the dinner takes place, the preparation proper begins: Three large loaves of bread are made for each blessing received and are given to three poor people of the village, who also receive invitations to attend the dinner and represent Joseph, Mary, and Jesus. On the eve of the feast the table is set and a large, colorful cloth, festooned with ivy, oranges, and lemons, is hung on one wall. An altar is set up next to the table, and on it a cross is placed with the now-sprouted wheat in two vases on either side. A large loaf of bread, made in the shape of a head with a beard and long hair, is placed at the foot of the altar. More bread, bunches of fennel, strawberries and other fruits, flowers

Dinner
on
Toti's
Terrace

(usually carnations, freesias, and stocks), and lots of cookies are placed nearby. Candles will be lit and must not be allowed to go out. By evening, meatballs, salt cod, toasted chick-peas, peanuts, and plates of pasta are set on the table, but nothing can be removed or eaten until the next day. The only exception to this rule is made for a pregnant woman who has a craving. During this time the person giving the feast is busy preparing Saint Joseph's staff, usually made of olive wood and decorated with ribbons, oranges, and a picture of the saint on top.

On the feast day the three poor people celebrated as living "saints," each wearing a laurel crown, take the staff and, accompanied by the feast giver and a band of musicians, set out for church to receive a blessing. When they return to the house, friends and relatives, who have all arrived by now, lock the front door. This is the cue for the "saints" to say: "Jesus, Joseph, Mary, either you open or I do." The relatives then open the door, the "saints" wash their hands with milk and wine and say the Lord's Prayer, and the "saint" representing Joseph gives a blessing. Finally everybody sits down to eat dinner.

Plan this meal for 10 and anticipate leftovers of *pasticcio*.

Pasticcio di San Giuseppe
SAINT JOSEPH'S PIE

This pie, a famous Palermo specialty, might well be served at a ritual Saint Joseph's feast like the one described above. It is typically Sicilian, made with many kinds of vegetables and a mixture of sweet and sour ingredients. Toti would part with the recipe only on the condition that it never be published in Sicily, since there is a man in Palermo who does nothing else but make these pies, which he sells at very high prices. This is not a quick recipe—it takes almost all day to prepare—but it is not difficult, and the spectacular results are worth the time it takes. It also feeds a lot of people.

SERVES 18

14-inch (36 cm) pizza pan,
heavily buttered and lightly
floured

FOR THE FILLING:

- 1   **pound spinach (450 grams)**
  salt and freshly ground black pepper to taste
- 1   **pound Swiss chard (450 grams)**
- 1   **cup packed fennel leaves and stems**
- 3/4   **cup diced celery heart**
- 6   **artichokes**
- 1   **lemon, cut in half**
- 1/2   **cup olive oil (125 ml)**
- 1   **small onion, finely chopped**
- 2-1/4   **cups frozen peas (300 grams)**
- 1   **large onion, finely chopped**
- 2   **tablespoons tomato puree**
- 5   **salt-packed anchovies, cleaned (see page 419), *or***
  10 oil-packed anchovy fillets, drained
- 2/3   **cup capers, rinsed and dried (110 grams)**
- 3/4   **cup pine nuts (120 grams)**

continued

1/2	pound (about 1-1/3 cups) dried currants *or* raisins (225 grams)
1/2	pound (about 1 heaped cup) spicy green Sicilian olives, pitted (225 grams)
1/3	cup (or less to taste) white wine vinegar (80 ml)
3	tablespoons (or to taste) sugar

FOR THE *PASTA FROLLA* (PASTRY):

7	cups flour (800 grams)
1	cup (1/2 pound) plus 2 tablespoons cool unsalted butter, cut into pieces (250 grams)
1/2	cup (1/4 pound) plus 2 tablespoons cool lard, cut into pieces (150 grams)
1-1/3	cups sugar (300 grams)
2	eggs
1/4	cup (or more) dry white wine (60 ml)
1	egg beaten with 1 tablespoon water for painting the crust

Make the filling. Wash the spinach, discard the tough stems, and cook it in a large pot, covered, in the water clinging to its leaves. Drain; when cool, squeeze it to remove excess moisture. Chop the spinach, adding salt and pepper. Reserve.

Cook the Swiss chard in boiling salted water for 5 or 6 minutes. Drain and squeeze out excess moisture. Chop and reserve.

Cook the fennel leaves and stems in boiling salted water for 2 minutes. Drain and squeeze out excess moisture. Chop and reserve.

Cook the celery in boiling salted water for 2 minutes. Drain and reserve.

Clean the artichokes (see page 420) and rub with lemon. Slice very thinly. Heat 3 tablespoons of oil in a skillet and add the artichokes. Cover and cook over low heat for about 25 minutes or until done, stirring often. Season with salt and reserve.

Sauté the small onion in 1 tablespoon oil in a medium saucepan over low heat. When transparent, add the peas, cover, and cook over low heat for about 25 minutes, stirring occasionally. Season with salt and pepper and reserve.

Heat the remaining 1/4 cup oil in a 13-inch (35 cm) sauté pan and in it sauté the large onion until transparent, adding water by the tablespoon as necessary to prevent burning. Add the tomato puree and cook for 1 minute.

In a bowl, mix together all the vegetables, the anchovies cut into pieces, capers, pine nuts, currants, and olives and add to the onion. Mix together the vinegar and sugar and add to the mixture. Simmer for 15 minutes. Remove from the heat and cool completely. (The vegetable mixture can be prepared a day before.)

Prepare the *pasta frolla*. Put the flour, butter, lard, sugar, eggs, and white wine in the large bowl of an electric mixer. Mix with the paddle attachment, covering the bowl with a kitchen towel to prevent the flour from scattering. Use more wine if necessary to make the dough hold together. Preheat the oven to 350° (180).

Divide the dough into 2 parts, one slightly larger than the other. Roll out the larger part to about 18 inches, drape it over the rolling pin, and carefully unroll it over the prepared tin. Trim, leaving a 1-inch overhang. Spoon the cooled filling into the crust. Roll out the top crust and lay it over the filling. Seal and crimp the edges decoratively. If desired, arrange pastry leaves or other shapes, made from the trimmings, on top. Paint the crust with the beaten egg.

Bake the *pasticcio* for 50 minutes to 1 hour or until the crust has browned. Cool on a rack, but do not turn out until completely cooled. Serve at room temperature.

NOTE: The quantity of vinegar and sugar in the filling can be reduced or increased to taste.

There will probably be some leftover pie. Serve it at room temperature, sliced and arranged on a platter garnished with parsley or small spinach leaves.

Falsomagro
FALSELY THIN

This well-known Sicilian dish (sometimes called *farsumagru*) has a confusing name. *Magro* is the name of a Lenten, therefore meatless, dish. *Falsomagro,* while it makes no pretense of being meatless, is not the simple piece of roasted veal it first appears to be. When the veal is carved, an elaborate stuffing made from a great number of ingredients—including hard-cooked egg yolks, which appear as golden circles in the center of each slice of meat—is revealed. To assure a properly dramatic effect, it is always sliced at the table.

SERVES 8 TO 10

Kitchen string

3/4	pound ground veal (330 grams)
2	tablespoons fine dry bread crumbs
2	small eggs
1/2	cup freshly grated *pecorino* cheese (65 grams)
	a handful of parsley, finely chopped
	salt and freshly ground pepper to taste
1	boneless veal slice, about 12 by 16 inches, about 1-3/4 pounds (800 grams)
1/4	pound *salame*, thinly sliced (110 grams)
3	small eggs, hard-cooked and peeled
1/2	cup chopped *provolone* cheese (70 grams)
1	small onion, finely chopped
4 to 5	tablespoons olive oil (60 to 75 ml)
1/4	cup dry white wine (60 ml)
1	tablespoon tomato paste
	parsley sprigs for garnish

Put into a small bowl the ground veal, bread crumbs, raw eggs, *pecorino,* parsley, salt, and pepper. Mix well with your hands.

Pound the slice of veal to flatten it, being careful not to tear it. Lay it out on a work surface and cover with the *salame* slices. Spread the ground meat mixture over the *salame* slices, leaving a 1-inch border around the sides, with a slightly wider border at the top.

Cut off the ends of the hard-cooked eggs and place them along the edge closest to you, about 3 inches inside. Sprinkle the *provolone* over all. Roll up the veal carefully and tie the roll with kitchen string to hold its shape.

Sauté the onion with a few tablespoons of water and a pinch of salt in a small pan over low heat until transparent. Add 1 tablespoon oil and cook for 30 seconds. Reserve.

In a pan in which the meat roll fits snugly, put enough oil to cover the bottom of the pan, about 3 tablespoons. Brown the roll, turning it carefully, over high heat. Add the wine and allow it to evaporate, turning the roll. Add the onion to the pan. Dilute the tomato paste in a little hot water and add to the pan. Lower the heat and add about 1/2 cup hot water. Simmer the meat, covered, for approximately 1 hour, adding hot water if the liquid becomes too thick. Allow to cool before serving and remove the string.

Cut the meat into 1-inch slices. A "gold coin" will show in the middle of each slice. The meat can also be reheated. Place the slices in an ovenproof dish, spoon the cooking liquid over them, and bake, uncovered, in a preheated 350° (180) oven for 20 minutes. Garnish with parsley.

Involtini di Melanzane Anzon
EGGPLANT ROLLS ANZON

Throughout Sicily *involtini* are a popular choice for a main course, and every cook has a favorite filling for these delicious little rolls. Usually they will be made of fish or meat, but here it's eggplant. This recipe originally came from Signorina Anzon, but Toti was so delighted with it that he insisted on serving these *involtini* at his own dinner party.

SERVES 8

    3 pounds eggplant (the long Japanese kind) (1.350 grams)
    salt
    olive oil for frying

FOR THE BÉCHAMEL:

    2 cups milk (500 ml)
  1/3 cup flour (50 grams)
    salt and freshly ground pepper to taste
    3 tablespoons unsalted butter (45 grams)
  1/2 cup freshly grated Parmesan cheese (65 grams)
    5 ounces *mozzarella* cheese, cut into small dice (about 1-1/4 cups) (150 grams)
2-1/2 ounces *provolone* cheese, cut into small dice (heaped 1/2 cup, approximately) (75 grams)

FOR THE SAUCE:

    2 pounds ripe fresh tomatoes, peeled, seeded, and cut into pieces (900 grams)
    salt to taste
  20 fresh basil leaves plus extra for garnish

    olive oil for the dish
    freshly ground pepper to taste

Peel the eggplant and slice it 1/2 inch thick lengthwise. Layer the slices in a colander, salting each layer. Weight them with a plate and leave for an hour.

Rinse and dry the eggplant with paper towels. Fry the eggplant in 1/2 inch of olive oil in a skillet over medium-high heat until lightly browned. Drain on paper towels and reserve.

Make the béchamel. In a blender, mix the milk, flour, salt, and pepper and blend for a minute. Melt the butter in a small saucepan and add the milk mixture. Bring to a simmer and cook for 5 minutes, stirring. Remove from the heat and add the Parmesan. Cover the surface of the sauce with plastic wrap and leave to cool. When cooled, add the *mozzarella* and *provolone* and refrigerate the béchamel until cold.

Make the tomato sauce. Put the tomatoes in a frying pan and cook over medium-high heat, stirring often, for 15 minutes. Add salt. Chop 7 of the basil leaves and add to the pan. If the sauce is still liquid, cook for another 5 minutes. Cool. Preheat the oven to 350° (180).

Oil an ovenproof dish in which the rolls will fit snugly. Lay out the eggplant slices on a work surface and spread the cold béchamel over the slices. Roll up rapidly and place in the dish close together so that the ends remain closed. Spoon the tomato sauce over the rolls and tuck the remaining basil leaves between the rolls. Grind black pepper over the top and bake for 25 minutes. Serve hot, garnished with basil.

Gelo di Caffè di Toti
TOTI'S COFFEE CREAM

Instead of serving after-dinner coffee to his guests, Toti prefers to give them a simple dessert with a rich espresso coffee flavor. Remember to make the dessert a day ahead.

SERVES 12

5-cup ring mold

> 1 **quart strong brewed espresso (1 liter)**
> 5 **tablespoons granulated sugar (75 grams)**
> 1/2 **cup plus 2 tablespoons wheat starch *or***
> **cornstarch (75 grams)**
> 1-1/2 **cups heavy cream (375 ml)**
> 1/4 **cup (or to taste) confectioners' sugar (30 grams)**
> **crushed coffee beans for garnish**

Sweeten the espresso with the granulated sugar.

Put the wheat starch or cornstarch in a large saucepan and add the coffee a little at a time, mixing with a wooden spoon. When all the coffee has been added, set the pan over low heat. Bring to a slow boil, stirring constantly, and simmer for 2 minutes. Cool.

Rinse out the mold with cold water and pour the cooled coffee into it. Refrigerate overnight.

Before serving, whip the cream until frothy and add the confectioners' sugar a little at a time. Beat until the cream is softly stiff. Unmold the dessert onto a round plate and put the whipped cream in the middle. Sprinkle the crushed coffee beans over the whipped cream. Serve very small portions. The coffee gelatin should be slightly bitter and the whipped cream sweet.

 *S I C I L Y*

Cena a Marsala alla Villa Rallo

DINNER IN MARSALA AT VILLA RALLO

*Dinner
in
Marsala
at Villa
Rallo*

Spuma di Fegatini Corleone
SIGNOR CORLEONE'S CHICKEN LIVER MOUSSE

Vitello Striato
STRIPED VEAL

Caponatina in Crosta
SWEET-SOUR VEGETABLE MÉLANGE IN A CRUST

Spumone
CHOCOLATE AND ZABAIONE ICE CREAM

WINES
Aperitivo: Marsala Vergine
Red: Etna DOC (Marsala); serve lightly chilled
Dessert: Marsala Riserva, Diego Rallo, DOC; serve cool

Gabriella and Giacomo Rallo's family has been in the wine business since 1860. Since they live in Marsala, it is not surprising that their specialty is Marsala wine. They produce eight different kinds of Marsala—the best is Riserva Vergine 1860. They also produce red and white wines, several dessert wines, and an excellent sparkling wine called Damaschino.

Gabriella also produces her own *Donnafugata* (white wine), named for the palace where the prince and his family spent three months every summer in Lampedusa's *The Leopard. Donnafugata* was not just Lampedusa's fictional creation; it really *did* exist and belonged to Gabriella's family until it was destroyed in an earthquake in 1968. All that remains is a beautiful garden, which now belongs to the state.

Spuma di Fegatini Corleone
SIGNOR CORLEONE'S CHICKEN LIVER MOUSSE

Signor Corleone lives in Palermo next door to Toti and recently celebrated his 90th birthday. Although he has a devoted cook who follows him around with infinite patience—collaborating, commenting, assisting, and cleaning up after him—Signor Corleone also likes to cook himself. Every day, accompanied by his faithful cook, he sets out for Palermo's famous Vucciria market in search of the best and freshest produce. This recipe for his chicken liver mousse is famous throughout the region and is proof of his lifelong passion for cooking and good food.

SERVES 8 TO 10

2	**pounds fresh chicken livers, cleaned (900 grams) very dry Marsala**
4	**bay leaves**
4	**cloves**
7	**tablespoons unsalted butter (100 grams)**
1	**tablespoon extra-virgin olive oil**
1	**large onion, thinly sliced**
1	**teaspoon (or to taste) salt**
1/3	**cup milk (80 ml)**
3	**tablespoons cognac**
1	**tablespoon gin**
1	**black truffle *or* 6 pitted black olives for decoration (optional)**

Put the livers in a bowl and pour over enough Marsala to cover them. Add the bay leaves and cloves and marinate, covered and refrigerated, overnight.

continued

In a large frying pan, heat 1/4 cup of the butter and the oil and in them sauté the onion over medium-low heat until transparent, adding a tablespoon of water now and then to prevent burning. Add the livers and brown lightly over high heat. Lower the heat and simmer for 1 hour, partially covered, stirring occasionally. Discard the bay leaves and cloves if you can find them.

Puree the livers with salt in a food processor or in a blender in batches. Add the milk, the remaining butter, melted, the cognac, and the gin. Put the *spuma* in 2 shallow rimmed serving dishes. The *spuma* can be decorated with the black truffle, sliced very thinly, or the black olives, cut lengthwise into 3 pieces, in the center or around the edge of the *spuma*. Serve the *spuma* at room temperature with Italian bread or toasted white or brown bread.

Vitello Striato
STRIPED VEAL

This is Gabriella Rallo's recipe for *scaloppine,* cooked in milk and, of course, Marsala. For this dinner you will need to make two striped veals.

SERVES 4 TO 5

Kitchen string

2/3	pound very thinly sliced veal **scaloppine** (300 grams) freshly ground black pepper and salt to taste
1/3	pound boiled ham, thinly sliced (150 grams)
1/3	pound **prosciutto or** tongue, thinly sliced (150 grams)
3	tablespoons unsalted butter (45 grams)

1	tablespoon olive oil
9	fresh sage leaves
4	3-inch rosemary branches
1/3	cup Marsala (80 ml)
1/3	cup milk (80 ml)

Trim the *scaloppine* of nerves and fat and flatten with a meat pounder until as thin as possible without tearing. Lay out the slices of veal on a work surface and grind black pepper over them. Salt only lightly as the ham will be salty. Put a slice of boiled ham over the veal and a slice of *prosciutto* over this. Repeat with all the veal and ham. Tie the stack of meat as evenly as possible—about every 2 inches—with kitchen string.

Melt the butter with the oil in a pan that will hold the meat snugly and add the sage and rosemary. Brown the meat over medium heat, turning as necessary to brown evenly.

When the meat has browned, add the Marsala and milk, cover, and lower the heat to low. Simmer for an hour, turning the meat every 10 or 15 minutes. The sauce will darken and thicken slightly.

Allow the meat to cool for 20 or more minutes before slicing. If necessary, reheat the sauce before serving and pour it over the meat. This dish can also be served cold.

Caponatina in Crosta
SWEET-SOUR VEGETABLE MÉLANGE IN A CRUST

Dinner in Marsala at Villa Rallo

"He who has not eaten a *caponatina* of eggplant has never reached the antechamber of the terrestrial paradise," exclaimed the Italian writer Gaetano Falzone in his book *Itinerari Palermitani*. And when a visitor arrives in Sicily and tastes his first *caponata* or *caponatina* (there appears to be little difference between them), which blends sweet with sour, nuts with vegetables, and raisins with capers, he is nearly always of the same opinion. This *caponatina* is unusual in that it is served in a crust. It should be made a day ahead and assembled at the last minute.

SERVES 8 TO 10

12-inch (30 cm) frying pan

> 5 **medium eggplants, about 2-1/2 pounds (1.100 grams)**
> **salt**
> **olive oil for frying, about 2/3 cup (160 ml)**
> 2 **pounds bell peppers, a mixture of green and yellow (900 grams)**
> 1 **cup diced celery**
> 1 **pound tomatoes, peeled, seeded, and chopped (1-3/4 cups) (450 grams)**
> **freshly ground pepper to taste**
> 1 **cup green Sicilian olives, pitted (200 grams)**
> **scant 2/3 cup capers, rinsed, soaked in cold water for 20 minutes, and drained (100 grams)**
> 2 **tablespoons sugar**
> 1/3 **cup white wine vinegar (80 ml)**
> 3 **tablespoons raisins, soaked in hot water until plump and drained (30 grams)**

   1/4   cup lightly toasted pine nuts (40 grams)
         Crosta per Caponatina **(recipe follows)**
     3   tablespoons toasted dried bread crumbs,
         approximately
     3   tablespoons coarsely chopped toasted almonds,
         approximately

Peel the eggplant if the skin is not shiny. Cut the flesh into 1-inch dice and layer in a colander, salting each layer. Weight the eggplant and leave for 3 hours.

Rinse and pat dry. In batches, fry in 1 inch of olive oil in a skillet over medium-high heat until lightly browned. Drain on paper towels. Reserve 1/3 cup of the oil.

Roast the peppers on a cookie sheet in a preheated 400° (200) oven for 20 minutes. Turn the peppers and roast for another 20 minutes or until the peppers are charred. Wrap each pepper in foil and cool. When cool enough to handle, remove stem, seeds, and peel. Cut into 1/2-inch-wide strips and set aside.

Blanch the celery in boiling salted water for 2 minutes. Drain and set aside.

Cook the tomatoes over medium heat in a small skillet for 25 minutes. Season with salt and pepper.

In a 12-inch (30 cm) frying pan, heat the reserved eggplant oil. Add the celery and fry it lightly over medium heat until it's a very light brown. Add the olives, capers, tomato sauce, sugar, vinegar, eggplant, and peppers. Simmer for 10 minutes. Taste and correct seasonings. Add the raisins and pine nuts and cook for 1 minute. Keep in a cool place until serving time.

When you're ready to serve the *caponatina,* spoon it into the cooled crust and sprinkle the bread crumbs and toasted almonds over it.

Crosta per Caponatina
CAPONATINA CRUST

11-inch (28 cm) buttered
quiche tin, foil, and dried
beans or pie weights

3-1/4   **cups flour (375 grams)**
1/2   **cup (1/4 pound) plus 2 tablespoons cold lard, cut into small pieces (150 grams)**
3   **tablespoons sugar**
2   **egg yolks**
1   **egg**
1/3   **cup (or more) Marsala (80 ml)**

Mix together the flour, lard, and sugar and mound on a marble slab or wooden pastry board. Make a well in the center and put one egg yolk and the whole egg into the well. Mix all together rapidly, and when the ingredients begin to crumble into small pieces, add the Marsala. Mix just enough to blend the ingredients, adding more Marsala if necessary.

Clean the board and wash your hands. Sprinkle the board with flour and roll out the pastry into a circle 1/4 to 1/8 inch thick. Pass a spatula under the pastry to detach it from the board and drape the pastry over a rolling pin. Unroll over the prepared pan. Trim and crimp the edges. Prick the bottom with a fork. Refrigerate until cold or put in the freezer for 30 minutes before baking.

Preheat the oven to 375° (190). Place foil and beans on the bottom of the crust to prevent the pastry from rising during baking. Bake for 30 minutes. Remove from the oven, remove the foil and beans, and paint the border with the remaining yolk beaten with 1 tablespoon water. Bake for 20 more minutes. Cool completely before filling with *caponatina*.

Spumone
CHOCOLATE AND ZABAIONE ICE CREAM

Signor Rallo likes rich desserts, and this *very* rich ice cream cake made of golden *zabaione* surrounded by chocolate ice cream is one of his favorites. The *spumone* is even more spectacular when made with praline, which is optional in the recipe. Save this dessert for special occasions and serve it with a glass of Marsala Riserva.

SERVES 8 TO 10

Dome-shaped 8-cup
(1.750 liters) *spumone* mold

FOR THE CHOCOLATE ICE CREAM:
- 1/2 **pound good-quality semisweet chocolate (225 grams)**
- 4 **large egg yolks**
- 1 **scant cup sugar (200 grams)**
- 2-1/2 **tablespoons unsweetened cocoa powder**
- 2 **cups milk (500 ml)**
- 1 **cup heavy cream (250 ml), plus additional for garnish (optional)**

FOR THE *CROCCANTE* (PRALINE) (optional):
- **vegetable oil**
- 1 **lemon**
- 1/3 **cup sugar (75 grams)**
- 2 **ounces (1/3 cup) shelled almonds, toasted (60 grams)**

FOR THE *ZABAIONE*:
- 5 **large egg yolks**
- 5 **tablespoons sugar (75 grams)**
- 5 **tablespoons dry Marsala (75 ml)**
- 3/4 **cup heavy cream (185 ml) plus 1/4 cup for rosettes (60 ml)**

continued

Put the mold in the freezer.

Make the chocolate ice cream. Melt the chocolate in a double boiler. Put the yolks, sugar, cocoa, and milk in a blender or a food processor fitted with the steel blade and blend until well mixed. Pour into a saucepan, add the chocolate and cream, and cook over low heat, stirring constantly, until the custard coats a metal spoon. *Do not boil.* Cool completely and process in an ice cream machine, following the manufacturer's instructions.

Remove the mold from the freezer and line the mold with chocolate ice cream, softening or freezing as necessary. Smooth the ice cream lining and push it into the curves, pressing with the back of a wooden spoon. Place in the freezer to harden for about an hour.

If you're using praline, make it at this point. Oil a marble surface or a platter and place the lemon nearby. Heat the sugar in a small, heavy saucepan and cook the sugar until it turns a golden caramel color. Add the toasted almonds and stir for a minute to coat them with caramel. Turn out onto the oiled surface and press with the lemon to flatten. When thoroughly hardened, chop coarsely. The praline will keep for weeks in an airtight container.

Make the *zabaione*. Whisk the yolks and sugar together in the top of a double boiler over barely simmering water. (Use a hand mixer if available.) Add the Marsala a tablespoon at a time. Continue whisking until the mixture is tripled in volume and thickened. Remove the top of the double boiler and set the *zabaione* in a basin of cold water, continuing to whisk until the *zabaione* is cool and very thick. Whip the cream until stiff but still soft and fold it into the yolks. Add half the praline, if you're using it, and fill the center of the chocolate ice cream with the *zabaione*. Freeze overnight.

Turn out the *spumone* onto a round platter and garnish with the remaining praline and whipped cream rosettes if desired. Soften in the refrigerator for at least 40 minutes before serving.

Picnic nel Vigneto

PICNIC IN THE VINEYARDS

**Picnic
in the
Vineyards**

Insalata Semplice di Riso
SIMPLE RICE SALAD

Polpettone con Pistacchi
VEAL LOAF WITH PISTACHIOS

Panzarotti con Ricotta
SWEET FRIED PASTRIES

WINE
White: Vigne di Gabri; serve cold

There are few trees or flowers in Marsala—the land is flat and barren, and all you can see for miles around are vines stretching into the distant horizon. This is wine country; vineyards have been cultivated here since the Greeks arrived in the eighth century B.C.

Gabriella Rallo prepared this menu for a picnic to be eaten at the height of the Sicilian spring, when the vines are full of green fruit just beginning to ripen and, although the sun is warm, there is always a refreshing breeze in the air.

Insalata Semplice di Riso
SIMPLE RICE SALAD

A simple rice salad is always the perfect standby for a summer picnic.

SERVES 6

> 1 **pound Arborio rice (450 grams)**
> 2 **tablespoons freshly squeezed lemon juice**
> 6 **tablespoons extra-virgin olive oil (100 ml)**
> 2 **teaspoons salt**
> **freshly ground pepper to taste**
> 1 **cucumber, about 1/2 pound (225 grams)**
> **coarse salt to taste**
> 1 **head of romaine lettuce, about 5 ounces**
> **(150 grams)**
> 3 **large ripe fresh tomatoes, about 1 pound**
> **(450 grams)**
> 1 **cup fresh basil leaves plus basil sprigs for garnish**

Cook the rice, uncovered, in boiling salted water to cover for 18 minutes, until *al dente,* stirring once or twice. Drain and rinse under cold water to cool. Drain and season with lemon juice, olive oil, 2 teaspoons salt, and pepper. Cover tightly and refrigerate for at least 2 hours.

Peel the cucumber and slice thinly. Layer the slices on a plate, sprinkling each layer with coarse salt. Refrigerate for about 2 hours. Pour off liquid. Do not rinse.

Shred the romaine. Peel and seed the tomatoes and slice thinly. Shred the basil.

Mix all ingredients together 1 hour before serving and taste for seasoning. Refrigerate until needed. Serve in a glass bowl garnished with basil sprigs.

Polpettone con Pistacchi

VEAL LOAF WITH PISTACHIOS

Pistachios and pine nuts add an exotic touch to this meat loaf, which is a perfect picnic dish.

SERVES 6

> 1 cup stale bread crumbs, soaked for 15 minutes in milk to cover
> 1 pound boneless veal, ground twice (450 grams)
> 1-1/2 tablespoons unsalted butter, melted (20 grams)
> 2 eggs
> 1/4 cup freshly grated Parmesan cheese (35 grams)
>   salt and freshly ground black pepper to taste
> 1 hard-cooked egg
> 1-1/2 tablespoons pine nuts (15 grams)
> 1/3 cup shelled unsalted pistachios, blanched, peeled, and lightly toasted (60 grams)
> 1/3 cup raisins, soaked in warm water until plump (60 grams)
> 5 thin slices of *pancetta,* about 1-1/2 ounces (45 grams)
> 1 tablespoon cold unsalted butter, cut into small pieces (15 grams)
> 1/3 cup dry white wine (80 ml)

Squeeze the bread crumbs tightly in your hands to remove excess milk. Mix with the meat, melted butter, raw eggs, 2 tablespoons of the Parmesan, and salt and pepper. Mix thoroughly with your hands.

Wet a work surface, preferably marble, and form a rectangle about 10 by 12 inches (26 by 30 cm) with the meat mixture, the shorter end toward you. Cut the hard-cooked egg into quarters and lay them on the shorter end 2 inches from the border. Sprinkle the pine nuts, pistachios, and raisins, drained and dried, evenly over the meat, leaving a 1-1/4-inch border all around. Sprinkle on the remaining Parmesan. Lay the slices of *pancetta* over the top, trimming to fit if necessary. Grind black pepper over the *pancetta*. Preheat the oven to 400° (200).

Dampen your hands with cold water. Starting with a short end, carefully roll up the loaf to about 11 by 2 to 2-1/2 inches (28 by 5 to 7 cm) with the help of 2 spatulas. Place a buttered ovenproof dish with low sides nearby and transfer the loaf to the dish. Dot with the cold butter. Bake for 40 minutes, uncovered, basting occasionally. Pour the wine over the loaf and cook 10 minutes longer. Cool. (The loaf usually absorbs all its liquid while cooling.)

The veal loaf should be served tepid or at room temperature. It is easier to slice, however, when completely cooled or refrigerator-cold. If you refrigerate the loaf, slice it and then allow it to come to room temperature before serving it.

Panzarotti con Ricotta
SWEET FRIED PASTRIES

Sicilians couldn't live without pastries and other sweets, and the national sweet tooth has been particularly susceptible to fried pastries ever since they were first introduced by the Arabs. These *panzarotti* would certainly be less fattening if they were baked and not fried, but there would be no comparison in taste. There is an old Latin proverb: *Semel in annum insanire licet*—once a year it is permitted to go crazy.

MAKES ABOUT 65

FOR THE FILLING:
 1 pound *ricotta* cheese, thoroughly drained (450 grams)
 1/2 cup plus 1 tablespoon sugar (125 grams)
 1/4 pound good-quality semisweet chocolate, chopped (110 grams)

FOR THE PASTRY:
 2 cups flour (225 grams)
 1/4 cup sugar (55 grams)
 3-1/2 tablespoons chilled lard (50 grams)
 1 tablespoon (or more) cold water

TO FINISH THE *PANZAROTTI:*
 peanut oil for frying, about 1-1/2 cups (375 ml)
 confectioners' sugar
 unsweetened cocoa powder

Make the filling. Sieve the *ricotta* and mix well with the sugar. Add the chocolate and refrigerate until needed.

Make the pastry. Put the flour, sugar, and lard in a food processor fitted with the steel blade. Process until crumbly. Add enough water to form a ball. Divide into 4 or 5 parts. Run through a pasta machine until very thin or roll out the pieces using a rolling pin. Cut the pastry into 3-inch rounds. (Scraps can be rerolled just once or twice to make more rounds.) Divide the filling among the pastry rounds, giving each about a heaped 1/2 teaspoon, and mounding the filling on one half of each round. Leave a border of pastry for sealing. Paint around the edges of the pastry with cold water and then fold the unfilled half of each round over the filled half, forming a half-moon shape. Press the edges with your fingers or with the tines of a fork to seal.

Heat the oil to a depth of about 1-1/2 inches (4 cm) in a sauté pan or skillet. When the oil reaches 375° (190), fry the *panzarotti* a few at a time until lightly browned, about 3 minutes, turning them once. Drain on paper towels. When cool, sift confectioners' sugar and then cocoa over the *panzarotti*. Serve at room temperature.

NOTE: Keep any leftovers in a cool place. They're particularly good served after a meal with a glass of sweet wine.

Una Cena in Famiglia a Messina

A FAMILY DINNER
IN MESSINA

A
Family
Dinner
in
Messina

Pasta con le Melanzane di Messina
PASTA WITH EGGPLANT

Pasta con Melanzane, Pomodoro, e Ricotta
PASTA WITH EGGPLANT, TOMATOES, AND RICOTTA

Pasta con Melanzane alla Napoletana
NEAPOLITAN EGGPLANT PASTA

Sarde a Beccafico alla Messinese
MESSINESE SARDINES

Pasticcio di Verdura
BAKED VEGETABLES

Pesche al Vino Rosso
PEACHES IN RED WINE

WINE
White: Taormina (Messina): serve cool

In Messina the frequent religious holidays are always occasions for elaborate celebrations and huge family meals. Violetta Speciale is Zia (Aunt) Irene's niece. Although she now lives in London, her childhood was spent in Messina, and she loves to use Sicilian recipes. Among her most vivid memories of growing up are the annual celebrations on August 15th, the Feast of the Assumption, the biggest religious holiday of the year. On Assumption Eve there is the traditional "Procession of the Giants," the "giants" being two huge equestrian statues made of wood and carried in solemn procession through the streets of Messina. One represents a Moorish prince called Grifone, the other his fair-skinned wife, Mata, who wears a tower-shaped crown. On the day of the feast there is another procession. This time the "giants" are accompanied by a huge wooden cart known as a *vara*. The cart carries a giant pyramid holding statues of angels, saints, patriarchs, and prophets. At the very top of this wobbling contraption is a representation of Jesus holding his mother's soul.

To bring back memories of this annual event and give her English friends a sampling of Messinese cooking, Violetta prepared this summer menu, typical of what would be served at a family dinner on the Feast of the Assumption. There are three variations on the pasta-with-eggplant theme; the second one, from Catania, includes *ricotta,* and the third, from Naples, is made with *mozzarella*. The choice is yours.

Pasta con le Melanzane di Messina
PASTA WITH EGGPLANT

This is almost a national dish in Sicily and southern Italy. Everyone has his or her own variation.

SERVES 4 TO 6

2 large eggplants, about 1-1/2 pounds (675 grams)
   salt
   olive oil for frying, about 1/3 cup, plus
   2 tablespoons (110 ml)
1 small onion, thinly sliced
4 pounds ripe fresh tomatoes, peeled, seeded, and
   cut into pieces (1.800 grams), *or* 2-3/4 cups
   canned Italian plum tomatoes with juice
   (750 grams)
   pinch of sugar
1 pound *rigatoni* (450 grams)
3/4 cup freshly grated Parmesan *or pecorino* cheese
   (105 grams)
   a handful of fresh basil leaves, washed, dried, and
   torn into pieces, plus basil for garnish
   freshly ground pepper to taste

Slice the eggplant lengthwise 1/3 inch thick and layer the slices in a colander, salting each layer. Put a weighted plate on top and leave for at least 1 hour. Rinse and pat dry.

Heat 1/2 inch of oil in a skillet and fry the eggplant over medium-high heat until browned. Drain on paper towels and salt lightly. When cool, break into strips with your hands. Reserve.

Make the tomato sauce. Cook the onion in a skillet over low heat with a tablespoon or 2 of water until transparent. Add the tomatoes, salt to taste, and a pinch of sugar. Simmer for 30 minutes if you're using fresh tomatoes, 20 minutes for canned tomatoes. Taste for seasoning and add 2 tablespoons oil. Reserve, but reheat before using.

Cook the pasta in boiling salted water until *al dente*. Drain and dress with the Parmesan, half the tomato sauce, half the eggplant strips, and half the basil. Mix well and turn out onto a serving platter. Pour the rest of the sauce on top and add the remaining eggplant strips and the rest of the basil. Garnish with basil and pass the pepper mill when serving.

Pasta con Melanzane, Pomodoro, e Ricotta

PASTA WITH EGGPLANT, TOMATOES, AND RICOTTA

This variation from Catania is often called *Pasta alla Norma*. As the story goes, in the 1920s a famous Sicilian actor complimented a Catanian cook on his eggplant pasta by saying that it was as good as *Norma*—an extravagant compliment since the composer Vincenzo Bellini is one of Sicily's most distinguished native sons. The name stuck, and today it regularly appears on every restaurant menu.

SERVES 4 TO 6

1   **pound eggplant, sliced lengthwise 1/4 inch thick (450 grams)**
   salt
   olive oil for frying
3   **pounds ripe fresh tomatoes, peeled, seeded, and cut into pieces (1.350 grams)**
1   **garlic clove**
   a handful of fresh basil leaves, washed and dried
1   **pound *ricotta* cheese, sieved (450 grams)**
1   **pound *pennette* or other short pasta (450 grams)**
1/3 **cup freshly grated Parmesan cheese (45 grams)**
1/3 **cup freshly grated *pecorino* cheese (45 grams)**
   freshly ground pepper

Layer the eggplant in a colander, salting each layer. Place a weighted plate on top and leave for at least an hour. Rinse and pat dry.

Fry the eggplant in an inch of hot oil in a skillet over medium-high heat until browned. Drain on paper towels and salt lightly while hot. When cool, tear into strips with your hands.

Put the tomatoes and garlic in a large frying pan and cook over medium-high heat, stirring often, for 15 minutes, mashing the tomatoes with the back of a wooden spoon. Add salt to taste and a few basil leaves, finely chopped. Remove the pan from the heat and add the *ricotta,* mixing well to make the sauce smooth.

Cook the *pennette* in boiling salted water until *al dente.* Drain and dress with the Parmesan and *pecorino.* Add the hot sauce, discarding the garlic if possible. Add the eggplant strips and toss well. Sprinkle the remaining basil over the pasta. Serve at once and pass the pepper mill.

Pasta con Melanzane alla Napoletana
NEAPOLITAN EGGPLANT PASTA

This Neapolitan variation naturally contains *mozzarella* since all the best *mozzarella* comes from Campania. The recipe gives a very simple version of this dish—for a spectacular presentation, see the variation below.

SERVES 4 TO 6

2-1/2   pounds eggplant, peeled and cut into 1/2-inch dice (1.100 grams)
         salt
         olive oil for frying, about 1 inch plus 1/4 cup
    3   pounds ripe fresh tomatoes, peeled, seeded, and cut into pieces (1.350 grams)
         a large handful of fresh basil leaves, washed and dried
    1   pound short pasta, such as *rigatoni or penne* (450 grams)
   14   ounces *mozzarella* cheese, diced (about 3 cups) (400 grams)
         freshly ground pepper

Layer the eggplant in a colander, salting each layer. Place a weighted plate on top and leave for an hour. Rinse and pat dry.

Fry the eggplant in an inch of hot oil in a skillet over medium-high heat until lightly browned. Drain on paper towels and salt lightly while hot.

Heat the 1/4 cup olive oil in a skillet and add the tomatoes. Cook over medium-high heat, stirring often, for 15 minutes, mashing the tomatoes with the back of a wooden spoon. Add 5 or 6 basil leaves and salt to taste. Reserve, but reheat before using.

Cook the pasta in boiling salted water until *al dente*. Drain and dress with the tomato sauce, the eggplant, and the *mozzarella*, tossing to mix thoroughly. Put into the serving dish and rapidly (to prevent the cheese from hardening) cover the pasta with basil leaves. Serve at once. Pass the pepper mill, but do not serve extra cheese with this pasta.

VARIATION: Instead of adding the *mozzarella* to the pasta, slice it thinly and prepare the pasta as directed. Mound it in a pyramid in an ovenproof dish or platter, possibly a *gratin* dish with low sides. Rapidly (to keep final cooking time short) place the *mozzarella* slices on the crown of the pasta and put the pasta in a preheated 450° (240) oven just until the *mozzarella* melts and runs. This is very dramatic and can be garnished quickly at the base with basil leaves.

Sarde a Beccafico alla Messinese
MESSINESE SARDINES

Plump fresh sardines are available year-round in Sicily (although most native Sicilians will tell you they taste best in the spring), so *sarde a beccafico* is a very common dish. A *beccafico* is a plump Sicilian songbird known to have a liking for figs, and usually *sarde a beccafico* means stuffed sardines, plump like the little birds, but not in Messina. Here, instead of being actually stuffed, the fish are coated with the stuffing mixture and then fried in olive oil. Delicious!

SERVES 4

2	pounds fresh sardines (900 grams)
2	tablespoons freshly squeezed lemon juice
	grated zest of 1 lemon
1/4	cup finely chopped parsley
1	garlic clove, finely minced
6	tablespoons fine dry bread crumbs
5	tablespoons freshly grated *pecorino* cheese (45 grams)
2	large eggs
	salt and freshly ground pepper to taste
1/2	cup (or more) olive oil (125 ml)
	lemon wedges for serving (optional)

Clean the sardines (see page 419) or have the fishmonger clean them. Rinse them in cold water and drain well. Pour the lemon juice over them and set aside while you prepare the rest of the recipe.

In a large plate, mix together the lemon zest, parsley, garlic, bread crumbs, and *pecorino*. In another bowl, beat the eggs with salt and pepper.

Dry the fish with paper towels and dip first in the beaten eggs and then in the bread crumbs, pressing to make the crumbs adhere. Prepare all the fish in this way and place on plates.

Heat the olive oil to a depth of 1 inch in a skillet, iron if possible, until hot but not smoking. Fry the fish in batches over medium-high heat for about 1 minute or until lightly browned, turn them gently, and fry for 50 to 60 seconds or until lightly browned. Drain on paper towels and serve very hot with lemon wedges if desired.

Pasticcio di Verdura
BAKED VEGETABLES

There is an old Sicilian saying, *di necessitá fai vertú* (of necessity make a virtue), and this certainly applies to the seemingly limitless variety of vegetable dishes eaten in Sicily. Meat is expensive, and Sicily's hot climate makes it easier to grow vegetables than to raise meat. Nearly every Sicilian vegetable recipe, regardless of what vegetable is used, is flavored with anchovies. Just as the trademark of Roman cooking is mint, so the sharp tang of the anchovy is characteristic of Sicilian cuisine. Make the *pasticcio* the day before you plan to serve it for best flavor.

SERVES 4 TO 6

9- by 13½-inch (23 by 34 cm) ovenproof glass dish, oiled

1-1/2	pounds eggplant, peeled and sliced crosswise, about 1/4 inch thick (700 grams)
2	garlic cloves, minced
	a large handful of parsley, finely chopped
1	large white onion or 2 medium, very thinly sliced
	salt and freshly ground pepper to taste
1/2	cup olive oil (125 ml)
1	pound yellow bell peppers, seeded and cut into 1/2-inch strips (450 grams)
3	large ripe fresh tomatoes, peeled, seeded, and thinly sliced
4	salt-packed anchovies, cleaned (see page 419) and cut into pieces, *or* 8 oil-packed anchovy fillets, drained and cut into pieces
1	cup green Sicilian olives, pitted and cut into pieces (200 grams)

Layer the eggplant in a colander, salting each layer. Put a weighted plate on top and leave for at least 1 hour. Rinse and squeeze dry.

Preheat the oven to 350° (180).

In a small bowl, mix together the garlic, parsley, onion, salt, pepper, and half the oil.

Put half the eggplant slices on the bottom of the prepared dish. Add salt and pepper and sprinkle on a little of the onion mixture. Layer half the peppers over this, add salt and pepper, and sprinkle on a little of the onion mixture. Add half the tomatoes, more salt and pepper, and sprinkle a few onions over the tomatoes. Strew on half the anchovies and half the olives. Repeat with the remaining vegetables, reserving enough onions to sprinkle all over the top of the *pasticcio*. Trickle the rest of the oil over the top.

Bake for 1 hour and 10 minutes. This is served hot or cold.

Pesche al Vino Rosso
PEACHES IN RED WINE

A wonderful, simple summer dessert that is particularly delicious with vanilla ice cream.

SERVES 4

4	large ripe yellow peaches
1-1/2	cups red wine (375 ml)
3	tablespoons freshly squeezed lemon juice
2	tablespoons (or to taste) sugar
1	clove
	a 1-inch strip of orange zest (optional)

Peel the peaches and cut in half. Discard the pits. Mix together the wine, lemon juice, and sugar and pour over the peaches. Add the clove, plus the orange peel if you're using it. Refrigerate for at least 1-1/2 hours before serving, removing the clove and orange peel.

Cena a Casa Tasca

DINNER AT CASA TASCA

Dinner
at
Casa
Tasca

Pasta con Ragù e Ricotta
PASTA WITH RAGOUT AND RICOTTA

Tonno con Capperi
FRESH TUNA WITH CAPERS

Frittedda
ARTICHOKES, FAVA BEANS, AND GARDEN PEAS

Melone al Marsala
MELON WITH MARSALA

WINES
White: Regaleali Bianco; serve cold
Red: Riserva del Conte; serve at cool room temperature

The ancestors of Count Giuseppe Tasca acquired the fiefdom of Regaleali in the Sclafani countryside near Palermo in 1830. The property boasts an extraordinary garden filled with bougainvillea vines, luxuriant magnolias, and tall cedar trees. There are 75 acres of walled vineyards, and over the years wine making has become the family's principal activity. Today it is a big business, and Tasca wines have an international reputation.

The present Count Tasca is in his late seventies but is still actively involved in the wine business, aided by his children and several of his grand-children. Countess Tasca is well known for her hospitality and for her knowledge of food, and the Tascas are one of the few remaining Sicilian families who still have their own *monzù*, Mario Lo Menzo. At the age of 18 he was apprenticed to the Tascas' previous *monzù*, Giovanni Messina, a legendary chef who had learned his craft during La Belle Époque and was by then in his eighties. Carrying on the noble tradition of his predecessor with a remarkable flair, Mario has been with the Tasca family for more than 40 years and now displays his cooking skills for a few select groups of cooking enthusiasts who combine a stay at Regaleali with a short cooking course. The count's three daughters run the school, and they share their parents' passion for the baronial cuisine so brilliantly executed by Mario.

Pasta con Ragù e Ricotta

PASTA WITH RAGOUT
AND RICOTTA

Fresh *ricotta,* made the same day at Regaleali, is the perfect complement to this hot ragout–sauced pasta.

*Dinner
at
Casa
Tasca*

SERVES 8

FOR THE *RAGÙ:*

1/4	cup olive oil (60 ml)
1	large onion, finely chopped
2	garlic cloves, finely chopped
4	hot sausages, about 9 ounces (250 grams)
1/2	pound ground pork (225 grams)
1/2	pound ground veal (225 grams)
1/2	cup dry red wine (125 ml)
	salt and freshly ground pepper to taste
	freshly grated nutmeg to taste
3	cloves
2	tablespoons tomato paste
1	quart tomato puree (1.100 grams)
3/4	teaspoon sugar

FOR THE PASTA:

1-1/2	pounds pasta, long or short (675 grams)
1	cup freshly grated *pecorino* cheese (135 grams)
1/2	pound *ricotta* cheese, sliced or crumbled (225 grams)

Make the *ragù*. Heat the oil in a saucepan, preferably terra-cotta, and in it sauté the onion and garlic over low heat until the onion is transparent, about 20 minutes. Remove the casings from the sausages and cut into pieces. Add the sausages to the onion and sauté for 3 or 4 minutes. Add the pork and veal and sauté until lightly colored and no longer pink. Add the red wine and cook for 6 to 7 minutes, until almost all the wine has evaporated. Season with salt, pepper, and nutmeg.

Add the cloves, tomato paste, tomato puree, and sugar. Mix well and cover the pan. Simmer very slowly for 3 hours, stirring occasionally and adding water or chicken or meat broth if the sauce thickens too much. Watch the sauce closely and stir more often during the last hour. Reserve. Reheat before using the sauce. (This sauce also freezes well.)

Cook the pasta in boiling salted water until *al dente*. Drain and dress with the *pecorino*. Pour two thirds of the sauce over the pasta, mix well, and pour onto a serving platter. Spoon the remaining sauce over the pasta and mound the *ricotta* over the pasta. Grind black pepper over the *ricotta* and serve hot.

Tonno con Capperi
FRESH TUNA WITH CAPERS

Throughout the south of Italy the fish markets are filled with fresh red tuna. In this recipe the tuna is lightly cooked in a skillet, piled high with capers, and served on a large platter. It looks spectacular and has a very delicate taste. The tuna can also be served cold the next day.

SERVES 8

13-inch (33 cm) skillet

1/2	**pound (1-1/3 cups) salt-packed capers, small Sicilian capers if possible (225 grams)**
1/2	**cup (1/4 pound) unsalted butter (110 grams)**
1-1/2	**tablespoons olive oil**
1	**3-1/2- to 4-pound wheel (crosswise-sliced steak) of tuna *or* swordfish (1.600 to 1.800 grams)**
7	**tablespoons white wine vinegar (110 ml)**

Rinse the capers thoroughly in cold water. Soak in cold water for an hour. Drain, rinse, and pat dry.

Heat the butter and oil in the skillet. Cook the fish on one side over moderate heat for 15 minutes. Then turn with care, using large spatulas. Cook on this side for 10 minutes. Add the capers and vinegar, cover, and simmer for 5 minutes. Remove the lid and simmer for another 5 or more minutes. The fish should look opaque when a fork is inserted near the bone. Serve on a heated round platter with the capers piled on top. The fish is also delicious at room temperature.

Frittedda
ARTICHOKES, FAVA BEANS, AND GARDEN PEAS

This dish—artichokes, fresh fava beans, and new peas gently cooked in olive oil—is much loved by Sicilians and thought to have ancient origins. There is no literal translation, a point of pride among the Sicilians. One recent Sicilian cookbook insists that this is a purely Sicilian dish and that there is no equivalent of *frittedda* on the mainland. But in fact *frittedda* is eaten all the way up to Rome. Using sugar and vinegar, however, is a strictly Sicilian touch. In Naples (see the variation below) *pancetta* is used, but no sugar or vinegar. Cook the dish the day before you plan to serve it.

SERVES 8

6	artichokes
1	lemon, cut in half
1/2	cup olive oil (125 ml)
3	scallions, thinly sliced
1	cup hot water (250 ml)
3	pounds fava beans, shelled (1.350 grams)
3	pounds fresh peas (1.350 grams)
1-1/2	teaspoons (or to taste) salt
1/4	teaspoon (or to taste) freshly ground black pepper
2	tablespoons white wine vinegar
	pinch of sugar

Prepare the artichokes (see page 420) and rub with lemon. Cut each artichoke into 6 pieces and put back in the cold water with the lemon halves until needed.

continued

Heat the oil and sauté the scallions over low heat until transparent. Drain the artichokes and add with 1/2 cup of the hot water. Bring to a boil and cook over medium heat for 2 minutes. Add the fava beans and the rest of the hot water and cook for 2 minutes over medium heat.

Add the peas, lower the heat, cover the pan, and simmer the vegetables for about 20 minutes or until tender, stirring occasionally. Season with salt and pepper, add the vinegar and sugar, and cook for 5 minutes, uncovered, stirring often. Refrigerate overnight and serve at cool room temperature.

NEAPOLITAN VARIATION: Using the same amounts of artichokes, fava beans, peas, scallions, salt, pepper, and hot water, prepare the vegetables as directed. Then heat 3 tablespoons olive oil and add the scallions and 6 ounces (170 grams) *pancetta,* diced. Cook over low heat until the onion is transparent and the *pancetta* is lightly browned. Add the artichokes and 1/2 cup hot water and cook for 2 minutes over medium heat. Add the fava beans and the rest of the water and cook for 2 more minutes.

Add the peas, cover, and bring the vegetables to a simmer. Simmer for about 25 minutes or until tender, stirring now and then. Add salt and pepper at the end of the cooking time. Serve as directed.

Melone al Marsala
MELON WITH MARSALA

Marsala is Sicily's best-known wine and is frequently used in the preparation of traditional Sicilian dishes—*zabaione* is the most famous. Marsala came into existence almost by accident. In the 17th century, when large quantities of Sicilian wine were being shipped to England, one part alcohol was added to 50 parts wine to fortify it for the long journey. Inevitably the wine casks were jogged, sloshed, and buffeted in the course of the voyage, and somehow this rough treatment helped to produce a wine with a most agreeable richness and smoothness. The English have always enjoyed fortified wine, and by the 17th century port, sherry, and Madeira were already highly valued imports. It was not for another century, however, that anyone decided to develop and commercially produce this Sicilian discovery. The Englishman who did so was John Woodhouse. In 1733 he went to Sicily, began to experiment with methods of production, and made the town of Marsala famous the world over for its wines.

In this recipe melon balls are sprinkled with sugar and allowed to soak in the Marsala before being served in cantaloupe halves. One large cantaloupe will serve three people.

1	or more large cantaloupes
1-1/2	cups Marsala for each melon (375 ml)
2	tablespoons sugar for each melon (30 grams)

Cut the cantaloupes in half. Remove and discard seeds and strings. With a melon baller, make little balls and put them in a bowl. Sprinkle the sugar over them and pour the Marsala over the melon. Put the melon balls back into the melon halves and refrigerate until ready to serve.

Una Colazione del Sabato al Palazzo

A SATURDAY LUNCH
AT THE PALAZZO

Torta Rustica
A COUNTRY PIE

Vitello Siciliano
SICILIAN VEAL

Pomodori al Forno
BAKED TOMATOES

Dolce Splendido di Pistacchi e Biancomangiare
SPLENDID PISTACHIO BLANCMANGE

WINES
Red: Cerasuolo di Mazzarino; serve cool
Dessert: Passito di Pantelleria DOC
or Mareate Passito di Pantelleria DOC; serve cool

Signorina Anzon lived her whole life in the same house, a 17th-century *palazzo* near the Chiesa della Casa Professa in Palermo, which had belonged to her family for many generations. Everything in the house, though polished and impeccably cared for, looked as if it had been set in place in the 1850s and never touched. The electrical cords were still covered in silk, and there were porcelain bellpulls to summon the maids.

After her sister's death many years ago Signorina Anzon continued to live in the house with her three maids—Vincella, Vitina, and Vicia—and even when she was very old she loved to entertain. But since two of the maids were her exact contemporaries, it is questionable how much real assistance they were still able to provide. So she reluctantly called a halt to her dinner parties, which were renowned throughout Palermo, and chose instead to receive her guests for lunch on Saturday or for tea during the week. Even then an invitation to her table was always much sought after.

In spite of having had help in the kitchen all her life, Signorina Anzon was an enthusiastic and accomplished cook and an avid collector of recipes. In addition to her "everyday" recipe book, she also had a trunkful of recipes, collected over the years, that she kept tucked away in a large closet. All of the recipes in the next three menus, with the exception of *Carciofi con la Salsa di San Bernardo,* come from her collection.

Torta Rustica
A COUNTRY PIE

Elaborate savory pies filled with all kinds of meats, cheeses, vegetables, herbs, and spices and baked in pastry crusts are unheard of in the dining rooms of northern Italy, but they are a venerable tradition in the South. These pies are a particular favorite for parties since they can feed a lot of people. In *The Leopard* Lampedusa provides a memorable description of the arrival of a procession of such pies at a grand banquet dinner:

> *Good manners apart, though, the appearance of those monumental dishes . . . was worthy of the quivers of admiration they evoked. The burnished gold of the crusts, the fragrance of sugar and cinnamon they exuded, were but preludes to the delights released from the interior when the knife broke the crust; first came a smoke laden with aromas, then chicken livers, hard-boiled eggs, sliced ham, chicken, and truffles in masses of piping-hot, glistening maccheroni, to which the meat juice gave an exquisite hue of suede.*

> *The Leopard*,
> trans. ARCHIBALD COLQUHOUN

*A
Saturday
Lunch
at
the
Palazzo*

SERVES 10 TO 12

9-inch (23 cm)
springform pan,
buttered and
floured

FOR THE FILLING:

- 1 pound *ricotta* cheese (450 grams)
- 1 cup freshly grated Parmesan cheese (135 grams)
- 2 ounces Gruyère cheese, cut into small dice (1/2 cup) (60 grams)

1/4   pound *provolone dolce* (see page 425), cut into
      small dice (3/4 cup) (110 grams)
1/4   pound *provolone piccante* (see page 425), cut into
      small dice (3/4 cup) (110 grams)
1/2   pound *mozzarella* cheese, cut into small dice
      (about 2 cups) (225 grams)
  5   ounces boiled ham, chopped (1-1/4 cups)
      (150 grams)
1/4   pound *salame*, chopped (1 scant cup) (110 grams)
      freshly ground black pepper
      salt to taste (optional)
  4   large eggs

FOR THE CRUST:
3-1/2   cups flour (400 grams)
  2/3   cup sugar (150 grams)
  1/2   cup (1/4 pound) plus 1 tablespoon cold unsalted
        butter, cut into pieces (125 grams)
    5   tablespoons cold lard, cut into pieces (75 grams)
    1   egg
    2   tablespoons (or more) dry white wine

    1   egg yolk beaten with 1 tablespoon water

Make the filling. In a large bowl, work the *ricotta* with a wooden spoon until soft. Add the rest of the filling ingredients in the order listed. Refrigerate the filling while you prepare the crust.

Make the crust. By hand or in a food processor or an electric mixer, rapidly mix together the flour, sugar, butter, lard, egg, and enough wine to hold the dough together. Form one third of the dough into a ball and refrigerate it. Preheat the oven to 375° (190).

Lightly flour a work surface and roll out the rest of the dough to about 16 inches (40 cm). Fit the bottom crust into the pan and trim the excess pastry. Fill the crust with the filling, smoothing it with a spoon.

continued

Roll out the top crust to about an 11-inch diameter (28 cm) so that you have a 1-inch overhang. Fit the crust over the filling and trim if necessary. Roll this overhang under to form an edge, sealing it to the bottom crust. Crimp decoratively and paint the *torta* with the egg yolk. If desired, decorate with pastry leaves or other designs made with the trimmings.

Bake for about 50 minutes. If the edges brown too rapidly, cover loosely with foil. Cool on a rack for 15 minutes. Remove the sides of the pan and then replace them until the *torta* has cooled. Serve tepid or at room temperature. Fillings may be varied as desired. Sprigs of parsley are a pretty addition.

NOTE: You'll undoubtedly have leftover *torta rustica*—it's wonderful served at room temperature for lunch, with a salad alongside. Or slice it thinly and serve with drinks.

Vitello Siciliano
SICILIAN VEAL

In this recipe the veal is stuffed with a mixture of spinach, pine nuts, cheese, and eggs. Then it is rolled, roasted, and served sliced on a bed of orange slices. The oranges are not just for decoration—they impart to the meat a very particular taste and piquant moistness.

SERVES 4 TO 6

Kitchen string and needle

	a large slice of boneless veal from the leg, about 1 pound 14 ounces, pounded as thin as possible (850 grams)
3/4	pound spinach *or* Swiss chard, cooked, drained, excess water squeezed out, and chopped (330 grams)
1/2	cup raisins, soaked in warm water until plump, drained, and chopped (80 grams)
1/3	cup plus 1 tablespoon pine nuts, chopped (65 grams)
2	ounces *caciocavallo* cheese, grated (about 1/2 cup) (60 grams)
1	hard-cooked egg, chopped
2	eggs
2	tablespoons finely chopped parsley
1/2	garlic clove, finely chopped salt and freshly ground pepper to taste
1/4	cup olive oil (60 ml)
3/4	cup Marsala (185 ml)
3/4	cup dry red wine (185 ml)
2	or 3 oranges, preferably organic parsley sprigs for garnish

Lay the veal slice on a work surface and with a meat pounder pound it as thin as possible without tearing. Mix together the spinach, raisins, pine

continued

nuts, *caciocavallo,* hard-cooked egg, raw eggs, parsley, garlic, and salt and pepper. Spread the mixture down the middle of the meat, leaving a wide border. Fold the edges over toward the center and roll up the entire slice of meat like a *salame*, being careful not to let the filling escape. Tie the roast and sew up the edges. Preheat the oven to 400° (200).

Put 1 tablespoon oil in a shallow ovenproof glass dish or a *gratin* dish with low sides. Place the veal in the pan and pour the rest of the oil over the meat. Cook the veal for 1-1/2 hours, alternating pouring Marsala and wine over it every 20 minutes, basting the meat with its juices. Turn the meat once. At the end of the cooking time the meat should be richly colored and have abundant sauce. Cool the roast completely.

When you're ready to serve, wash and dry the oranges. Slice thinly, removing any seeds.* Remove the meat from the sauce and slice the cold meat thinly. Make a bed of orange slices on a platter. Put a layer of meat on top of the oranges. Decorate the dish with orange slices and parsley. Heat the sauce and serve with the meat. The meat should be at room temperature and the sauce very hot.

---

* If you think the oranges may have been heavily sprayed or colored, peel them and slice after peeling. Do this at the last minute.

Pomodori al Forno
BAKED TOMATOES

These baked tomatoes are excellent with any kind of roast meat, and they can be served either hot or at room temperature.

MAKES ABOUT 6

Ovenproof dish large enough
to hold tomatoes snugly, oiled

2	pounds (about 6) tomatoes (900 grams)
1/2	cup freshly grated *pecorino* cheese (65 grams)
1	(or more to taste) garlic cloves, finely chopped
5	tablespoons finely chopped parsley
5	tablespoons finely chopped fresh basil
6	oil-packed anchovy fillets, drained and finely chopped, *or* 1 tablespoon anchovy paste
	salt and freshly ground black pepper to taste
1/3	cup olive oil (80 ml)
1	tablespoon fine dry bread crumbs

Preheat the oven to 350° (180). Wash and dry the tomatoes. Cut off about 1/2 inch from the stem end of the tomato and discard. With a sharp knife, remove all the green stem part. Turn the tomatoes cut sides down on a rack to drain while you prepare the filling.

Mix together the *pecorino,* garlic, parsley, basil, and anchovies. Season with salt and pepper and add 3 tablespoons oil. Mix well.

Place the tomatoes in an ovenproof dish in which they fit snugly. Divide the filling among the tomatoes, covering the tops completely. Sprinkle the bread crumbs over the filling and trickle the remaining oil over the crumbs. Bake for 1 hour. Serve hot or at room temperature.

Dolce Splendido di Pistacchi e Biancomangiare
SPLENDID PISTACHIO BLANCMANGE

Signorina Anzon was particularly proud of this recipe, which in Sicily is sometimes called a "triumph of gluttony." Upon first seeing this exquisite blancmange, elaborately decorated with pistachios in the shape of flowers and served on a rare porcelain platter, her guests would always gasp in admiration and appreciation. Sicilian pistachios are considered the best in Europe. Signorina Anzon liked to offer her guests a glass of *Passito di Pantelleria* with this dessert.

SERVES 8

Shallow 2-quart dish or
platter with a rim, concave
part 13 by 8 inches
(33 by 20 cm)

> 1/2   **pound shelled unsalted pistachios (225 grams)**
> 1   **cup sugar, superfine if possible (225 grams)**
> 1-1/3   **cups citron, soft, not dry (225 grams)**
>   **slices of *pan di Spagna* (page 139) to line the dish**
>   **shelled unsalted pistachios for garnish**

FOR THE *BIANCOMANGIARE* (BLANCMANGE):

> 1   **quart milk (1 liter)**
>   **peel of 1 medium-large lemon**
> 1   **cup sugar (225 grams)**
> 1   **cinnamon stick, about 2 inches (5 cm)**
> 1/2   **cup plus 2 tablespoons wheat starch *or* cornstarch (75 grams)**

Put the pistachios in boiling water for a minute, drain, and remove the skins. Pass the pistachios and sugar through a food mill, using the disk with the largest holes. Chop the citron finely and add it to the pistachios.

Line the dish or platter with thin slices of *pan di Spagna.* Spoon the pistachio mixture over it, leveling with a spatula. Cover tightly while you prepare the blancmange.

Make the blancmange. Pour 3 cups of the milk into a heavy saucepan and add the lemon peel, sugar, and cinnamon stick. Dissolve the wheat starch or cornstarch in the remaining milk and pass it through a sieve into the saucepan. Bring slowly to a simmer, stirring constantly, and simmer for 2 minutes.

Discard the peel and cinnamon and spoon the blancmange over the pistachio mixture. Decorate the top of the dish with pistachios made into flowers. Refrigerate until needed, covered. Serve cool but not cold.

Il Compleanno della Signorina Anzon

SIGNORINA ANZON'S BIRTHDAY LUNCH

Carciofi con la Salsa di San Bernardo
ARTICHOKES WITH SAINT BERNARD SAUCE

Pasticcio di Pollo con Mandorle e Pistacchi
CHICKEN PIE WITH ALMONDS AND PISTACHIOS

Insalata Verde
GREEN SALAD

La Cassata della Signorina Anzon
SIGNORINA ANZON'S CASSATA

WINES
White: Alcamo DOC; serve cold
Dessert: **Marsala Vergine Diego Rallo DOC**; serve cool

This menu, assembled by Signorina Anzon, is typical of what she would serve at a luncheon celebrating her birthday.

Signorina Anzon liked to entertain at lunch on Saturdays. First there would be aperitifs in one of her smaller drawing rooms—only a glass of white wine, to preserve your appetite. With her soft voice and gentle ways, she presided over lunch in the formal dining room. Coffee was served on a beautiful small terrace overlooking Casa Professa, the first church built by the Jesuits in Palermo.

Carciofi con la Salsa di San Bernardo
ARTICHOKES WITH SAINT BERNARD SAUCE

Artichokes are grown all over Italy, but the *spinelli* variety, which has a very sweet flavor, is found only in Sicily. It is small and pointed, with a silvery gray color. Try to find small artichokes for this recipe—the artichokes are marinated in a richly aromatic sauce of almonds, anchovies, and honey. The variation on the *San Bernardo* sauce includes an even more exotic taste—cocoa.

SERVES 6

6	artichokes
1	tablespoon freshly squeezed lemon juice
	salt to taste
1/4	cup olive oil (60 ml)
2/3	cup diced dry bread
1/3	cup peeled almonds (60 grams)
1-1/2	tablespoons (or more to taste) honey
1/4	cup (or more) white wine vinegar (60 ml)
2	tablespoons plus 2 teaspoons anchovy paste
	freshly ground black pepper to taste

Clean the artichokes (see page 420), removing the stems. Cook in boiling water with the lemon juice and salt until tender—15 to 25 minutes, depending on the size of the artichokes. Drain, cut side down, on paper towels.

Make the sauce. Heat 2 tablespoons of the oil in a small, heavy frying pan and fry the bread over medium heat until golden brown. Drain on paper towels. In the same oil, fry the almonds until browned and drain on paper

continued

towels. Cool and pulverize the bread and almonds in a food processor fitted with the steel blade or in a blender in batches.

Put the bread and almonds into a bowl and add the honey, mixing. Add the vinegar a tablespoon at a time. Dissolve the anchovy paste in the remaining oil and add slowly. When all has been amalgamated, season with pepper and more vinegar if desired.

Cut the artichokes carefully into 2 or 4 pieces, depending on size. Spread the sauce over the cut parts of the artichokes and re-form the artichokes; place on a serving platter, stem parts up. If there is any sauce remaining, spread it over the stem parts. Leave at room temperature until serving time.

VARIATION OF THE *SALSA DI SAN BERNARDO*

1/2	**cup finely chopped almonds (80 grams)**
8	**oil-packed anchovy fillets, drained and finely chopped**
1	**tablespoon unsweetened cocoa powder**
3	**tablespoons sugar (45 grams)**
1/2	**cup dry bread crumbs**
	white wine vinegar as needed

Mix together the almonds, anchovies, cocoa, and sugar. Add the bread crumbs and, beating with a fork, add enough vinegar to form a spreadable sauce. Taste for seasoning and heat in a double boiler before pouring it over the boiled and quartered artichokes.

Signorina Anzon's Birthday Lunch

Pasticcio di Pollo con Mandorle e Pistacchi
CHICKEN PIE WITH ALMONDS AND PISTACHIOS

Here is another of Signorina Anzon's beloved pies. No ham or cheese in this one—just a delectable combination of chicken, nuts, and capers.

SERVES 6

8-inch (20 cm) springform
pan, buttered and floured

FOR THE FILLING:
- 3 tablespoons olive oil
- 1 chicken, about 2-2/3 pounds (1.200 grams)
- 2 cups broth, approximately (500 ml)
- 2 ounces (heaped 1/3 cup) shelled unsalted pistachios, peeled (60 grams)
- 2 ounces (heaped 1/3 cup) shelled almonds, peeled (60 grams)
- 2 cups fresh bread crumbs
- 2 eggs
- 1/4 cup finely chopped parsley
- 1-1/2 tablespoons capers, rinsed and patted dry
- 1/4 cup freshly squeezed lemon juice (60 ml)
  freshly ground black pepper and salt to taste

FOR THE CRUST:
- 2-2/3 cups flour (300 grams)
- 5 tablespoons sugar (70 grams)
- 6 tablespoons cold unsalted butter, cut into pieces (90 grams)

continued

1/4 **cup cold lard, cut into pieces (60 grams)**
1 **egg**
1 **tablespoon (or more as needed) dry white wine**

1 **egg yolk beaten with 1 tablespoon water**

Make the filling. Heat the oil in a saucepan into which the chicken fits snugly. Brown the chicken over moderate heat, turning it to brown it evenly, keeping the pot covered. This will take 15 to 20 minutes.

Add 1/2 cup broth and continue cooking the chicken over low heat, covered, turning it every 15 minutes. Add broth as necessary when it has thickened or been absorbed. When the chicken is done and the meat falls from the bones, leave it in the pan to cool.

When the chicken has cooled, discard the skin and bones and shred the meat coarsely. Pour the sauce and meat into a bowl and reserve. (There should be about 6 tablespoons thick sauce.)

While the chicken is cooling, prepare the rest of the filling.

Toast the pistachios lightly and chop coarsely. Toast the almonds until light brown and chop coarsely. Soak the bread crumbs in 1 cup broth. Add the nuts, bread crumbs, eggs, parsley, capers, lemon juice, and freshly ground black pepper to the chicken. Mix well and taste for salt. Reserve. Preheat the oven to 375° (190).

Make the crust. Put the flour, sugar, butter, lard, and egg in a large bowl. Add enough white wine to make a pastry that is not too damp or crumbly. (Or use an electric mixer with the paddle attachment or food processor fitted with the steel blade.) Refrigerate one third of the pastry and roll out the larger part to form a circle large enough to line the pan. Drape it over the rolling pin and unroll it over the pan. Cut away the extra pastry, leaving a 1/2-inch overhang.

Spoon the filling into the crust and roll out the remaining pastry in a circle to cover the *pasticcio*. Drape the top crust over the rolling pin and unfold it over the filling. Trim the crust, leaving a 1/2-inch overhang. Roll the overhang under to seal the crust edge and crimp decoratively. Make a hole in the center and decorate the *pasticcio* with pastry leaves or other shapes, cut from the trimmings, if desired. Paint the crust with the beaten egg yolk.

Bake for 50 minutes or until browned. Cool for 15 minutes before removing the sides. Cool for 10 minutes more before serving. This is usually served hot.

Insalata Verde
GREEN SALAD

SERVES 6

1 **pound mixed greens, preferably field greens
(450 grams)
salt and freshly ground pepper to taste**
5 **to 6 tablespoons extra-virgin olive oil
(75 to 100 ml)**
2 **tablespoons freshly squeezed lemon juice**

Clean the greens, removing tough leaves and trimming the stems. Wash several times in cold water. Drain and then dry in a salad spinner or tie in a kitchen towel and swing it vigorously back and forth to remove the water. Refrigerate in the damp cloth until needed.

When you're ready to serve the salad, put salt and pepper in a small bowl. Pour the olive oil over and beat with a fork. Add the lemon juice. Put the greens in a serving bowl and pour the dressing over them. Toss well and serve at once.

La Cassata della Signorina Anzon
SIGNORINA ANZON'S CASSATA

Signorina Anzon's Birthday Lunch

Cassata, an elaborate concoction of sponge cake combined with a rich cream of *ricotta* cheese and chocolate, iced and decorated with candied fruit, is *the* Sicilian dessert for Christmas, Easter, and all other important occasions. It is also the most famous Sicilian dessert to have an Arab name—*cassata* comes directly from the Arabic word *qas'ah,* meaning a round bowl or pan—and was first introduced to Sicily by the Arabs. *Cassata* is nothing less than a national obsession—during a time of famine in 1575 there was great consternation when a public decree was issued forbidding *cassata* and announcing that anyone found preparing it would be severely punished.

Signorina Anzon was famous throughout the region for her *cassata* and took immense care with its preparation. The differences between her recipe and dozens of others are small but extremely significant—this is an extraordinary *cassata.* Two days ahead of time she would make the cake (*pan di Spagna*) and the *ricotta* filling, allowing the vanilla and the chocolate to blend fully with the cheese. The next day she would assemble it in a traditional round *cassata* pan with sloping sides, place a round marble weight on top, and store it overnight in a cool place. (A *cassata* is easier to slice if it is a day old.) The final decoration of the *cassata* would be done at the last minute: swirls of angelica, slivers of candied orange, citron, and candied cherries would be arranged around the side and a small candied tangerine placed in the center. The final effect was a masterpiece of baroque elegance.

SERVES 10 TO 12

9-inch cake pan with 2-inch-
high sides (24 by 6 cm),
lined with plastic wrap

FOR THE *PAN DI SPAGNA* (ITALIAN SPONGE CAKE):
- **4 eggs, separated**
- **2/3 cup sugar (150 grams)**
  grated zest of 1 small lemon
- **7/8 cup cake flour (100 grams)**

FOR THE FILLING:
- **2 pounds best-quality *ricotta* cheese (900 grams)**
- **2 cups sugar (400 grams)**
- **1/2 teaspoon vanilla extract**
- **1 scant cup (1/4 pound) good-quality chopped semisweet chocolate (110 grams)**
- **3/4 cup (1/4 pound) *zuccata or* citron, cut into tiny dice (120 grams)**
- **1/3 cup candied orange peel, cut into tiny dice (60 grams)**

FOR THE ICING:
- **1 cup sugar (225 grams)**
- **6 tablespoons water (100 ml)**
- **2 tablespoons freshly squeezed lemon juice**

  candied fruit for decoration: citron, angelica, cherries, a tangerine, orange and lemon peel, etc.

Make the *pan di Spagna*. Butter and flour an 8-inch (20 cm) square cake pan. Preheat the oven to 325° (160). Beat the egg yolks and sugar together until thick and lemon-colored. Add the lemon zest. Whip the egg whites until stiff but not dry and fold them into the yolks. Sift the flour over the mixture and fold it in carefully. Pour the batter into the prepared pan. Bake for 45 to 50 minutes or until a straw inserted in the middle comes

continued

out clean. Cool on a rack for 10 minutes, turn out, and cool completely before using—it's best the next day.

Make the filling. Sieve the *ricotta* and, using a wooden spoon, mix it with the sugar until creamy. Cover and refrigerate overnight. When you're ready to use it, add the vanilla, chocolate, *zuccata* or citron, and orange peel.

Slice the *pan di Spagna* thinly and line the bottom and sides of the prepared pan. Spoon in half the *ricotta* mixture. Put strips of cake over the filling. Spoon in the rest of the *ricotta* and cover with more strips of cake. Reserve the remaining crumbs, even if few. Put a round of cardboard over the *cassata* and put a weight of about 2 pounds on top. Cover and refrigerate, weight and all, overnight.

Make the icing when you're ready to finish the cake. In a small saucepan, mix together the sugar and water and, stirring occasionally, allow it to come to a simmer. Simmer for 15 to 20 minutes or until the liquid no longer smokes but makes large bubbles. (If you put a drop in a saucer and take it between your fingers, it will stick to your fingers.) Remove from the heat and add the lemon juice. Beat the mixture with a wooden spoon (or a hand mixer) until white and spreadable. Use the icing at once, adding a little water if necessary to keep the icing fluid.

To finish the *cassata,* turn it out onto a serving plate and remove the plastic wrap. Cover it with the icing using a small spatula. In a blender or a food processor fitted with the steel blade, pulverize the remaining crumbs from the *pan di Spagna* and put them around the bottom of the *cassata.* Decorate the top with strips of *zuccata* or citron, candied lemon and orange peel, and angelica placed as spokes on top, the tangerine in the center and the cherries in between the strips.

Tè dalla Signorina Anzon

TEA WITH
SIGNORINA ANZON

*Tea
with
Signorina
Anzon*

Arancini
LITTLE ORANGES

Cassata Infornata
SICILIAN BAKED RICOTTA PIE

Signorina Anzon invited me to tea to delve into her famous recipe collection. Tea in Sicily is uncommon, but those who serve it bring out everything—sandwiches, pastries, cakes, ice creams, sweet wines, dry wines, even tea. The dishes are placed on the dining room table and someone, usually one of the young girls in the family, serves you a cup of tea on a small tray with sugar, cream, and lemon. On this occasion we were sampling two of Signorina Anzon's most acclaimed recipes—both Sicilian classics. The food was not at all typical of what one would expect to be served for tea in an Italian household. First came a dish of *arancini*, served on a silver dish covered with a white napkin, and then a *cassata infornata*.

Arancini
LITTLE ORANGES

Arancini is one of those dishes that can be found in every part of Sicily. The literal translation is "little oranges," but they are actually rice croquettes, flavored with cheese and sometimes containing chopped meat. Every housewife in Sicily has her own recipe for *arancini*, and they are also sold at almost every Sicilian bar. When *arancini* are fried to a golden brown and served piping hot, crispy on the outside and delicate on the inside, they are *very* good.

Signorina Anzon's *arancini* can be prepared a day in advance and refrigerated, but they should not be fried until just before serving. At one time Signorina Anzon served *arancini* as a first course at dinner, but she found that people would eat so many they had no room for anything else. Her solution: serve them only at tea or for drinks.

MAKES ABOUT 28 2-INCH ARANCINI,
*SERVING 8 TO 10 AS A FIRST COURSE
OR 12 AS HORS D'OEUVRES*

> coarse salt
> 1 **pound Arborio rice (450 grams)**
> 3 **tablespoons unsalted butter (45 grams)**
> 6 **tablespoons freshly grated Parmesan cheese
> (50 grams)**
> 2 **eggs, beaten**
> **salt and freshly ground pepper to taste**
> **several gratings of nutmeg**

continued

FOR THE BÉCHAMEL:

    2   tablespoons unsalted butter (30 grams)
    3   tablespoons flour (30 grams)
    1   cup milk (250 ml)
        salt and freshly ground pepper to taste
        freshly grated nutmeg to taste
    2   tablespoons freshly grated Parmesan cheese

FOR THE PEAS:

    1   tablespoon unsalted butter (15 grams)
    1   small onion, finely chopped
1-1/3   cups fresh or frozen peas (180 grams)
  1/4   pound boiled ham, fat removed, coarsely chopped
        (about 1 scant cup) (110 grams)

TO FINISH THE *ARANCINI*:

    2   eggs
        salt to taste
        fine dry bread crumbs, about 1-1/2 cups
        olive oil for frying

Bring a large saucepan of water to a boil, add coarse salt, pour in the rice, and stir once or twice. When the water comes back to a rolling boil, lower the heat and cook at a low boil for 20 minutes. Drain and mix with the butter and cheese. Cool a bit, stirring, and add the eggs and salt, pepper, and nutmeg to taste. Spread on a large platter to cool completely. Refrigerate until very cold.

Make the béchamel. Melt the butter in a small saucepan. Put the flour, milk, salt, pepper, and nutmeg in a blender and blend for 30 seconds. Pour the milk over the butter and bring to a simmer, stirring. Simmer for 5 minutes. Remove from the heat and add the Parmesan. Place plastic wrap directly on the surface and cool completely. Refrigerate until cold.

Tea
with
Signorina
Anzon

Prepare the peas. Melt the butter in a small saucepan and sauté the onion over low heat until transparent. Add the peas, lower the heat, cover, and simmer, stirring occasionally, until done, about 20 minutes for frozen peas, 10 minutes for fresh. Let the peas and onions cool and then add them to the béchamel along with the ham. Refrigerate until needed.

When you're ready to prepare the *arancini*, beat the eggs with salt in a soup bowl. Place the bread crumbs in another bowl. Take up a tablespoon of cold rice and put it in the hollow of your hand. Place a teaspoon of cold béchamel on top and cover with another tablespoon of rice. Form a small ball with your hands. Dip the ball first in the eggs and then in the bread crumbs. Prepare all the *arancini* in this way. At this point they may be refrigerated or frozen.

Heat about 2 inches of oil in a deep skillet until about 375° (190). Fry the *arancini* (defrosted if they were frozen) until golden brown, turning as necessary. Drain on paper towels and keep warm until ready to serve.

VARIATIONS: Instead of béchamel, put a 1/2-inch cube of *mozzarella* wrapped in a strip of *mortadella* in the center of each ball or use *mozzarella* alone, *ragù*, or chicken livers cooked in Marsala.

Cassata Infornata
SICILIAN BAKED RICOTTA PIE

This is a simple, everyday version of *cassata*. Here the cooked *ricotta* cream is served in a crust of *pasta frolla*. It is unusual for a piecrust to be made with white wine, but Signorina Anzon always took great pleasure in doing things just a little differently.

*Tea
with
Signorina
Anzon*

SERVES 8

11-inch (26 cm) tart pan
with removable sides,
buttered and floured

FOR THE FILLING:

1	pound *ricotta* cheese (450 grams)
1-1/2	cups plus 1 tablespoon sugar (360 grams)
2	ounces good-quality semisweet chocolate, cut into small dice (60 grams)
2	tablespoons *zuccata or* candied citron in small dice
2	tablespoons candied orange peel in small dice

FOR THE *PASTA FROLLA* (PASTRY):

3	cups plus 1 tablespoon flour (350 grams)
2/3	cup plus 1 tablespoon sugar (160 grams)
1/2	cup (1/4 pound) cool unsalted butter, cut into pieces (110 grams)
1/4	cup cool lard, cut into pieces (60 grams)
1	egg
2	tablespoons (or more as needed) dry white wine

confectioners' sugar

Prepare the filling. Puree the *ricotta* in a food processor fitted with the steel blade or pass it through a food mill. Add the sugar and mix well. Refrigerate. When you're ready to use it, add the rest of the filling ingredients. Preheat the oven to 350° (180).

Make the *pasta frolla*. Mix together the flour, sugar, butter, lard, and egg in a bowl. Add enough white wine to form a ball, making a pastry neither too sticky nor too crumbly. (The pastry can also be made in a food processor fitted with the steel blade.) Divide the pastry into 2 parts, one slightly larger. Roll out the larger piece into a circle large enough to line the bottom of the tin. Trim the overhang and crimp the edges.

Spoon in the filling and level it. Roll out the remaining pastry and cut it into strips about 3/4 inch wide. Use the strips to make a lattice on top of the pie, crimping the edges to seal.

Bake the *cassata* for about 50 minutes or until slightly browned. Serve warm or at room temperature. Sift confectioners' sugar over the pie before serving.

 *S I C I L Y*

Cena a Trapani al Palazzo d'Alì

DINNER AT THE PALAZZO D'ALÌ IN TRAPANI

*Dinner
at the
Palazzo
d'Alì
in
Trapani*

Couscous di Pesce con Polipi Fritti
FISH COUSCOUS WITH OCTOPUS

Pescespada a Sfincione
BAKED SWORDFISH

Patate con Olive e Pomodori
POTATOES, OLIVES, AND TOMATOES

Gelatina di Frutta
FRUIT GELATIN

WINE
White: Bianco di Alcamo DOC (Province of Trapani); serve cold

DOPO CENA (AFTER DINNER)
Cannoli Siciliani (Sicilian Cannoli)

WINE
Dessert: Marsala Vergine DOC; serve cool

Antonio d'Alì and his wife live in their family *palazzo* in Trapani, on the northwest coast of Sicily. Their extraordinary cook, Rosa Parisi Bruna, has been with them for 40 years; now in her 90s, she's planning to open a boardinghouse when she retires.

Rosa's specialty is *couscous di pesce*, a traditional Trapanese dish seldom found on restaurant menus but frequently served in private homes. Trapani, just 90 miles from Africa, where the Arab influence is most evident, is the only region in Sicily where couscous is made. However, although the Arab origins of this dish are beyond dispute, Trapani couscous is not at all the same as North African couscous. Here the couscous grains are covered and steamed very slowly. A sauce is then added, and the dish is always made with fish, never meat.

Couscous di Pesce con Polipi Fritti
FISH COUSCOUS
WITH OCTOPUS

*D i n n e r
a t   t h e
P a l a z z o
d ' A l ì
i n
T r a p a n i*

Rosa makes her couscous in a terra-cotta couscousière and was shocked by the very idea of using one made of steel. Her couscous is not quick to make, but don't be deterred; it's not complicated, and the results are well worth it. (Part of Rosa's technique is to make the sign of the cross and wave her hands at certain key points in the cooking process, but these steps have been reluctantly omitted from her recipe.) She also wraps the couscous in a wool blanket for a final rest before serving. Don't be put off by the look of this dish—couscous is one of those dishes that never look absolutely wonderful, but it has a very special taste.

This procedure is not as involved as it seems. The first part of the couscous and the sauce can be prepared the day before. However, the octopus or shrimp must be fried at the last minute so that it's served very hot on top of the tepid couscous. It is lovely on a large terra-cotta platter.

SERVES 8

TO PREPARE THE COUSCOUS:

   2   **pounds couscous, preferably not precooked
       (900 grams)**
   1/2 **cup salted water (125 ml)**
   1/2 **medium onion, very thinly sliced**
   3/4 **teaspoon ground cinnamon
        freshly ground black pepper**
   1/2 **cup olive oil (125 ml)**

FOR THE FISH BROTH:

         2 quarts water (2 liters)
         1 teaspoon peppercorns
         2 bay leaves
       1/2 medium onion
         2 sprigs parsley
            salt to taste
     2-1/4 pounds fish—rockfish, red mullet, John Dory
            (1 kilogram)

FOR THE SAUCE:

       1/2 cup olive oil (125 ml)
       1/2 medium onion, very thinly sliced
     1-1/2 cups drained canned Italian plum tomatoes
            (400 grams)
         2 garlic cloves
     1-1/2 teaspoons salt
         3 tablespoons finely chopped parsley
       1/3 cup peeled almonds, finely chopped (60 grams)
            hot red pepper flakes to taste

TO COOK THE COUSCOUS:

         1 medium-large onion, 1/2 very thinly sliced
         5 bay leaves
         4 ripe fresh tomatoes *or* 5 canned Italian plum
            tomatoes, drained
            salt to taste

TO FINISH THE COUSCOUS:

         1 cup olive oil for frying (250 ml)
     1-1/3 pounds cleaned baby octopus (2 pounds/900
            grams before cleaning) *or* peeled shrimp (2-2/3
            pounds with shells) (600 grams)
            flour for dredging
            salt to taste
            parsley sprigs for garnish

continued

A day ahead, prepare the couscous, using a large platter with a raised rim. Work 1 tablespoon salted water into 1 cup couscous. Rub the couscous through your hands and "knead" it to help it absorb the water. Repeat, and when all the water has been absorbed into the couscous, sprinkle the onion, cinnamon, and pepper over it and mix well. Add the olive oil a little at a time, stirring. When all the oil has been worked in, cover the platter with a clean cloth and set aside overnight.

Make the fish broth. Put the water in a large saucepan and add the peppercorns, bay leaves, whole onion, parsley, and salt. Bring to a simmer and cook, covered, for 15 minutes. Add the fish and simmer, covered, for 45 minutes. Leave the fish in the broth and reserve until ready to complete the dish. (The broth can be prepared in advance and refrigerated, covered.)

Make the sauce. Heat the olive oil in a sauté pan and sauté the onion over medium-low heat until transparent. Add the tomatoes, mashing them with the back of a spoon, and simmer for 15 minutes. Mash the garlic to a pulp with the salt and add to the tomatoes with the parsley, almonds, and hot red pepper flakes. Reserve.

When you're ready to serve the dish, strain the fish broth, pressing on the fish to extract all the liquid. Add the broth to the tomato sauce and discard the fish. Reheat the sauce before using it.

Cook the couscous. Put the unsliced onion half, 3 bay leaves, tomatoes, and salt into the bottom part of a couscousière. Add enough water to come within 4 inches of the top part of the couscousière. Cover and simmer for 30 minutes.

Put a bed of the thinly sliced onion and 2 bay leaves into the top part of the couscousière and pour the couscous over this. Cover and steam for 20 minutes for precooked couscous, 1-1/2 hours for uncooked.

Remove the couscous and put it back onto the platter. Pour 2/3 cup of the liquid used to steam the couscous over it and work it into the couscous, stirring. Now add, from the top of the hot tomato and fish broth sauce, 2-1/3 cups of the sauce, 1/2 cup at a time, mixing rapidly so that the

couscous does not cool. Cover the platter with a clean cloth, wrap in a wool blanket, and leave for an hour before serving.

Fifteen minutes before serving the couscous, heat the tomato sauce, uncovered, to a simmer to thicken it slightly. Meanwhile, heat the olive oil in a skillet. It should be hot but not smoking. Dredge the octopus in salted flour and fry in 2 or 3 batches until lightly browned. Drain on paper towels and keep hot in a turned-off oven with the door open—they'll hold for 10 minutes. Make a mound of the couscous on its platter and put the hot octopus on top. Serve at once, garnished with parsley. Pass the tomato sauce separately.

Pescespada a Sfincione
BAKED SWORDFISH

This simple recipe for swordfish baked with tomatoes and bread crumbs has a curious name. *Sfincione* generally means some kind of fried pastry and comes either from the Greek *sfoggia*, meaning "little sponge," or from the Arab word *isfang*, which refers to a fried pastry sweetened with honey. But none of this explains why a swordfish recipe bears the name of *sfincione*, and the confusion doesn't end here. In Catania *sfinci* are sweet fried *ravioli*, but in eastern Sicily the same name is given to a salty pizza bread.

Dinner at the Palazzo d'Alì in Trapani

SERVES 6 TO 8

10- by 15-inch (25 by 40 cm)
ovenproof glass dish

2-1/2	pounds swordfish, cut into 1/2-inch steaks (1.100 grams)
1	cup fine dry bread crumbs
	salt and freshly ground black pepper to taste
1/2	cup olive oil (125 ml)
1	pound onions, thinly sliced (450 grams)
1-1/2	pounds ripe fresh tomatoes, peeled, seeded, and cut into pieces (675 grams)
1	tablespoon anchovy paste
2	tablespoons chopped fresh basil
1	teaspoon dried oregano

Remove the skin and central bone from the fish slices and pound lightly. Put the bread crumbs in a shallow dish. Salt and pepper the swordfish and roll it in the bread crumbs, pressing to make the crumbs adhere. Reserve the remaining bread crumbs.

Use 1 tablespoon of the oil to oil the baking dish and place the fish in one layer in the dish. Preheat the oven to 450° (230).

Blanch the onions in boiling salted water for 2 minutes. Drain. Put all but 1 tablespoon of the oil in a skillet and cook the onions over medium-low heat for 10 minutes. Add the tomatoes. Dissolve the anchovy paste in the reserved tablespoon of oil and add to the sauce. Add salt and pepper to taste.

Sprinkle the basil over the fish. Spoon the sauce over it and sprinkle the oregano on top. Cover with the remaining bread crumbs. Bake for 10 minutes.

VARIATION: This dish can be made without the onions, using thin slices of seeded tomato, dressed with anchovies mashed and dissolved in oil, using only oregano. The dish is also made both ways with fresh tuna.

Patate con Olive e Pomodori

POTATOES, OLIVES, AND TOMATOES

This potato dish is very simple to make and can be served with just about anything. If they are available, use waxy yellow potatoes—they absorb the flavor of the oregano and the olives so much better than other varieties of potatoes.

SERVES 6 TO 8

7- by 13-inch (18 by 33 cm)
ovenproof dish

5	tablespoons olive oil (75 ml)
2	pounds potatoes (see above), sliced 1/2 inch thick (900 grams)
2/3	pound onions, thinly sliced (300 grams)
1	pound ripe fresh tomatoes, peeled, seeded, and cut into pieces (450 grams)
3/4	cup black Gaeta olives, pitted (150 grams)
1	tablespoon plus 1 teaspoon dried oregano *or* 3 tablespoons chopped fresh oregano
	salt and freshly ground black pepper to taste

Preheat the oven to 375° (190). Put a tablespoon of oil on the bottom of the ovenproof dish. Put one third of the potatoes over the bottom of the dish and cover with half the onions. Add half the tomatoes and then half the olives. Sprinkle on half the oregano and add salt and pepper. Trickle 1 tablespoon oil on top.

Repeat, reserving a pinch of oregano, then add the remaining third of the potatoes last. Add salt, pepper, and the reserved pinch of oregano. Trickle over the remaining 2 tablespoons of oil. Cover tightly with aluminum foil.

Bake for 1 hour or until the potatoes are tender. Uncover and bake for 10 to 15 minutes more. Cool. This dish is served tepid or at room temperature but is also good hot.

Gelatina di Frutta
FRUIT GELATIN

In Sicily this Trapanese specialty is done in a particularly attractive way: prepared in a mold and then turned out on a bed of lemon leaves and decorated with fresh flowers. Many Sicilian families have their own, much prized collections of antique terra-cotta molds, and when Rosa prepares her *gelatina* the d'Alìs have a great number of beautiful ones for her to choose from.

SERVES 8

6- or 7-cup (1.5 liters) mold

> 1/2 **cup sugar (110 grams)**
> 1/2 **cup water (125 ml)**
> 4 **1/4-ounce envelopes unflavored gelatin**
> 2-1/2 **cups freshly squeezed orange juice (625 ml),**
>   **about 9 or 10 oranges**
> 1/4 **pound (1 cup) tiny strawberries *or fraises du bois***
>   **(110 grams)**
> 5 **ounces (1 cup) fresh raspberries (150 grams)**
>   **extra strawberries and raspberries and mint**
>   **leaves for garnish**

Put the sugar and water in a small saucepan and bring to a simmer over low heat, swirling the pan until the sugar dissolves. Simmer the syrup for 5 minutes.

While the syrup is cooking, prepare the gelatin. Put the gelatin in a small bowl with 1/2 cup orange juice. When the syrup is ready, put the softened gelatin into the hot syrup, stirring to dissolve. Add the remaining orange juice to the gelatin and cool. Refrigerate the gelatin until syrupy.

continued

Wash the strawberries and raspberries rapidly in cold water and drain on paper towels. When the gelatin is almost set, fold in the fruit. Dampen the mold with cold water and pour in the gelatin. Chill overnight.

Turn out onto a serving platter and decorate with the extra fruit. Mint leaves are attractive at the base of the dessert.

Cannoli Siciliani
SICILIAN CANNOLI

When dinner is finished and their other guests arrive, the d'Alìs like to serve a large dish of *cannoli* with chocolates and coffee in the living room. Sicilians adore *cannoli*—sweet pastry cylinders with each filling sweeter than the next—and Rosa's are the best! Traditionally *cannoli* are rolled on wooden sticks; Rosa was shocked to find that most people today use metal tubes. At one time *cannoli* were associated with Easter, but now they are eaten year-round, and no holiday is complete without them. During Carnival time it is still very much the tradition to send one's close friends no fewer than 12 *cannoli* as a gift.

Beautiful the Cannoli of Carnival.
No better sweet in the world.
They are a blessed way to spend money:
Each Cannoli a king's scepter.
Women miscarry for Cannoli, the staff of Moses,
He who eats not should have himself killed,
Who despises them, is a big cuckold!

ANON.

Metal or wooden tubes for *cannoli*

1-1/3 cups flour (150 grams)
    2 teaspoons unsweetened cocoa powder
    1 tablespoon sugar
       pinch of salt
    3 tablespoons (or more) Marsala
    1 to 2 tablespoons white wine vinegar
    1 tablespoon plus 2 teaspoons lard, cut into pieces
       (25 grams)
       egg white
       peanut oil for frying

Sift the flour on a wooden or marble surface and make a well in the center. Put in the cocoa, sugar, salt, 3 tablespoons Marsala, and 1 tablespoon vinegar. Add the lard and work the dough until firm, adding vinegar or Marsala as needed. (The dough may also be made in a mixer or a food processor.) Knead until smooth. Wrap in plastic wrap and allow to rest for 1 hour.

Divide the dough into 4 parts. Each part should yield about 6 *cannoli*. Run enough dough for 1 *cannoli* through a pasta machine on number 6, then 5, 4, 3, stopping on number 2. Cut a square of dough to 3-1/2 inches (8 cm) and wrap it diagonally around the *cannoli* tube so that opposite corners meet. Paint the corners with egg white and press carefully to seal tightly. Rework all the dough. There should be about 22 *cannoli*.

In a skillet, preferably iron, heat enough peanut oil to enable the *cannoli* to float. When the oil is hot but not smoking, fry 3 or 4 at a time, seam side down, until golden brown, turning to brown evenly. Drain on paper towels and, as soon as they can be handled, gently twist the *cannoli*, using a paper towel, out of the tubes. Set aside to cool completely. When cooled, they can be stored in an airtight tin up to a week. The shells must be filled at the last minute.

continued

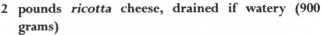

**Dinner
at the
Palazzo
d'Alì
in
Trapani**

> 2 pounds *ricotta* cheese, drained if watery (900 grams)
> 1 cup plus 1 scant cup (225 grams) confectioners' sugar
> 2-1/2 ounces semisweet chocolate, chopped (75 grams)
> 3 tablespoons diced candied orange peel (45 grams)
> 3 tablespoons finely chopped shelled and peeled unsalted pistachio nuts (30 grams)
> candied cherries (optional)
> 1 cup plus 1 scant cup (225 grams) confectioners' sugar
> confectioners' sugar to dust the finished *cannoli*

Beat the *ricotta* in a bowl until smooth. Add the sugar and mix thoroughly. Mix in the chocolate and orange peel and refrigerate, covered, until needed. The filling gains from a few hours of refrigeration.

When you're ready to prepare the *cannoli*, fill a pastry bag with the mixture and, using a 3/4-inch (2 cm) tip, pipe the *ricotta* into the shells. (Or use a demitasse spoon.) Sprinkle pistachios on one end of the *cannoli* and place half a candied cherry on the other end. Sift confectioners' sugar over the *cannoli* and serve at once—the *cannoli* cannot wait.

SICILY

Una Colazione Siciliana Informale

AN INFORMAL SICILIAN LUNCH

Penne alla Siracusana
PENNE FROM SIRACUSA

Polpettine in Agrodolce
MEAT OVALS IN A SWEET-SOUR SAUCE

Melanzane Scapece
MARINATED EGGPLANT

Crostata delle Suore di Clausura
THE CLOISTERED NUNS' TART

WINE
White: Milazzo (Messina); serve cool

Ada Parasiliti was the first person to have a cooking school in Italy, long before cooking became fashionable. Ada was born in Sicily, was reared in Naples, studied in Rome, and now teaches in Milan, but her heart has always remained with southern food, particularly Sicilian food. Over the years she has collected a large number of traditional Sicilian recipes, several of which she put together for this menu.

Penne alla Siracusana
PENNE FROM SIRACUSA

Siracusa, on the eastern or "Greek side" of Sicily, is known not only for its beautiful blue skies and temperate climate but also for its excellent food. This pasta has all the ingredients of a classical Mediterranean dish— peppers, eggplant, tomatoes, and basil.

SERVES 6

3	large bell peppers, a mixture of red and yellow if possible
2	pounds eggplant, peeled and cut into 1/2-inch dice (900 grams)
	salt
1/2	cup olive oil (125 ml)
2	garlic cloves
	freshly ground pepper to taste
1-3/4	cups tomato puree (450 grams)
2	tablespoons finely chopped fresh basil
1	pound *penne or* other short pasta (450 grams)
	freshly grated *pecorino* cheese for serving

Roast the peppers in a 400° (200) oven for about 40 minutes, turning once or twice, or until they are blistered and browned. Wrap them in foil and leave to cool. When completely cooled, peel, seed, and cut them into narrow strips. Reserve.

Sprinkle the eggplant with salt and layer in a colander. Put a weighted plate on top and leave for an hour. Rinse and pat dry.

continued

Heat the oil and garlic in a skillet. Add the eggplant and brown slightly over medium heat. Add the peppers and season with salt and pepper. Pour the tomato puree over the vegetables and simmer for 50 minutes, covered, stirring frequently. Remove from the heat and add the basil.

Cook the *penne* in boiling salted water until *al dente*. Drain and mix with the sauce. Serve at once, passing the *pecorino* separately.

Polpettine in Agrodolce
MEAT OVALS IN A
SWEET-SOUR SAUCE

These oval meatballs served with a piquant sweet-sour sauce can be eaten either hot or at room temperature. They seem to improve with age—they're even better the next day, if any are left to be eaten.

In Italy, instead of pickle relish, we use the pickled carrots, cauliflower, pearl onions, and small gherkins that are packed in vinegar. Don't substitute a sweet pickle relish or you'll unbalance the dish.

SERVES 4 TO 6

9   ounces ground veal (250 grams)
1   cup freshly grated *pecorino* cheese (135 grams)
5   tablespoons fine dry bread crumbs
2   tablespoons finely chopped parsley
1   garlic clove, finely chopped
2   small eggs
1   tablespoon (or more) water
   olive oil for frying, about 1/2 cup (125 ml)

An Informal Sicilian Lunch

1	small onion, finely chopped
	salt to taste
1/2	cup finely chopped dill pickle relish (70 grams)
1/4	cup sugar (55 grams)
1/4	cup water (60 ml)
2	cups tomato puree (500 grams)
1/4	cup white wine vinegar (60 ml)
	freshly ground pepper to taste

Mix together the first 6 ingredients, adding 1 tablespoon of water or more until you have a soft but manageable mixture. Form 25 ovals of meat (divide the mixture in half after making the first oval and then make 12 ovals per batch). Heat the olive oil in a skillet, preferably iron, and fry the ovals over medium heat in 2 batches until they are browned. Drain on paper towels. Reserve the oil.

Cook the onion with salt and a few tablespoons of water in a skillet over low heat. When transparent, add 5 tablespoons of the reserved oil. Add the pickle relish and sauté for a few minutes. In a small saucepan, dissolve the sugar in the 1/4 cup water over low heat and add to the onion. Add the tomato puree and vinegar and simmer for 5 minutes. Add pepper and taste for salt, adding if necessary.

Add the ovals to the tomato sauce and simmer for 30 minutes. If the sauce is too liquid (it should be thick enough to coat the ovals), cook for a few minutes longer, stirring to coat the meat. Cool and serve at room temperature.

Melanzane Scapece
MARINATED EGGPLANT

Here is another recipe from the vast repertoire of Sicilian eggplant dishes. Simpler than a *caponata* but also delicious, this is a perfect summer dish. It is best prepared a day in advance. It improves with age, and you'll enjoy having leftovers.

*An
Informal
Sicilian
Lunch*

SERVES 8

13-inch (30 cm) skillet

   4   **pounds eggplant, sliced crosswise 1/2 inch thick
       (1.800 grams)
       salt
       olive oil for frying, about 1-1/4 cups (310 ml) plus
       2 tablespoons**
   1   **large onion, thinly sliced**
   2   **tablespoons sugar (30 grams)**
 1/2   **cup white wine vinegar (125 ml)**
   1   **pound ripe fresh tomatoes, peeled and seeded
       (450 grams)
       a large handful of mint leaves plus mint for
       garnish**
 1/4   **pound *caciocavallo* cheese, cut into small dice
       (about 1 cup) (110 grams) (optional)
       freshly ground pepper to taste**

Layer the eggplant in a colander, salting each layer. Put a weighted plate on top and leave for an hour. Rinse and pat dry.

Heat 1 inch of oil until hot and fry the eggplant in batches over medium-high heat until lightly browned. Drain on paper towels.

Cook the onion with a few tablespoons of water in a 13-inch skillet over medium-low heat until transparent. Add 2 tablespoons olive oil and the eggplant and cook over medium-high heat for 10 minutes, shaking the pan occasionally. Mix together the sugar and vinegar and add to the eggplant; cook over fairly high heat for 4 minutes.

Puree the tomatoes in a food processor fitted with the steel blade or put them through a food mill and add to the eggplant. Simmer for 10 minutes, shaking the pan every now and then. Add the mint and cheese if desired and mix delicately. Simmer for 1 or 2 minutes and remove from the heat. Taste for seasoning and add pepper to taste. Serve cold, garnished with mint.

Crostata delle Suore di Clausura
THE CLOISTERED NUNS' TART

Since so many Sicilian sweets are connected to religious feasts, many of them have traditionally been made not in bakeries but in convents. Enrichetta Caracciolo's account of life in the cloister, published in 1874, provides some fascinating insights into the intense rivalry and competition over this sweet making, which rose to a fever pitch at Easter time:

> *The principal occupation, the summa rerum of the convent, lies in the preparation of sweets. . . . Each nun is the mistress of the pastry oven for an entire day . . . but since at times this is not sufficient, the nun takes recourse to a second and a third, so that the poor lay sisters are dying for want of sleep. . . . More than one elderly lay sister, grown hoary in the cloister, has said to me that she had never seen the Holy Week services, not having ever had a free minute during that period.*
>
> MISTERI DEL CHIOSTRO NAPOLITANO

Although particular sweets used to be made in honor of a particular saint or were known to be the specialty of a particular convent, they are now eaten year-round. At one time these sweets were a significant source of revenue for a convent, and many religious orders would guard their secret recipes with extreme ferocity. The original recipe for this *crostata* came from the Poor Clare Sisters in Palermo. It has a marmalade filling and a pastry cover composed of a pattern of four larger circles in the center of the tart surrounded by 21 smaller circles of pastry. This design must have had some religious significance, but, alas, we no longer know what it symbolizes. If you are in a hurry and don't want to fuss with the circles, use a simple lattice pattern instead.

SERVES 6 TO 8

10-inch tart tin with 1-inch
sides (26 by 2¹/₂ cm) and
removable bottom, buttered

FOR THE FILLING:

- **1 cup (3/4 pound) good-quality orange marmalade (330 grams)**
- **1/8 teaspoon ground cinnamon**
- **3/4 cup (1/4 pound) candied citron in small dice (120 grams)**
- **grated zest of 1 large lemon**
- **1/4 cup orange liqueur (60 ml)**
- **1/2 pound shelled almonds, peeled, toasted, and coarsely chopped (225 grams)**

FOR THE CRUST:

- **2-2/3 cups flour (300 grams)**
- **1/2 cup plus 1 tablespoon sugar (125 grams)**
- **1/2 cup (1/4 pound) plus 2 tablespoons unsalted butter, cut into pieces (150 grams)**
- **3 large egg yolks**
- **grated zest of 1/2 lemon**

Make the filling. Put the marmalade, cinnamon, citron, and zest in a bowl. Add the liqueur and mix thoroughly. Add the almonds just before using the filling. Preheat the oven to 350° (180).

Put the flour on a wooden or marble surface and make a well in the center. Add the sugar and butter to the center and rub in the butter until the flour is coated with butter. Add the yolks and zest and mix rapidly until the pastry forms a ball. (The dough may also be made in a food processor fitted with the steel blade.)

Roll out two thirds of the pastry and line the tin, leaving an overhang of 1/2 inch. Trim to make the edge even. Pour in the filling and smooth.

continued

Carefully turn down the edge onto the filling all the way around, using a sharp knife to detach the dough from the tin's sides.

Roll out the remaining pastry and cut 4 circles 2-1/2 inches (7 cm) in diameter and put these in the center of the tart. Now cut about 21 1-inch (2-1/2 cm) circles and place all around the turned-down edges and over the filling.

Bake the tart for 1 hour and 10 minutes or until lightly browned. Cool on a rack for 10 minutes and remove the sides. When cooled but not cold, run a sharp knife around the edges of the tart and turn out on a rack. Cool completely. Serve at room temperature.

Una Colazione Vegetariana Data da Ada

A VEGETARIAN LUNCH
GIVEN BY ADA

Penne al Cavolfiore
PASTA AND CAULIFLOWER

Peperoni Ripieni
STUFFED PEPPERS

Zucchine Scapece
MARINATED ZUCCHINI

Biancomangiare con Salsa di Fragole
BLANCMANGE WITH STRAWBERRY SAUCE

WINE
Red: Calabrese d'Avola (Province of Siracusa); serve cool

Given the wealth of vegetables in the diet, there is probably nowhere a vegetarian would rather live than in Sicily or southern Italy. Ada Parasiliti has a number of vegetarian friends, and she put together this lunch menu with them in mind.

Penne al Cavolfiore
PASTA AND CAULIFLOWER

An old Sicilian proverb says that after Easter, sermons and cauliflowers lose their flavor. The moral of this bit of wisdom is to be sure to use a fresh, young cauliflower whenever possible. Cauliflower may seem a surprising companion for pasta, but this Catanian recipe proves otherwise. If you want to prepare this recipe in advance, pour a cup of cold water over the pasta to stop the cooking process once it is cooked and cool the cauliflower before adding it to the pasta. Complete the dish, cover and refrigerate, then bring the dish to room temperature before reheating and serving.

SERVES 6

13½- by 9-inch (34 by
23 cm) ovenproof glass oval
dish, oiled

1	medium onion, finely chopped
1/2	cup plus 1 tablespoon olive oil (140 ml)
3	pounds cauliflower (1.350 grams)
	salt
2/3	pound *pennette* (300 grams)
2/3	cup freshly grated *pecorino* cheese (90 grams)
	freshly ground black pepper to taste

Cook the onion with a few tablespoons water in a small skillet over medium-low heat until transparent. Add 2 tablespoons oil and sauté for another minute or 2. Reserve.

Wash the cauliflower and break into flowerets. Cook in boiling salted water until *al dente*. Remove with a slotted spoon, reserving the cauliflower water. In a skillet large enough to hold the cauliflower, heat the

continued

remaining oil and sauté the cauliflower gently for 5 minutes. Preheat the oven to 375° (190).

Cook the *pennette* in the boiling cauliflower water until *al dente*. Drain and dress with all but 3 tablespoons of the cheese, add the onion, and grind black pepper over it generously. Mix thoroughly and put the pasta in the prepared dish. Cover with the cauliflower and sprinkle the remaining cheese over it. Bake for 20 to 25 minutes. Serve hot.

Peperoni Ripieni
STUFFED PEPPERS

Peppers and eggplant, grown in such abundance in southern Italy and Sicily, are often stuffed and served roasted, grilled, baked, or fried. Among the hundreds of different recipes this tasty one features capers, olives, basil, and parsley.

SERVES 4 TO 6

Ovenproof glass dish, about
7 by 13 inches (18 by 32 cm)

5	large (about 3 pounds) bell peppers, a mixture of red and yellow (1.350 grams)
1	pound eggplant, cut into 1/2-inch dice (450 grams)
	salt
1/2	cup olive oil (125 ml)
1/2	cup black Sicilian olives, pitted and cut into pieces (100 grams)
3	tablespoons capers, rinsed, dried, and finely chopped (30 grams)

1 garlic clove, finely chopped
2 tablespoons finely chopped parsley
1 tablespoon finely chopped fresh basil
  freshly ground black pepper to taste
2 tablespoons fine dry bread crumbs

Oil the baking dish with 1 tablespoon olive oil. Roast the peppers in a 400° (200) oven for about 40 minutes or until charred and blistered. Wrap each pepper in foil and cool. When cold, remove the stems, seeds, and skin, taking care not to break the peppers. Cut each pepper in half lengthwise. Set aside.

Put the eggplant in a bowl of well-salted cold water and put a weight on top. Leave for 1 hour. Drain and pat dry.

Heat 7 tablespoons of the olive oil and sauté the eggplant slowly until browned, about 15 to 20 minutes. Salt lightly and cool. Preheat the oven to 350° (180).

In a bowl, mix together the cooled eggplant, olives, capers, garlic, parsley, basil, black pepper, and bread crumbs. Lay the pepper halves on a flat work surface and divide the filling among them. Roll up the peppers and place in the prepared dish "seam" side down. Bake for 40 minutes. Serve at room temperature.

Zucchine Scapece
MARINATED ZUCCHINI

Here zucchini is preserved in sugar and vinegar flavored with mint and garlic. It will keep for up to a week and absorbs more flavor the longer you leave it. In southern Italy and Sicily—and elsewhere—this dish is a godsend for all those whose gardens are overwhelmed with zucchini.

SERVES 6 TO 8

> 4-1/2 **pounds zucchini, sliced crosswise 1/4 inch thick**
> **(2 kilograms)**
> **salt**
> **olive oil for frying**
> **freshly ground black pepper to taste**
> **a handful of fresh mint leaves plus mint for**
> **garnish**
> 2 **garlic cloves, thinly sliced**
> 1-1/2 **tablespoons sugar**
> **scant 1/2 cup white wine vinegar (100 ml)**

Sprinkle the zucchini with salt and set in the sun on a large, flat wicker tray or screen for an hour, if possible, or leave in a colander. Rinse and dry the zucchini.

Heat 3/4 inch of oil in a skillet and fry the zucchini over medium-high heat until browned. Drain on paper towels. Reserve 3 tablespoons of the cooking oil.

Make a layer of zucchini in a serving dish. Grind black pepper over it and sprinkle it with mint leaves. Repeat, using all the zucchini and mint leaves except the garnish.

In a small saucepan, boil the garlic, sugar, and vinegar for 1 minute. Add the reserved oil and pour the mixture over the zucchini. Cover with plastic wrap and marinate in a cool place, unrefrigerated, for 2 or 3 days. Serve at room temperature, garnished with mint.

Biancomangiare con Salsa di Fragole
BLANCMANGE WITH STRAWBERRY SAUCE

Cool, soothing cornstarch puddings are popular throughout the Middle East, and it is most likely that *biancomangiare* was another present brought to Sicily by the Arabs. Nowadays it is often used as a filling in pastries, but it can also be served on its own, as it is here. *Biancomangiare* is traditionally made in individual patterned terra-cotta molds passed down through the generations in a family; when each pudding is set, it is turned out onto a bed of lemon leaves. Ada Parasiliti uses this recipe with her least experienced students because it's so simple to make and never fails to please.

SERVES 6 TO 8

5-cup (1.250 ml) ring mold
or 6 to 8 small cups, rinsed
with cold water

    1   **quart milk (1 liter)**
1/2   **cup wheat starch *or* cornstarch (60 grams)**
1/2   **cup plus 2 tablespoons sugar (140 grams)**
       peel of 1 lemon
       ***Salsa di Fragole* (recipe follows) *or* 9 ounces**
       (1 cup plus scant 1/4 cup) strawberries
       (250 grams)
       fresh flowers for garnish, if available

continued

Put half the milk along with the wheat starch or cornstarch and sugar in a blender or a food processor fitted with the steel blade and blend for a minute. Pour the milk mixture into a saucepan with the rest of the milk and the lemon peel. Bring to a boil and simmer for 5 minutes, stirring constantly. Discard the lemon peel. Pour the mixture into the prepared mold and cool. Refrigerate, tightly covered, overnight.

When you're ready to serve the dessert, turn it out onto a platter and decorate with fresh flowers. Serve with Strawberry Sauce or with berries.

SALSA DI FRAGOLE (*STRAWBERRY SAUCE*)

    9 **ounces (1 cup plus scant 1/4 cup) strawberries (250 grams), pureed**
    2 **tablespoons (or more to taste) sugar (30 grams)**
  3/4 **cup heavy cream (185 ml)**

Alternate strawberry puree, sugar, and cream in a serving bowl; do not mix. Refrigerate and serve cold with the *biancomangiare*.

SICILY

Cena a Palermo

DINNER IN PALERMO

Dinner
in
Palermo

Pasta con le Sarde
PASTA WITH FRESH SARDINES

Ruota di Tonno con Salsa Origanata
WHEELS OF TUNA WITH OREGANO

Peperonata
PEPPERS IN A SKILLET

Crostata di Pomodori e Pistacchi
TOMATO AND PISTACHIO TART

WINE
White: Solunto (Palermo); serve very cold

The recipes that make up this menu are all specific to Palermo and come from a number of different sources.

Pasta con le Sarde
PASTA WITH FRESH SARDINES

Legend has it that when the Arabs landed on the coast of Sicily in 827 their leader, Euphemius, ordered his cooks to look around for something to eat. Finding fresh sardines in the water and wild fennel growing on the hills, they tossed them together, added raisins, pine nuts, and saffron, and came up with what has become almost the national dish of Sicily and a particular obsession in Palermo.

Pasta con le sarde exemplifies all that is special about Sicilian cookery—the combination of this particularly Mediterranean fish with the slightly bitter taste of fennel, embellished with those spices and nuts so dear to the Arab palate. There are, not surprisingly, innumerable variations of this dish, some of which are considered downright blasphemous by those who prepare it differently. This one comes from Signor Corleone, who considers it *the* classical version—but then again, he has a slightly different version he serves only for lunch. This is such an extraordinary dish that I think the Sicilians are quite right to be obsessive about it.

SERVES 6 TO 8

15- by 8½-inch ovenproof
glass dish, oiled

1-1/2	pounds fresh sardines or smelts, about 1 pound after cleaning (450 grams)
1	pound wild herb fennel, if available, *or* 2 heaped cups feathery leaves and tender stems of fresh bulb fennel (450 grams)
5	quarts water
	salt
3/4	teaspoon fennel seeds
2/3	cup olive oil (160 ml)
1/4	cup finely chopped parsley

continued

1 medium onion, finely chopped
7 oil-packed anchovy fillets, drained and cut into small pieces
2/3 cup raisins, soaked in hot water until plump and drained (110 grams)
2/3 cup pine nuts (110 grams)
  freshly ground black pepper
1 teaspoon saffron threads
  flour for dredging
1 pound *pennette or bucatini* (broken into 3 pieces) (450 grams)
1/2 cup shelled almonds, peeled, lightly toasted, and coarsely chopped (80 grams)

Have the fishmonger clean the fish if possible. If not, it is easily done (see page 419).

Wash the fennel leaves and stems and cut into 1-inch pieces. Boil the water with salt and 1/2 teaspoon fennel seeds. Cook the fennel leaves and stems in this water for about 3 minutes or until the stalks are tender. Remove with a strainer when done. Reserve the water for cooking the pasta.

Heat 2 tablespoons of the oil in a small skillet and add half the sardines, the parsley, salt to taste, and 1 or 2 tablespoons water. Cook over medium heat for a few minutes and reserve.

Heat 3 tablespoons of the oil in another skillet and sauté the onion over low heat for 5 minutes. Chop the fennel (do not puree) and add it to the onion. Add salt to taste and a tablespoon or so of water if necessary to prevent burning. When the onion is transparent, add the anchovies, remaining fennel seeds, raisins, and pine nuts. Season with salt and pepper. Simmer over very low heat for 10 minutes and add the saffron. Reserve the sauce.

Heat 1/4 cup of the oil. Dredge the remaining sardines in flour and fry in the hot oil over medium-high heat until lightly browned—about 1 minute on one side and 50 to 60 seconds on the other side. Drain on paper towels. Preheat the oven to 375° (190).

Bring the reserved fennel water to a boil and cook the pasta until *al dente*. Drain and dress with the remaining 2 tablespoons oil. Add the reserved sauce and mix well.

Place half the pasta on the bottom of the prepared dish. Put all the fried sardines on this layer and the rest of the pasta on top. Bake for 15 minutes. Serve hot, sprinkled with almonds, or pass the almonds separately.

This dish is best freshly assembled and cooked; however, the sauce may be prepared in advance and gently reheated. Add the saffron when reheating. Leftover *pasta con le sarde* is also eaten cold.

Ruota di Tonno con Salsa Origanata
WHEELS OF TUNA WITH OREGANO

This is Signorina Anzon's recipe for a simple baked tuna cooked with diced fresh tomatoes. It also works very well with swordfish.

SERVES 6

2-1/2	**pounds fresh tuna, skinned and cut into slices (1.100 grams)**
1/2	**cup olive oil (125 ml)**
3	**ripe fresh tomatoes, peeled, seeded, and cut into tiny dice**
1	**heaped tablespoon capers, rinsed and dried**
1	**garlic clove, finely chopped**
	salt and freshly ground black pepper to taste
1	**tablespoon plus 1 teaspoon dried oregano**

Preheat the oven to 350° (180). Rinse the tuna and pat it dry. Using 1/4 cup of the oil, oil an ovenproof dish into which the fish fits snugly in one layer. Fit the tuna into the dish and cover with the remaining oil. Sprinkle the tomatoes, capers, and garlic over it. Season with salt and pepper. Sprinkle the oregano over the fish.

Bake for 25 to 30 minutes. When the fish is done, it will flake in the center when touched with a fork. This dish is usually served hot.

Peperonata
PEPPERS IN A SKILLET

This popular Sicilian dish can be eaten hot or cold. The recipe was given to me about 10 years ago by a woman who does remarkable embroidery, specializing in Sicilian drawn work.

SERVES 6

2-1/2	pounds bell peppers, a mixture of red, yellow, and green (1.100 grams)
6	tablespoons olive oil (100 ml)
1	pound white onions, thinly sliced (450 grams)
	salt
1	scant teaspoon (or to taste) hot red pepper flakes (optional)
1	pound ripe fresh tomatoes, peeled and seeded (450 grams)
3	tablespoons white wine vinegar
3/4	cup spicy green Sicilian olives, pitted (150 grams)
	a handful of fresh basil leaves plus basil for garnish (optional)

Cut the peppers into 4 (or more, according to their size) 1-1/2- to 2-inch pieces each. Heat the oil in a skillet and cook the onions over medium-low heat with salt, pepper flakes if desired, and a spoonful of water to prevent browning. When the onions are transparent, add the peppers. Cut the tomatoes into pieces the size of the peppers and add to the skillet. Cover and simmer for 1 hour.

Add the vinegar and cook at a brisk simmer for 5 to 10 minutes or until thickened slightly. Add the olives and simmer for 3 minutes. If you're using basil, add it with the olives or sprinkle it over the *peperonata* after the dish is completed. Serve hot or cold. If you've used basil, garnish the dish with more basil.

Crostata di Pomodori e Pistacchi
TOMATO AND PISTACHIO TART

This *crostata* is one of those closely guarded secret recipes from a Sicilian convent, shared on the strict understanding it would never appear in print in Sicily. It is a most unusual recipe, for although green tomatoes are often eaten in salads in and around Rome, you would rarely, anywhere but in Sicily, find them cooked and then mixed with pistachios and oranges, and served in a tart. It sounds bizarre, but it is perfectly delicious.

SERVES 8

10-inch (30 cm) tart pan
with removable sides,
buttered and floured

FOR THE FILLING:

2	pounds green tomatoes (900 grams)
1-3/4	cups sugar (400 grams)
	grated zest of 1/2 lemon
	grated zest of 1/2 small orange
1/2	cup plus 1 tablespoon shelled unsalted pistachios (90 grams)
2	large oranges *or* 1 small grapefruit *or* 2 cups peeled, halved, and seeded large green grapes *or* a combination

FOR THE CRUST:

1-3/4	cups flour (200 grams)
1/3	cup plus 1 tablespoon sugar (90 grams)
7	tablespoons cool unsalted butter, cut into pieces (100 grams)
2	large egg yolks
	grated zest of 1/2 lemon
2	tablespoons orange marmalade

Peel and seed the tomatoes and cut them into very small pieces. Put them in a stainless-steel saucepan, add the sugar, and mix well. Cover and cook over low heat for 30 minutes. Remove the lid and simmer for 1-1/2 hours or until the tomatoes are transparent and syrupy. Cool. (The tomatoes can be cooked several days in advance.)

When you're ready to use the tomatoes, add the grated zests, mixing well. Chop the pistachios in a food processor in batches or, better still, grind them in a nut grinder. Do not chop too finely. Reserve until needed.

Make the crust. If you're using a food processor, put the flour, sugar, butter, yolks, and lemon zest in the bowl fitted with the steel blade. Process on and off until the dough masses. Or make the dough by hand, mixing all the ingredients together as quickly as possible.

Roll the dough into a circle large enough to fit the pan. Drape the dough over the rolling pin; unroll it over the prepared tin and fit it into place. Trim and crimp the edges. Refrigerate until ready to use.

Preheat the oven to 350° (180). If you're using oranges or grapefruit, peel them using a sharp knife; remove the peel and white pith and slice 1/4 inch thick.

Spoon the tomato preserves into the crust. Sprinkle the pistachios over the preserves and arrange the oranges or other fruit over the top as desired. Bake for 55 minutes or until the crust has browned. Cool on a rack for 10 minutes. Remove the sides and cool completely on the rack. Turn out on a serving plate. If desired, the fruits may be painted with orange marmalade, melted and cooled, to keep the fruit shiny. Serve at room temperature.

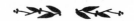

Una Colazione nella Campagna Siciliana

LUNCH IN THE SICILIAN COUNTRYSIDE

*Lunch
in the
Sicilian
Countryside*

Pasta con i Broccoli Rimestati
SAFFRON CAULIFLOWER PASTA

Polpettine Avvolte in Melanzane
EGGPLANT-WRAPPED VEAL MEATBALLS

Insalata di Finocchi, Cipolle, e Olive
FENNEL, ONION, AND OLIVE SALAD

Dolce di Ricotta
RICOTTA TORTE

WINE
Red: Rapitalà Rosso; serve at cool room temperature

Pasta con i Broccoli Rimestati
SAFFRON CAULIFLOWER PASTA

In Palermo cauliflower is known as *broccoli* and the vegetable we call broccoli is known as *sparaceddi*. You might think that there would be only one way to serve pasta with cauliflower—not so; there are many recipes to choose from. This Palermo version adds currants, pine nuts, and saffron to the pasta, raising the humble cauliflower to a new level of exoticism. It makes a satisfying winter dish that's a meal in itself.

SERVES 8 AS A FIRST COURSE

4	quarts water (4 liters)
	salt
2	pounds cauliflower, broken into flowerets (900 grams)
1/2	cup extra-virgin olive oil (125 ml)
1/2	teaspoon (or more to taste) hot red pepper flakes
2/3	cup dried black currants *or* raisins, soaked in warm water until plump and drained (110 grams)
2/3	cup pine nuts, lightly toasted (110 grams)
1	tablespoon anchovy paste
1	pound *bucatini*, broken into 3 pieces, *or* whole *pennette* (450 grams)
1/2	cup grated Parmesan cheese
1	teaspoon saffron threads
1/2	cup grated *pecorino* cheese (65 grams) plus extra for serving
	freshly ground black pepper

Salt the water, bring it to a boil in a large pot, and cook the cauliflower until tender. Remove from the water with a slotted spoon; reserve the water for cooking the pasta.

continued

Heat the oil in a skillet large enough to hold the pasta. Add the pepper flakes, currants, pine nuts, and cauliflower. Dissolve the anchovy paste in a little cauliflower water and add it to the skillet. Cook over low heat for 10 minutes, adding cauliflower water if needed to prevent cauliflower from drying out and mashing the flowerets with the back of a wooden spoon.

Heat the cauliflower water to a boil and cook the pasta until very firm. Drain, reserving 1 cup of pasta water.

Add the pasta to the cauliflower in the skillet. Dissolve the saffron in a tablespoon or 2 of the pasta water and add it to the skillet. Mix all together over low heat for a minute or 2, using the remaining pasta water only if the mixture is too dry.

Sprinkle the *pecorino* over the pasta, cover, and allow to rest for 1 minute. Serve with additional *pecorino* and pass the pepper mill.

Polpettine Avvolte in Melanzane
EGGPLANT-WRAPPED VEAL
MEATBALLS

This recipe—spicy meatballs wrapped in eggplant and baked in a simple tomato sauce—comes from Catania. It's a dish that works marvelously for a crowd and can be prepared in advance with no problem; it's also delicious at room temperature.

MAKES 30 MEATBALLS, SERVING 8

30	Japanese eggplant slices cut lengthwise, a little more than 1/3 inch thick, about 3-1/3 pounds (1.500 grams)
	salt
	olive oil for frying
	flour for dredging

FOR THE MEATBALLS:

1-1/3	pounds ground veal (600 grams)
1	scant cup fresh bread crumbs
1/2	cup less 1 tablespoon milk (110 ml)
3	tablespoons finely chopped parsley
1	egg
1	egg yolk
3/4	cup freshly grated Parmesan cheese (105 grams)
1-1/2	tablespoons unsalted butter, melted (20 grams)
1-1/2	teaspoons (or to taste) salt
	freshly ground black pepper to taste
1/4	cup pine nuts (40 grams)
1/3	cup raisins, plumped in warm water (60 grams)

continued

FOR THE TOMATO SAUCE:

2 **tablespoons olive oil**
1 **small onion, finely chopped**
2 **pounds ripe fresh tomatoes, peeled, seeded, and
   cut into pieces (900 grams)
   salt and freshly ground pepper to taste
   pinch of sugar**

**freshly ground pepper to taste
parsley sprigs for garnish**

Layer the eggplant in a colander, salting each layer. Place a weighted plate on top and leave for an hour. Rinse and pat dry.

Heat 1 inch of oil in a skillet. Dredge the eggplant in flour and fry over medium-high heat until lightly browned. Drain on paper towels.

Make the meatballs. Put the ground veal in a bowl. Soak the bread crumbs in the milk and, when soft, add to the meat. Add the parsley, egg, egg yolk, Parmesan, butter, salt, and pepper. Mix thoroughly with your hands. Add the pine nuts and raisins. Wet your hands with cold water and form 30 small balls.

Make the sauce. Heat the oil in a skillet and cook the onion over medium-low heat until transparent. Add the tomatoes and cook over medium-high heat, stirring occasionally, for 15 minutes. Season with salt and pepper, plus sugar if necessary (if the sauce is too tart). The sauce should be dense; if it is too thin, cook until thickened. Puree in a food processor fitted with the steel blade or pass it through a food mill. Preheat the oven to 350° (180).

Put 2 tablespoons sauce on the bottom of an ovenproof dish large enough to hold the meatballs. Wrap each meatball in an eggplant slice and place in the prepared dish. Grind black pepper over the meatballs and spoon the remaining sauce over them. Bake for 50 minutes. Serve hot or at room temperature. Garnish the dish lavishly with parsley.

Insalata di Finocchi, Cipolle, e Olive
FENNEL, ONION, AND OLIVE SALAD

Italians love fennel for its aromatic scent, its crisp texture, and its anisey taste. Eaten raw, finely slivered and served with olives, a generous amount of black pepper, and a little oil drizzled over the top, fennel is a simple culinary pleasure hard to equal.

SERVES 8

2-2/3	**pounds cleaned bulb fennel, about 5-1/2 pounds before cleaning (1.200 grams cleaned, 2.450 grams before cleaning)**
4	**scallions, thinly sliced**
1-1/3	**cups black Gaeta olives, pitted (275 grams) salt to taste**
5	**tablespoons extra-virgin olive oil (75 ml) freshly ground black pepper to taste**

Slice the fennel 1/4 inch thick and put in a salad bowl. Divide the scallions into rings and add along with the olives. Toss and add a little salt. Dress with the olive oil and grind black pepper over the salad. Toss again and serve at once.

Dolce di Ricotta
RICOTTA TORTE

It is unlikely that the South could survive without *ricotta*. It is eaten fresh, used in sauces and stuffings, and is a frequent ingredient in sweets and desserts. *Ricotta* ice cream is a Sicilian specialty. Here the sweetness of the creamy *ricotta* is arrested by the tartness of the citron and just the barest hint of rum.

SERVES 8

10-inch (25 cm) nonstick
cheesecake-type pan,
heavily buttered

2/3	pound *ricotta* cheese (300 grams)
2/3	cup sugar (150 grams)
6	eggs, separated
1/4	pound cold cream cheese, cut into 1/2-inch dice (110 grams)
1/2	cup raisins, soaked for 2 hours in white rum to cover (80 grams)
	pinch of ground cinnamon (optional)
1/2	teaspoon vanilla extract
1/2	cup candied citron in 1/4-inch dice (80 grams)
	pinch of salt
1/4	cup finely chopped shelled and peeled almonds (40 grams)
	confectioners' sugar and chopped toasted almonds for garnish

Beat the *ricotta* in an electric mixer until smooth. Add the sugar and beat until creamy. Add the egg yolks, one by one, beating well after each addition. Add the cream cheese, raisins with the rum, cinnamon if you're using it, vanilla, and citron, mixing by hand. Beat the egg whites with a pinch of salt until stiff but not dry and fold them into the *ricotta*. Preheat the oven to 325° (160).

Dust the inside of the prepared pan with the finely chopped almonds, rotating the pan so that they adhere to the surface. Pour the *ricotta* mixture into the pan and smooth the surface gently. Bake for about 45 minutes or until the dessert is lightly browned and pulls away from the sides. Cool for 15 minutes in the pan and then turn it out onto a serving platter. Sift confectioners' sugar over the dessert and sprinkle it with the toasted almonds.

*Una Colazione al Sole a Conca
dei Marini da Ersilia*

ERSILIA'S LUNCH
IN THE SUN
IN CONCA DEI MARINI

Polpette di Melanzane con Salsa di Pomodoro
EGGPLANT BALLS WITH TOMATO SAUCE

Coniglio al Limone
LEMON RABBIT

Capriolata
BAKED TOMATOES

Melanzane al Cioccolato
CHOCOLATE EGGPLANT

WINE
White: Episcopio Ravello; serve chilled

Ersilia Lucibello planned this menu with recipes collected from her own family and her fiancé's family, who all come from the Amalfi coast. Conca dei Marini is about halfway between Amalfi and Praiano. You may think a menu with two eggplant dishes would be monotonous—but virtually no one will be able to identify the eggplant in the dessert.

Polpette di Melanzane con Salsa di Pomodoro

EGGPLANT BALLS WITH
TOMATO SAUCE

These delicious little eggplant balls are best served as a first course and can be made ahead of time and reheated at the last minute. They should be served with a simple tomato sauce, a recipe for which is given below.

MAKES ABOUT 25 LITTLE CAKES,
SERVING 6 TO 8

> 3 **pounds eggplant (1.350 grams)**
>   **salt and freshly ground black pepper to taste**
> 2 **cups fresh bread crumbs**
> 3/4 **cup freshly grated Parmesan cheese (105 grams)**
> 2 **egg yolks**
> 1 **cup olive oil for frying (250 ml)**
>   ***Salsa di Pomodoro* (recipe follows)**
>   **fresh basil leaves for garnish (optional)**

Peel and cut the eggplant into pieces. Cook in boiling salted water for about 10 minutes or until well done. Drain in a colander for at least 30 minutes.

Pass the eggplant through a food mill and put the puree into a bowl. Add salt, pepper, the bread crumbs, Parmesan, and egg yolks. Mix thoroughly. The mixture will be soft and will stick to the fingers. Form little balls, about 2 inches (5 cm) in diameter, flattened slightly. You should have around 25 little cakes.

continued

Heat the oil in a 10-inch (25 cm) skillet and fry the *polpette* over medium-high heat in batches until golden. Drain on paper towels. Serve hot with the *salsa di pomodoro* or at room temperature. Garnish the *polpette* with basil.

NOTE: The *polpette* may be prepared in advance and reheated in a 400° (200) oven for 10 to 15 minutes.

Salsa di Pomodoro
TOMATO SAUCE

1   **small onion, finely chopped**
    salt to taste
1   **2-pound can Italian plum tomatoes with juice (900**
    grams) *or* **3 pounds ripe fresh tomatoes, peeled,**
    seeded, and cut into pieces (1.350 grams)
6   **fresh basil leaves, finely chopped**
    freshly ground black pepper to taste

Cook the onion in a skillet over low heat with a few tablespoons of water until transparent. Add salt and the tomatoes, pureed in a food processor or put through a food mill, with the finely chopped basil leaves. Cook for 15 minutes, more if the sauce is watery. (This depends on the type of tomatoes used.) Season with pepper and taste for salt. Serve the sauce hot in a sauceboat to accompany the *polpette*.

Coniglio al Limone
LEMON RABBIT

Rabbit, versatile and inexpensive, is eaten up and down the Amalfi coast and lends itself to all kinds of preparations—boned, stuffed, often mixed with olives and served with pasta. In this recipe chunks of rabbit are wrapped in lemon leaves and baked. The result: a succulent dish with the barest edge of lemon.

SERVES 6

Toothpicks

> 1 2-2/3-pound rabbit, cut into 10 pieces (1.200 grams)
> 1 large lemon
> 9 tablespoons extra-virgin olive oil (140 ml)
>   salt to taste
> 2 tablespoons chopped fresh rosemary
> 1/2 cup fine dry bread crumbs
> 1/3 cup freshly grated Parmesan cheese (45 grams)
> 1 small garlic clove, finely chopped
> 3 tablespoons finely chopped parsley
>   freshly ground black pepper to taste
> 10 large lemon leaves, unsprayed

Rinse and dry the rabbit and put it in a bowl with the juice of the lemon. Cover with cold water and leave for an hour. Drain and dry the pieces of rabbit.

In a large skillet, heat 1/4 cup of the olive oil with 1 teaspoon salt and 1 tablespoon of the rosemary. Brown the rabbit quickly, adding oil if necessary. Set aside. Preheat the oven to 350° (180).

continued

Put the bread crumbs, Parmesan, garlic, parsley, remaining rosemary, salt, and pepper in a small bowl. Mix well. Put 2 tablespoons of the olive oil in a soup plate. Rub the rabbit pieces and the lemon leaves with oil. Roll the rabbit pieces in the bread crumb mixture, pressing to make the crumbs adhere. Wrap each piece in a large lemon leaf and secure with a toothpick.

Put the rabbit pieces in an oiled ovenproof dish that holds them snugly, one next to the other, toothpicks underneath. Trickle the remaining oil over them. Bake for 50 minutes. Turn the pieces over and cook for another 10 minutes. Serve hot.

Capriolata
BAKED TOMATOES

A simple baked tomato dish that can either be served with the rabbit or used to dress pasta. Refrigerated, the sauce keeps for two or three days; it also freezes well and tastes marvelous served at room temperature with cold meat.

SERVES 6

> 5 tablespoons olive oil (75 ml)
> 2 pounds ripe fresh tomatoes, plum if possible (900 grams)
> 2 garlic cloves, cut into slivers
> salt and freshly ground pepper to taste
> dried oregano to taste
> 1/2 cup freshly grated Parmesan *or pecorino* cheese (65 grams)
> a handful of fresh basil leaves, chopped

Preheat the oven to 350° (180).

Put 1 tablespoon of the oil in the bottom of an ovenproof glass dish large enough to hold the tomatoes in 2 layers. If the tomatoes are small, cut them in half; if large, cut them into 4 pieces. Cover the bottom of the dish with the tomatoes, cut sides up. Put a sliver of garlic in each one. Sprinkle salt and pepper, 2 tablespoons of the oil, oregano, half the Parmesan, and half the basil over the tomatoes.

Place the remaining tomatoes on top to form another layer, cut side up. Repeat with the remaining ingredients. Cover tightly with foil.

Bake for 30 minutes. Remove the foil and cook for another 35 to 45 minutes. The tomatoes will be tender and slightly browned.

Melanzane al Cioccolato
CHOCOLATE EGGPLANT

Eggplant for dessert? Only in southern Italy. This seems the oddest possible combination, but this Amalfi specialty actually tastes wonderful.

SERVES 6 TO 8

Round serving plate with
8-inch (20 cm) center

1-1/3	pounds Japanese eggplant (600 grams)
	salt
	olive oil for frying, about 1 cup or more as needed (250 ml)
1	cup sugar (225 grams)
1/2	teaspoon ground cinnamon
	grated zest of 1 large lemon
	flour for dredging
2	eggs
1/2	pound good-quality semisweet chocolate (225 grams)
3	tablespoons water
2/3	cup unsweetened cocoa powder (50 grams)
1/2	cup plus 2 tablespoons red vermouth (150 ml)
3	tablespoons candied lemon *or* orange peel in tiny dice plus candied peel for garnish (45 grams)
2	tablespoons toasted peeled almonds (30 grams), plus extra almonds for garnish

Peel the eggplant and slice lengthwise about 1/4 inch thick: there should be about 20 slices, large and small. Salt and layer in a colander. Put a weighted plate on top. Leave for an hour. Rinse and pat dry.

Heat the olive oil and fry the eggplant over medium-high heat until lightly browned. Drain on paper towels.

In a soup plate, mix together 3/4 cup of the sugar, the cinnamon, and the grated lemon zest. Reserve. In another soup plate, put the flour for dredging and in another beat together the eggs.

Roll the eggplant slices in the flour and then in the eggs. Fry in hot olive oil over medium-high heat again, adding oil if necessary, until lightly browned. Drain on paper towels. While still hot, roll the fried eggplant in the sugar mixture and set aside on paper towels.

Put the chocolate, water, cocoa, and vermouth in the top of a double boiler over simmering water and melt, stirring occasionally, until dense and shiny. Remove from the heat and add the candied peel.

Put a few tablespoons of chocolate sauce over the bottom of the serving plate. Lay one third of the eggplant slices over the sauce and cover with more sauce. Sprinkle 1-1/2 teaspoons of the almonds over the sauce. Add another layer of eggplant, sauce, and almonds. Add a final layer of eggplant, the remaining sauce, and remaining almonds. Cover with plastic wrap and refrigerate for at least 3 hours. Bring to cool room temperature before serving. Decorate the dessert with candied peel and extra almonds.

CAMPANIA

Le Specialità del Signor Vuilleumier

SIGNOR VUILLEUMIER'S SPECIALTIES

*Signor
Vuilleumier's
Specialties*

Gnocchi di Semolino Soufflé
SOUFFLÉED SEMOLINA GNOCCHI

Sogliole all'Arancio
SOLE FILLETS WITH ORANGE SAUCE

Insalata Verde
GREEN SALAD (*page 137*)

Cremolata d'Arancio
ORANGE ICE

WINE
White: Episcopio Ravello; serve chilled

This menu comes from Ravello, just in from the Amalfi coast. The cathedral there is especially known for its mosaic-encrusted pulpit, supported by four slender, twisted columns held up by four of the most appealing stone lions in the world and topped by a majestic eagle. The local townspeople, however, are more interested in the sacred phial of Saint Pantaleone's blood that is kept locked away in one of the cathedral's side chapels. Every year, on July 27th, Saint Pantaleone's feast day, the blood is said to liquefy, and there are great celebrations with bands of musicians coming from as far away as Gioia Tauro and Potenza. In the evening there are fireworks, and each family prepares a banquet feast. Signor Pasquale Vuilleumier, who lives in one of the most beautiful palaces of Ravello, Il Palumbo, now a hotel, takes great care with his menu for this occasion. These are his recipes.

Gnocchi di Semolino Soufflé
SOUFFLÉED SEMOLINA GNOCCHI

Gnocchi can be made with potatoes, polenta, flour, or, as in this recipe, semolina. Sometimes they can be a little heavy, but not these. Here egg whites are beaten and folded into the semolina mixture to produce exquisitely light *gnocchi* with the most delicate flavor.

SERVES 6

13½- by 18½-inch (34 by
22 cm) ovenproof glass dish,
buttered

3-1/4	cups milk (800 ml)
	salt and freshly ground pepper to taste
	freshly grated nutmeg to taste
6	tablespoons unsalted butter (90 grams)
1	cup plus 2 tablespoons semolina (200 grams)
5	eggs, separated
1/4	pound Gruyère cheese, chopped (about 3/4 cup) (110 grams)
3/4	cup freshly grated Parmesan cheese (105 grams)

In a saucepan, bring the milk to a boil with the salt, pepper, and nutmeg. Add half the butter to the hot milk. When boiling, add the semolina "like rain," as Signor Vuilleumier's recipe says, stirring to prevent lumps from forming. Cook for 7 minutes or until the spoon stands straight in the mixture (again, as the recipe says).

Remove the pan from the heat and add the egg yolks one at a time, then half the Gruyère and half the Parmesan, mixing well.

continued

When the semolina has cooled slightly, beat the whites with a pinch of salt until stiff and fold the whites into the semolina. Fold in the remaining Gruyère. Dampen a marble surface or a large platter and turn out the *gnocchi* on it to cool completely. Preheat the oven to 375° (190).

Using 2 spoons, take up the semolina by the tablespoon and put it into the prepared dish in one layer. Melt the remaining butter and trickle it over the *gnocchi*. Sprinkle the remaining Parmesan over the *gnocchi*.

Bake for 20 minutes. Raise the oven temperature to 425° (220) and bake for 10 minutes more or until browned. Serve hot.

Sogliole all'Arancio
SOLE FILLETS WITH ORANGE SAUCE

Nature seems to have lavished all her gifts on the countryside around Ravello, which is perched high in the hills of Campania, not far from Positano. The rich black volcanic soil is so extraordinarily fertile that local farmers even plant crops of vegetables between their fruit trees. Grapes, citrus trees, and figs grow side by side; orchards and gardens lead down to the clear blue sea below. Oranges grow in profusion and, as they cost less than bread, are used to great effect in all kinds of local dishes. In this recipe the clean, fresh astringency of the orange sauce is particularly well matched to the delicate flavor of the sole.

SERVES 6

Ovenproof glass dish, about
15 by 8 inches (38 by 20 cm),
buttered

6	**soles, about 9 ounces each (250 grams), cleaned and filleted**
	flour for dredging
	salt to taste
5	**tablespoons (or more as needed) unsalted butter (75 grams)**
1	**tablespoon olive oil**
1/2	**cup freshly squeezed orange juice (125 ml)**
1	**heaped tablespoon orange zest in tiny julienne**
5	**tablespoons heavy cream (75 ml)**
	freshly ground pepper to taste
	orange sections and orange peel for garnish

continued

Preheat the oven to 375° (190).

Dry the fillets with paper towels and dredge them lightly in flour. Put a large pinch of salt in a frying pan, preferably iron, and add the butter and oil. When the fat is hot, add the fillets. Do not overcrowd the pan; fry the fillets over medium-high heat, in batches if necessary, adding more butter if needed. When the fillets have browned on one side, turn gently and brown on the other side. Remove carefully with a large spatula and place in the prepared dish. Add the orange juice to the frying pan, turn the heat to high, and scrape up the browned particles from the bottom of the pan. Cook for 1 minute and add the zest. When the juice is reduced by half, add the cream, season with salt and pepper, and lower the heat. Simmer the sauce for 2 minutes. Pour evenly over the sole.

Bake for 10 minutes. Serve hot, garnished with orange sections and "roses" made of curled orange peel.

Signor Vuilleumier's Specialties

Cremolata d'Arancio
ORANGE ICE

A soft, sweet orange ice, its flavor intensified by a generous helping of orange liqueur, makes the perfect ending to a summer meal and has been served in this part of the world for centuries. Look for an Italian orange liqueur, such as *aurum*.

SERVES 6

>   1   cup sugar (225 grams)
>   2   cups water (500 ml)
>   grated zest of 6 oranges
>   grated zest of 1 lemon
>   2-1/2   cups freshly squeezed orange juice (625 ml),
>   about 10 oranges
>   6   tablespoons freshly squeezed lemon juice (100 ml)
>   5   oranges
>   1/4   cup orange liqueur, preferably Italian (60 ml)
>   tiny strips of candied orange peel for garnish

Put the sugar and water in a saucepan and simmer for 5 minutes. Put the zests in the syrup and steep (off the heat) for 45 minutes. Add the orange and lemon juice to the syrup and strain. Process in an ice cream machine according to the manufacturer's instructions. Spoon the ice into a bowl and put in the freezer.

When the ice is frozen but manageable, use an ice cream scoop to make balls of ice and place in a serving bowl. Replace in the freezer.

Using a sharp knife, peel the oranges, removing both peel and white pith. Cut out the orange sections, carefully removing all skin. Put the sections in a bowl and pour the liqueur over them. Refrigerate until needed.

Serve the orange ice in its bowl accompanied by the orange sections. Decorate the ice balls with the candied orange peel strips.

Una Colazione Autunnale in Bisceglie

AN AUTUMN LUNCH
IN BISCEGLIE

Zuppa di Fave e Cicoria
FAVA BEAN AND DANDELION SOUP

Polipi di Bisceglie
OCTOPUS FROM BISCEGLIE

Insalata Pugliese
APULIAN SALAD

Pizzette
LITTLE PIZZAS

WINES
White: Locorotondo Bianco Secco; serve cold
Dessert: Aleatico di Puglia DOC (Puglia); serve cool

Across Italy on the Adriatic coast is Bisceglie, an old port town north of Bari in the region of Puglia (Apulia). The long, narrow coastal area on the northeast side of the boot of Italy is steeped in history and known for its small seaports and fishing towns, many of them complete with Norman castles. Before the Normans conquered southern Italy, however, the Greeks had settled here, and their influence, too, can still be felt. Puglia is one of the richer sections of southern Italy, but the food is simple, being, as Waverley Root put it, "resolutely peasant in spirit." Lina Alferi, a native of Bisceglie who now lives in Rome, assembled the next two menus. She chose only those recipes that are typical of her part of the country.

Zuppa di Fave e Cicoria
FAVA BEAN
AND DANDELION SOUP

This "poor man's" soup is made from dried fava beans, which are cultivated all over southern Italy, and dandelion greens growing wild in the fields. The combination, served throughout Puglia, is marvelous, and it is, according to Lina, short on price and long on time. If dandelion greens are not available, use chicory instead.

SERVES 4 TO 6

1 pound dried fava beans, soaked in cold water for
   24 hours (450 grams)
1/2 medium carrot, finely chopped
1 medium onion, finely chopped
1 4-inch celery stalk, finely chopped
1/4 cup olive oil (60 ml)
1 cup pureed Italian plum tomatoes (drained if
   canned, peeled and seeded if fresh) (250 grams)
1 beef bouillon cube
2 pounds dandelion greens, wild if possible, cleaned
   and chopped (900 grams)
   salt and freshly ground pepper to taste

After soaking, remove and discard the outer skin from the fava beans. Put the peeled fava beans in a saucepan with cold water to come 1 inch over the beans. Bring to a boil and cook over low heat for about 45 minutes. Pass the beans through a food mill or puree them in a blender or in a food processor fitted with the steel blade, in batches if necessary. Reserve.

continued

In another saucepan, cook the carrot, onion, and celery in the olive oil over medium-low heat. Add a little water if necessary to prevent browning. Add the tomato puree and bouillon cube. Add this mixture to the fava bean puree in a saucepan large enough to hold the greens too. Reserve.

In a large stockpot, cook the greens in boiling salted water until tender, about 20 to 25 minutes. Drain. Bring the fava beans to a boil and add the greens, mixing. Simmer for 15 minutes. Serve in soup bowls; pass the pepper mill and a little pitcher of extra-virgin olive oil.

Polipi di Bisceglie
OCTOPUS FROM BISCEGLIE

Bisceglie is now an important fishing town, but when Lina was a child it was still a small village where the fishermen brought in their local catch every morning. Sea bass, sole, squid, octopus, and red mullet are all fished in this part of the world, and there are any number of local octopus recipes. The most popular method is to gently sauté them in garlic-flavored oil and hot red pepper flakes and then add a little wine.

This dish, which can be served hot or cold, can also be made with squid, but since squid gives off more liquid than octopus it should be cooked uncovered. Depending on the size of the squid, you may need to increase the amount of cooking time. Be careful, however, not to overcook it; although you might think that the more it is cooked the more tender it will become, this is simply not the case with squid and there is nothing more disheartening to the palate than overcooked, rubbery squid.

SERVES 4

2-1/2	pounds small octopus (1.100 grams)
5	tablespoons olive oil (75 ml)
4	garlic cloves
1/2	teaspoon (or to taste) hot red pepper flakes
	scant 1/2 cup dry white wine (100 ml)
	salt to taste
1/2	cup finely chopped parsley

Clean the octopus (see page 419). If they are baby octopus, leave them as they are. If they are larger, cut them lengthwise into 4 or more pieces. Soak in cold water until you are ready to prepare them.

Heat the oil in a pan large enough to hold the octopus. Add the garlic and hot red pepper flakes and cook over medium-low heat until the garlic browns. Discard the garlic and add the octopus. Cover and cook over low heat for 30 minutes. Add the wine and cook, still covered, for 15 minutes. Test for tenderness and season with salt. If the octopus is not tender when tested, cook for a few more minutes. Unlike squid, octopus won't become rubbery if overcooked. Sprinkle the parsley over the octopus before serving.

Insalata Pugliese
APULIAN SALAD

SERVES 4

2 medium-size ripe fresh tomatoes, about 2/3 pound
(300 grams)
1 small head romaine lettuce, washed and dried
1/4 cup drained capers, washed and dried (40 grams)
3/4 cup green olives packed in brine, pitted
(150 grams)
1 garlic clove, minced
1 scant tablespoon (or to taste) dried oregano
salt and freshly ground pepper to taste
5 tablespoons extra-virgin olive oil (75 ml)
2 tablespoons freshly squeezed lemon juice

Wash and dry the tomatoes and cut them into wedges. Cut the lettuce
into bite-size pieces and put into a salad bowl with the tomatoes. Add the
capers and olives. Put the garlic, oregano, salt, and pepper in a small bowl
and mix in the olive oil. Add the lemon juice, beating with a fork. Pour the
dressing over the salad and toss to mix well. Serve at once.

Pizzette
LITTLE PIZZAS

In Italy the word *pizza* is used to mean any flat, round, baked pastry. When Lina was a child, she remembers, her mother made huge quantities of these hard, chocolate-coated, almond- and coffee-flavored cookies called *little pizzas* and then took them to the town baker to be baked in his wood-fired oven. Each family would stamp its initials on its *pizzette* to be sure it got its own batch back. Nowadays these cookies, traditionally served on flat straw trays, are made at home. They are delicious served with a sweet wine for dessert.

MAKES ABOUT 30

1	pound unpeeled shelled almonds, finely chopped but not pulverized (about 2-3/4 cups) (450 grams)
2	cups flour (225 grams)
1-1/4	cups sugar (280 grams)
	pinch of baking soda
	grated zest of 1 large lemon
1/4	teaspoon ground cinnamon
1/4	teaspoon ground cloves
5	tablespoons (or more as needed) brewed *espresso* (75 ml)
1	cup plus 3 tablespoons water (300 ml)
1	cup plus 2 tablespoons sugar (250 grams)
2	tablespoons unsweetened cocoa powder

Preheat the oven to 375° (190). Mix together the almonds, flour, sugar, baking soda, lemon zest, cinnamon, and cloves. Add the coffee a tablespoon at a time, adding enough to make the dough hold together. Make rolls of the dough the size of sausages (about 1 inch thick). Cut 2-inch (5 cm) cookies on the bias. Place the cookies on a buttered sheet of foil on a cookie sheet and bake for 30 minutes. Remove to a rack and cool.

continued

Put the water, sugar, and cocoa in a small saucepan and simmer for 20 minutes or until a drop of syrup placed on a saucer strings when held between 2 fingers. Let the syrup cool. Dip the cooled cookies in the syrup and roll them around to coat them in the syrup. Place on foil and allow to dry.

Pass the cookies through the syrup a second time. Place on foil and leave to dry completely. These will keep for a month in an airtight container.

An Autumn Lunch in Bisceglie

La Festa dei Tre Santi a Bisceglie

DINNER TO CELEBRATE THE FEAST OF THE THREE SAINTS

*Dinner
to
Celebrate
the Feast
of the
Three
Saints*

Antipasto di Mare
SEAFOOD HORS D'OEUVRES

Pasta al Forno di Bisceglie
BAKED BISCEGLIE PASTA

Agnello al Calderotto
LAMB CASSEROLE

Fagiolini in Insalata
GREEN BEAN SALAD

Morzapany
MARZIPAN BALLS

WINES
White: Rivera (Bari); serve very cold
Red: Torre Giulia (Foggia); serve at room temperature
Dessert: Moscato di Trani (Bari); serve chilled

The biggest celebration of the year in Bisceglie comes at the beginning of August. It is the Patronal Feast of the Three Martyred Saints, and since the town has three patron saints rather than the usual one, the festivities last for three days. Saints Mauro, Sergio, and Pantaleone have been venerated in Bisceglie for many centuries and are believed to have saved the townspeople from cholera, plague, earthquakes, and wars. The three saints date back to the Roman period, when they were martyred as Christians. Several times in the intervening centuries their remains disappeared, only to reappear after a few hundred years. Like most religious feasts in Italy, this one is an occasion for music, dancing, fireworks, religious processions, and, of course, celebratory food.

The recipes come from a brilliant Bisceglie cook, Lina Alferi. For the *fagiolini*, simply boil green beans until they're tender, drain, then dress them with olive oil, salt, and lemon juice to taste.

Antipasto di Mare
SEAFOOD HORS D'OEUVRES

*Dinner
to
Celebrate
the Feast
of the
Three
Saints*

Traditionally each family gets together for a celebratory meal on the second day of the festivities. Although *antipasto* is not eaten that frequently in the South, on a festive occasion it is customary to begin with an *antipasto di mare*—a wonderful assortment of local seafood marinated in lemon juice and olive oil. Start this *antipasto* a day ahead.

SERVES 4 TO 6

3/4	**pound fresh anchovies* (330 grams)**
1/2	**cup plus 2 tablespoons freshly squeezed lemon juice (150 ml)**
	salt and freshly ground black pepper to taste
1-1/2	**pounds mussels (675 grams)**
1	**pound octopus (450 grams)**
3/4	**pound squid (330 grams)**
5	**cups water (1.250 ml)**
3	**garlic cloves**
3/4	**pound shrimp (330 grams)**
5	**tablespoons olive oil (15 ml)**

Clean the anchovies (see page 419). Rinse them under cold water and drain well. Put into a soup bowl with 3 tablespoons of the lemon juice and salt and pepper. Reserve.

Clean the mussels. Remove the beards and scrub well, scraping with a knife if necessary. Rinse in cold water. Put the mussels in a frying pan over high heat. Discard those that don't open and put the open ones in a bowl, discarding the shells. Strain and reserve the mussels' liquid.

---

* If fresh anchovies are not available, use double the quantity of squid.

Clean the octopus (see page 419) if not already cleaned. Rinse and soak in cold water until needed.

Clean the squid if necessary. Rinse and soak in cold water.

Boil the water with 3 tablespoons of the lemon juice, the garlic, and salt. Cook the shrimp in the simmering water just until pink, about 3 minutes. Remove with a slotted spoon and cool.

Add the octopus to the simmering water and cook for 13 to 15 minutes or until tender when pierced. Remove with a slotted spoon and cool.

Add the squid to the simmering water and cook for 8 to 10 minutes or until tender. Remove and cool.

Peel the shrimp and put them in a serving bowl. Cut the squid and octopus into 1/4-inch slices and add to the bowl. Add the mussels and their liquid and the drained anchovies. (Discard the marinade.) Add the remaining lemon juice and the olive oil. Season with salt and pepper. Toss well and cover with plastic wrap. Refrigerate until the next day.

Pasta al Forno di Bisceglie
BAKED BISCEGLIE PASTA

A true Biscegliean likes to eat this elaborate pasta dish lukewarm. Perhaps this custom dates back to the time when a large baked pasta dish such as this would have been prepared at home, cooked by the local baker in one of his large ovens, and then carried home to be eaten. Most of the old-timers in Bisceglie remember having their holiday pasta cooked by the baker and are quick to tell you that nothing tastes quite so good as pasta baked in a wood-burning oven.

SERVES 8 TO 10

9- by 13-inch (23 by 34 cm)
ovenproof glass dish, oiled

FOR THE *RAGÙ*:

1/4	**cup olive oil (60 ml)**
1	**small celery stalk, finely chopped**
1	**medium carrot, finely chopped**
1	**medium onion, finely chopped**
1	**garlic clove, finely chopped**
1-1/2	**ounces *prosciutto* (1 thick slice), finely chopped (45 grams)**
	salt and freshly ground pepper to taste
1/2	**pound ground beef (225 grams)**
1/2	**cup dry white wine (125 ml)**
1	**tablespoon tomato paste**
1	**quart tomato puree (1 kilogram)**

FOR THE MEATBALLS:

1/2	**pound ground beef (225 grams)**
1/2	**cup freshly grated *pecorino* cheese (65 grams)**
2	**tablespoons fine dry bread crumbs**
6	**tablespoons finely chopped parsley**
2	**eggs**
	salt and freshly ground pepper to taste
1/4	**cup olive oil (60 ml)**

*Dinner
to
Celebrate
the Feast
of the
Three
Saints*

TO ASSEMBLE THE DISH:

    1   **pound *rigatoni* (450 grams)**
    1   **cup freshly grated Parmesan cheese (135 grams)**
  1/3 **pound *mortadella*, finely chopped (150 grams)**
  3/4 **pound *mozzarella* cheese, finely chopped (about
        2-3/4 cups) (330 grams)**
        freshly ground pepper to taste

Make the *ragù*. Heat the olive oil in a saucepan, preferably terra-cotta. Add the vegetables, *prosciutto,* salt, and pepper. Cook over low heat, stirring occasionally, for about 20 minutes or until the vegetables begin to brown. Add the ground beef and brown, about 10 minutes. Add the wine and cook for 5 minutes.

Add the tomato paste, mixing well, and the tomato puree. Bring back to a boil and simmer, covered, for 1 hour, stirring every now and then. Season with salt and pepper. (The *ragù* can be prepared the day before.)

Make the meatballs. Mix together the meat, *pecorino,* bread crumbs, parsley, and eggs. Season with salt and pepper. Make 3/4-inch (2 cm) meatballs. Heat the oil in a skillet and fry the meatballs in 2 batches over moderately high heat. Drain on paper towels. Reserve. Preheat the oven to 400° (200).

Cook the *rigatoni* in boiling salted water until *al dente*. Drain and dress with half the Parmesan. Add 1 cup of the *ragù* and mix.

Assemble the dish. Put 2 or 3 tablespoons of the *ragù* on the bottom of the prepared dish. Put one third of the pasta over the *ragù*, then half the *mortadella,* half the *mozzarella*, half the meatballs, a third of the *ragù,* and a third of the Parmesan. Grind pepper over the top. Make another layer of one third *rigatoni* and the remaining *mortadella, mozzarella,* and meatballs. Spoon over another third of the *ragù* and sprinkle with another third of the Parmesan. Add another grinding of pepper. Spread the remaining pasta, *ragù,* and Parmesan on top. Bake for 45 minutes. Let the pasta rest at least 15 minutes before serving.

Agnello al Calderotto
LAMB CASSEROLE

*Dinner
to
Celebrate
the Feast
of the
Three
Saints*

In this part of Italy lamb is invariably served as the main course on a big holiday. While many families opt for a lamb roasted on a spit, some prefer to serve this wonderfully aromatic casserole dish—the recipe was given to Lina by Paola Pettini, who runs a cooking school in Bari.

SERVES 6

10-inch (26 cm) flameproof
casserole, preferably terra-cotta

1	small hind leg of lamb with part of the rib cage, about 3 pounds (1.350 grams)
1	large onion, finely chopped
1	garlic clove, finely chopped
1/2	cup freshly grated *pecorino* cheese (65 grams)
3	sweet sausages, about 9 ounces (250 grams)
3	tablespoons finely chopped parsley
2	bay leaves
2	3-inch fresh rosemary sprigs
	salt and freshly ground pepper to taste
4	canned Italian plum tomatoes *or* peeled, seeded fresh tomatoes
1/2	cup dry white wine (125 ml)

Have the butcher cut the lamb into 2-inch pieces, reserving all bones. Rinse the lamb in cold water and pat dry. Put the lamb, bones, onion, garlic, and *pecorino* in the casserole.

Remove and discard the casings and crumble the sausages into the casserole. Add the parsley, bay leaves, and rosemary and season with salt and pepper.

Gently squeeze the liquid from the tomatoes and add to the casserole with the wine. Cover and cook over medium-low heat for 1 hour, covered, stirring occasionally. Test the meat at the end of the cooking time. The sauce should be slightly thickened; if it is too thin, cook, uncovered, for a few minutes. Serve the lamb hot, in the casserole.

Morzapany
MARZIPAN BALLS

*Dinner
to
Celebrate
the Feast
of the
Three
Saints*

The love of marzipan gets stronger the farther south you go in Italy, but when you reach Sicily it really takes off! This passion is nowhere stronger than in Palermo. Should you happen to be there at the end of October, you will see in every pastry shop window an incredible assortment of fruit, vegetables, and even snails, all exquisitely fabricated out of marzipan. These delicacies are made in preparation for All Souls' Day, when they are given to all children who have prayed for the souls of the dead during the past year.

Gastone Vuillier, in his book *La Sicilia*, published in Milan in 1897, gives a charming description of these confections:

> *Most marvelous of all is the fruit that . . . [the shops] exhibit, such as figs just opened from which a crystalline drop is oozing, little strawberries, pears, bananas, walnuts with the shell broken so that the inside is visible, roast chestnuts sprinkled with a faint trace of ashes; nor do they forget the legumes. . . . And all this in almond paste that melts in your mouth . . . the imitation is of an amazing exactness.*

The recipe for these traditional marzipan balls came from Lina's cousin, who still lives in Bisceglie. But after testing the recipe, Lina was not happy with how the marzipan balls looked and must have used up 10 pounds of almonds making tiny adjustments and refinements to her cousin's recipe. Finally she was ready to let them out of her kitchen. Rich and chewy, these little marzipan delicacies keep for weeks and are particularly good served with a sweet dessert wine.

MAKES 75 TO 85

Ovenproof paper cases,
1½ inches (about 4 cm)
across the bottom

> **1** **pound 1 ounce shelled almonds, peeled (about**
> **3 cups) (475 grams)**
> **2** **cups sugar (450 grams)**
> **grated zest of 1 large lemon**
> **3** **eggs**
> **1** **teaspoon vanilla extract**
> **1** **egg white**
> **sugar**

In a food processor, a small one if possible, fitted with the steel blade, chop the almonds in batches, each time with some of the sugar. They must be very finely pulverized. Put in a bowl and add the lemon zest. Beat the eggs with the vanilla and add, mixing well with the hands. The mixture must be soft and moist but not wet. Preheat the oven to 425° (220) and place a rack in the upper third of the oven.

Put the egg white in a plate. Rub your palms with egg white and form small balls with 1 teaspoon of the mixture, dividing the total so that there are 75 to 85 balls. Place in the paper cases and put on a cookie sheet. Bake for 14 or 15 minutes, watching carefully. They must be slightly browned. Remove from the oven and, while still hot, sprinkle sugar over the *morzapany*. Cool on cake racks.

When completely cold and hardened, peel off the paper cases. If too brown on the bottom (Lina says they always are), grate them gently across the bottom with a fine grater to remove the dark part. Store in tin boxes.

Un Matrimonio nella Campagna Molisana

A WEDDING PARTY
IN THE
MOLISE COUNTRYSIDE

A
Wedding
Party
in the
Molise
Countryside

Poncia per Natale
CHRISTMAS PUNCH

Fegato e Scarola
LIVER AND ESCAROLE

Pasta al Ragù
PASTA WITH RAGOUT

Braciola al Ragù
ROLLED VEAL IN RAGOUT SAUCE

Agnello Arrosto con Patate
ROAST LAMB WITH POTATOES

Taralli col Naspro
ICED HARD BISCUITS

Taralli Salati
SALTED HARD BISCUITS

WINES
White: Molise (Campobasso); serve cold
Red: Marsicano (Isernia); serve at cool room temperature
Dessert: Moscato; serve chilled

Even today a country wedding in southern Italy is steeped in ritual and tradition. The first rite that takes place when two young people decide to get married is for the future groom to bring his parents to visit the bride's family. There the two exchange rings and the bride's future mother-in-law presents her with a ring, earrings, and a gold necklace—a gift known as a *concerto*. Two days before the wedding, which always takes place on a Saturday, an engagement party is held at the bride's home. Her trousseau (the wedding dress is provided by her family; the veil and wedding bouquet come from the groom's mother) is displayed in a bedroom where the bed has been made with new linens and a coverlet, both embroidered and edged with handmade lace. The *concerto* is placed on the bed together with the bride's nuptial nightgown, the groom's pajamas, a handful of money, an Easter egg, and a wreath of olive twigs decorated with sugar-coated almonds. The groom's wedding clothes, a present from the bride's family, are placed on a table. That evening the bride's future mother-in-law presents her with a quilted bed cover, a black coat, shoes, gloves, a handbag, and an umbrella. Then the couple, their families, and invited guests enter the bedroom and throw rice, sugar-coated almonds, and money on the *primo letto* (first bed). Everyone dances, and homemade rolls filled with *prosciutto,* cookies, and sweets are served. If it is summer, the guests will be offered a lemon liqueur to drink; in winter a *poncia* or punch is served.

The next day the bride's trousseau is moved to the groom's house and the *primo letto* is remade by the bride's godmothers. On the wedding day, following the church ceremony, an elaborate wedding feast is held, with dancing and toasts. At home later, the couple is serenaded, and the newlyweds respond by offering the serenaders wine and *prosciutto* sandwiches. For one day following the wedding the groom's parents bring them food, for the bride must remain at home and not be seen. During this time it is the bridegroom's responsibility, perhaps for the only time in his life, to do the shopping. On the following Sunday the bride puts on the coat and shoes given by her mother-in-law, takes the umbrella if it is raining, and goes to Mass with her husband. And so her married life officially begins.

Maria Bonicori prepared and served this menu for her own daughter's wedding in Campobasso, the capital of the Molise region, which is south of Abruzzi. The recipes are taken from *La Cucina Molisana,* a book published in 1986, that is full of traditional recipes from Molise, compiled by Anna Maria Lombardi and Rita Mastropaolo.

Poncia per Natale
CHRISTMAS PUNCH

Italians like to bring out this punch on special occasions, such as baptisms, engagements, weddings, and at Christmas. They also serve it mixed with hot milk for breakfast and sometimes use it as a sauce to pour over a steaming bread pudding. Note that this liqueur takes three weeks to ripen, so start well ahead.

MAKES MORE THAN 1 GALLON

> **peel of 1 large lemon**
> 1 **quart spirits for homemade liqueurs *or* vodka (1 liter)**
> 4 **pounds sugar (1.800 grams)**
> 5 **cups water (1.250 ml)**
> **coffee beans**

Put the lemon peel in the spirits and let sit for 24 hours.

In a heavy saucepan, put 2-1/4 pounds of the sugar; put the rest of the sugar in another heavy saucepan. Put the water in the pan containing 2-1/4 pounds sugar and bring to a boil. Begin to heat the sugar in the other pan. (The pans must be close to each other.) When the sugar in the second pan begins to turn a darkish golden brown, begin adding the boiling syrup, a ladleful at a time. Add all the syrup to the caramel in this manner. Cool.

Discard the peel and add the spirits to the cooled syrup. Put the liqueur in bottles, adding 2 or 3 coffee beans per bottle. Let the liqueur rest for 20 days before serving.

Fegato e Scarola
LIVER AND ESCAROLE

Liver dishes are not often found in the South, but L'Aquila, the capital of Abruzzi, is particularly noted for two liver dishes: *fegati dolci* (sweet liver) and *fegati pazzi* (crazy liver). The first is cooked with honey, the second with very hot red peppers. Here liver is cooked with escarole and hot red pepper flakes—a variation on crazy liver.

SERVES 6 AS ANTIPASTO

1/3	**cup olive oil (80 ml)**
1	**medium onion, thinly sliced**
1	**pound lamb's liver *or* pork liver, cut into 3/4-inch dice (450 grams)**
1/2	**cup dry white wine (125 ml)**
1/2	**teaspoon (or to taste) hot red pepper flakes**
	salt to taste
2	**pounds escarole, washed (900 grams)**
	freshly ground pepper to taste
4	**eggs**
2	**tablespoons finely chopped parsley**
3/4	**cup freshly grated *pecorino* cheese (105 grams)**

Heat the oil in a skillet and cook the onion over low heat until transparent. Add the liver and cook over high heat until the meat "speaks" (makes a frying noise). Add the wine a little at a time, then the pepper flakes and salt. Lower the heat and finish cooking the liver over low heat. All this will take about 20 minutes.

Cook the escarole in boiling salted water for 10 minutes or until *al dente*. Drain and, when cool, squeeze out excess moisture. Chop coarsely. Reserve a little of the cooking water. Add the escarole to the liver with a little of the reserved water if the mixture seems too dry. Season with salt and pepper. Cover and cook over low heat for 15 minutes, stirring occasionally.

In a small bowl, beat together the eggs, parsley, *pecorino,* and a pinch of salt. Pour the eggs over the liver and mix well. Cook, covered, over low heat for 2 or 3 minutes, stirring every now and then. Serve hot. This is also an excellent main course.

Pasta al Ragù
PASTA WITH RAGOUT

At a country wedding in southern Italy it is still the custom for the bride's female relatives, including her most distant cousins, to help prepare the wedding feast and be on hand to serve the meal and clean up afterward. If the wedding is large, several lambs and even a calf or two will be butchered beforehand and the meat used to make several dishes. One of these will invariably be based on a rich, hearty *ragù* sauce. As befits a wedding, this is a very fancy *ragù* sauce made from tomatoes that are cooked with the rolled veal in the next recipe.

SERVES 6

> 1-1/3 pounds *rigatoni* (600 grams)
> 3/4 cup freshly grated *pecorino* cheese (105 grams)
>   the *ragù* sauce from *Braciola al Ragù* (recipe
>   follows)
>   freshly ground pepper

Cook the pasta in boiling salted water until *al dente.* Drain and dress with the *pecorino* and *ragù* sauce. Serve hot and pass the pepper mill.

Braciola al Ragù

ROLLED VEAL IN
RAGOUT SAUCE

Here veal stuffed with hard-cooked eggs and sausage meat is gently simmered in a rich tomato sauce, which is then used to dress the pasta accompanying the veal.

SERVES 6

Kitchen string

- 1 large slice of boneless veal, about 2-1/2 pounds, trimmed to about 11 by 15 inches (28 by 38 cm) (1.100 grams)
- 5 fairly thick slices *prosciutto,* about 5 ounces (150 grams)
- 3 hard-cooked eggs, shelled
- 2 sweet or hot sausages, about 1/4 pound (110 grams)
- 1/4 cup finely chopped parsley
- 2 garlic cloves
- 2 teaspoons finely chopped fresh mint *or* 1-1/2 teaspoons dried mint
- 1/4 cup freshly grated *pecorino* cheese (35 grams) salt and freshly ground black pepper to taste
- 1 medium onion
- 1/2 cup olive oil (125 ml)
- 1/3 cup dry red wine (80 ml)
- 1-1/2 quarts tomato puree (1-1/2 liters)

Trim tendons and excess fat from the slice of veal and pound with a meat pounder until of even thickness. Lay 4 of the *prosciutto* slices over the veal, leaving a 1-inch border all around. Lay the hard-cooked eggs in a row over the *prosciutto*. Remove and discard the sausage casings and crumble the sausages. Sprinkle them evenly over the veal.

Chop together 2 tablespoons of the parsley, 1 garlic clove, and 1 teaspoon of the mint. Sprinkle the herb mixture, *pecorino,* salt, and pepper over the veal. Roll up the veal and tie it tightly with kitchen string.

Chop together the remaining *prosciutto,* parsley, garlic, and onion. In a saucepan large enough to contain the veal, preferably terra-cotta, heat the oil and sauté the *prosciutto* mixture over low heat until limp, about 15 minutes. Add the veal roll and brown, turning it, over medium heat. Add the red wine a tablespoon at a time.

When all the wine has evaporated, add the tomato puree and the remaining mint; season with salt. Cover and simmer for 2 hours, turning the meat every now and then. The tomato puree will be dark and dense. Allow the meat to cool completely.

When you're ready to serve, preheat the oven to 400° (200). Slice the meat and arrange it in an ovenproof dish. Spread a little sauce over it, cover with foil, and bake for 15 minutes. Serve with some of the hot sauce in a sauceboat.

NOTE: Leftover *ragù* can be frozen or refrigerated, covered, for up to 3 days.

Agnello Arrosto con Patate
ROAST LAMB WITH POTATOES

In the south of Italy a wedding without lamb is unheard of. Here is the classic Molise way of doing it: roasted lamb with lashings of garlic and rosemary, alongside potatoes roasted to a crispy finish in the same pan.

SERVES 4

Large roasting pan, about 11 by 14 inches (28 by 36 cm)

2-1/4	pounds lamb, leg and part of loin (1 kilogram)
3	garlic cloves, sliced
	salt and freshly ground pepper to taste
1/4	cup chopped fresh rosemary
2	pounds potatoes, cut into 1-inch wedges and soaked in cold water (900 grams)
1/4	cup olive oil (60 ml)
1/2	teaspoon (or to taste) hot red pepper flakes

Have the butcher cut slashes in the meat every inch or so without cutting through completely. Wash and dry the meat. Put garlic slices into the cuts in the meat, reserving one sliced clove for the potatoes. Season the meat with salt and pepper and rub 2 tablespoons rosemary over it. Preheat the oven to 325° (160).

Drain and dry the potatoes and put them in a bowl. Pour 2-1/2 table-spoons of the oil over them, along with the reserved garlic slices, 1 tablespoon of the rosemary, salt, and the pepper flakes, tossing to mix well. Put the meat in the roasting pan with half the potatoes on each side. Trickle the remaining oil over the meat, brushing it over the entire surface of the meat, and sprinkle on the remaining rosemary.

Roast for 50 minutes. Turn the heat up to 425° (220) and cook for 20 more minutes. Serve hot.

Taralli col Naspro
ICED HARD BISCUITS

Everyone has his own special recipe for these hard little biscuits that are shaped like bagels and covered with a plasterlike white icing. They are very popular in the South and always brought out on special occasions. For a baptism the icing would be tinted blue or pink.

MAKES ABOUT 65

>   2/3   **pound (2-2/3 cups) flour (300 grams)**
>   3   **large egg yolks**
>   **pinch of salt**
>   1   **tablespoon plus 1 teaspoon olive oil**
>   1   **cup plus 2 tablespoons sugar (250 grams)**
>   1   **cup water (250 ml)**

Mound the flour on a pastry board or marble surface and make a well in the center. Put the egg yolks, salt, and oil in the well. Beat the eggs with a fork, gradually incorporating the flour. When the eggs have absorbed enough flour to be difficult to beat, begin kneading by hand. Work the dough until it has absorbed the flour.

Cut off a small piece of dough at a time, leaving the rest under an overturned bowl. Shape the dough into pencils about 3-1/2 inches long. Bring the ends together to make a circle and press the ends to seal. Make all the *taralli* this way. Preheat the oven to 425° (220).

Bring a large pan half full of water to a boil. Put in the *taralli* 4 or 5 at a time. When they float to the top, remove them with a slotted spoon and drain on a tea towel. When cold, make a shallow cut all around the middle of the *taralli,* using a very sharp knife. Cool completely. When cold, put them on a cookie sheet and bake for 14 to 15 minutes or until golden. Cool on racks.

continued

Put the sugar and water in a heavy saucepan over medium-high heat and bring to a boil. Continue to cook until the mixture makes large bubbles and no longer smokes, about 15 minutes. Test a drop of the syrup on a saucer; pinch it between your fingers; it should stick. Beat the syrup until it forms a white spreadable icing, adding water if necessary. Dip the *taralli* in the icing at once and allow them to dry on a rack overnight. Store in an airtight tin.

A Wedding Party in the Molise Countryside

Taralli Salati
SALTED HARD BISCUITS

This recipe is a savory variation on the previous one. Most Italian families keep a ready supply of salted *taralli* biscuits on hand—if you store them in a tight container, they keep for ages. They are often served as a snack between meals, sometimes with a glass of wine on the side. This recipe comes from Paola Pettini, who likes to collect recipes from little old ladies dressed in black. She teaches these traditional Barese recipes in her cooking school in Bari.

MAKES ABOUT 90

> 1 **pound (4 cups) flour (450 grams)**
> 6 **tablespoons olive oil (100 ml)**
> 3/4 **teaspoon salt**
> 3 **tablespoons (or more as needed) dry white wine**
> 1-1/4 **teaspoons baking powder**

Mound the flour on a pastry board or marble surface and make a well in the center. Put the oil and salt in the well and mix. Add the wine and baking powder and knead the dough until smooth and silky.

Roll the dough into finger-size cylinders and bring the ends together to make circles about 2 inches (5 cm) in diameter. Press the ends to seal. Preheat the oven to 400° (200).

Bring a large pot of water to a boil and put the *taralli,* a few at a time, in the boiling water. When they float on the surface, remove with a slotted spoon and drain on a tea towel.

Put the *taralli* on a cookie sheet and bake for about 20 minutes. Cool on racks. Store in airtight tins.

Una Cena Festiva in Poggetello

A FESTIVE MEAL
IN POGGETELLO

A
Festive
Meal
in
Poggetello

Fiaoni
LITTLE BASKETS

Agnello alla Cacciatora
HUNTER'S LAMB

Patate Abruzzesi
POTATOES FROM ABRUZZI

Pane Rozzo
ROUGH BREAD

WINE
Red: Cerasuolo d'Abruzzo Rosso; serve cool

Giovanni and Assunta Grossi come from Poggetello, a farming village high in the mountains of Abruzzi, a small region of southern Italy that borders on the Adriatic coast. Most Italians agree that for some reason the Abruzzi produces the best chefs in the whole of Italy. For many generations Giovanni's family has raised sheep and vegetables, and Giovanni grew up learning to butcher hogs, cure his own *prosciutto,* smoke his own fish, and make his own *salame,* sausages, and lard. (His mother even wove the sheets and towels for her wedding trousseau from homegrown flax.) His wife, Assunta, is also steeped in country ways. She is an exceptional cook and chose this menu to include the kind of dishes that would be served on a special occasion in her hometown.

Fiaoni
LITTLE BASKETS

These little tarts in the shape of baskets are traditionally served in Abruzzi either as a first course or in the afternoon with a glass of sweet wine. (In Calabria they are called *fragone.*) *Pecorino,* a cheese made from sheep's milk, is the favorite cheese of the Abruzzi region and is used for both eating and cooking. The little pastry baskets, filled with a mixture of *pecorino, ricotta,* goat cheese, and raisins, served warm, puffed and lightly browned, are the most delicious treat imaginable.

MAKES ABOUT 32,
SERVING 8 AS A FIRST COURSE

FOR THE PASTA:
    2-1/4 to 2-3/4 cups flour (250 to 320 grams)
       3 large eggs
       1 tablespoon olive oil

FOR THE FILLING:
    2/3 pound fresh *caciotta or* firm fresh goat cheese, chopped (300 grams)
    1/2 pound *ricotta* cheese (225 grams)
    1/2 pound freshly grated *pecorino* cheese (225 grams)
      3 eggs
      1 cup raisins (160 grams)
        freshly ground black pepper to taste

Put 2 cups of the flour on a wooden or marble surface and make a well in the center. Break the eggs into the well and add the oil. Beat the eggs and oil with a fork, gradually incorporating flour. When all the flour has been absorbed, knead the dough, using as much of the remaining flour as needed to make a pasta of fairly soft consistency, softer than that used for *fettuccine.* Put the pasta under an overturned bowl.

continued

Prepare the filling. Mix the *caciotta* with the *ricotta* and *pecorino*. Add the eggs one at a time, mixing well. Add the raisins and add a generous grinding of pepper. Reserve. Preheat the oven to 350° (180).

Roll out the pasta by hand to 1/8-inch thickness or by machine to number 4. Cut circles 3-1/2 inches (9 cm) in diameter. Put 1 tablespoon of the filling in the center of each circle and pinch the pasta on opposite sides, pulling it up slightly to form an edge. Pinch all around the circles in this way, forming little round baskets. Pinch the pasta carefully; the edges of the baskets will have a raised, pointed border.

When all the baskets are formed, cut strips 1/4 inch wide and place 2 strips on top of the baskets, crossed. Seal the strips to the edges. Oil a cookie sheet lightly and put the baskets on it, 2-1/2 inches apart.

Bake for 18 to 20 minutes or until puffed and lightly browned. Serve hot.

NOTE: These can also be cut with a 2-1/4-inch cookie cutter and served hot with white wine as an aperitif.

Agnello alla Cacciatora
HUNTER'S LAMB

Abruzzi is renowned for its excellent lamb and exports it in great quantities to the north of Italy. Each town or village in the region boasts its own lamb recipes, and on a drive through Abruzzi on a holiday or during a fair it is not uncommon to find a lamb being roasted on a large outdoor wooden spit, giving off its unforgettable aroma. But for those of us who don't often have the opportunity to eat lamb cooked this way, here is the next best thing—chunks of lamb cooked in wine and garlic and, when almost done, coated with a sauce made from marjoram, rosemary, anchovy paste, and vinegar. It's a dazzling combination. This dish is served with a lettuce salad, dressed with oil and vinegar.

        2 **pounds 14 ounces lamb shoulder (1.300 grams)**
      1/3 **cup olive oil (80 ml)**
        3 **garlic cloves**
      1/2 **teaspoon (or to taste) hot red pepper flakes**
           salt to taste
      1/2 **cup dry white wine (125 ml)**
    1-1/2 **teaspoons dried marjoram *or* 1 heaped tablespoon**
           fresh marjoram leaves
        1 **heaped tablespoon fresh rosemary leaves**
        1 **teaspoon anchovy paste**
        2 **tablespoons wine vinegar**

Cut the lamb into pieces about 2 inches long and 1-1/2 inches wide. Heat the oil in a skillet large enough to hold the lamb. Add the garlic and pepper flakes and brown the lamb over medium-high heat. Season with salt. Pour the wine over the lamb and allow half to evaporate. Cover and turn the heat to low. Cook for 20 minutes, stirring occasionally. Skim off any fat that has risen to the surface.

In a mortar, pound together the marjoram and rosemary. Add the anchovy paste and vinegar, mixing. Pour this sauce over the lamb and cook over medium heat, stirring constantly, for 5 minutes. Serve hot.

Patate Abruzzesi
POTATOES FROM ABRUZZI

Potatoes with their skins on, roasted with rosemary, garlic, and olive oil and served fiery hot, straight from the oven, are one of life's nicest pleasures. After 50 years, they're still one of Giovanni Grossi's favorite potato dishes.

SERVES 6

Large ovenproof dish, about
9 by 15½ inches (23 by
40 cm), oiled

> 2-2/3 pounds new potatoes (1.200 grams)
> 2 teaspoons salt
> 1/2 teaspoon (or to taste) hot red pepper flakes
> 2 tablespoons fresh rosemary leaves
> 3 garlic cloves, sliced or whole
> 1/4 cup olive oil (60 ml)

Preheat the oven to 400° (200). Do not peel the potatoes. Scrub them and cut them into thick pieces about 2 inches long and 3/4 inch thick, similar to orange sections. Sprinkle the salt, pepper flakes, and rosemary over the potatoes. Add the garlic and oil and toss to mix well.

Put the potatoes in the prepared dish and roast for 1 hour or until browned. If you left the garlic cloves whole, remove them. Serve hot.

Pane Rozzo
ROUGH BREAD

Signora Grossi cannot remember exactly how her mother prepared this traditional Abruzzi bread pudding, so the recipe given here comes from Ada Boni's *Talismano della Felicità*.* The recipe includes a chocolate icing, which, in Signora Grossi's family, would have been added only on very special occasions—in a small mountain village chocolate was an expensive luxury. Prepare this dessert two days before you plan to serve it.

SERVES 6

Domed 6¹/₂-inch 4-cup
(16¹/₂ cm, 1 liter) mold,
buttered heavily and floured

> 1 **scant cup lightly toasted peeled almonds (125 grams)**
> 2/3 **cup sugar (150 grams)**
> 5 **eggs, separated**
> 1 **tablespoon flour**
> 1 **tablespoon ground cinnamon**
> 1 **teaspoon vanilla extract**
> 5 **ounces good-quality semisweet chocolate (150 grams)**
> 1/2 **cup grated or very finely chopped semisweet chocolate, approximately (40 grams)**

In batches, chop the almonds very finely in a food processor with two thirds of the sugar. Put an egg yolk in a bowl and add the remaining sugar. Mix well and add another yolk. When that has been absorbed, add a third

* Recipe from *Il Talismano della Felicità,* page 752, XXIII edition, published by Sa Editrice Carlo Colombo.

yolk, working the mixture with a wooden spoon. Add the almonds and mix well. Refrigerate overnight.

The next morning, preheat the oven to 325° (160). Add the remaining egg yolks one at a time, then the flour, cinnamon, and vanilla. Beat the egg whites until stiff but not dry and fold carefully into the almond mixture. Spoon the batter into the prepared pan.

Bake for about 45 minutes. Remove to a cake rack, top down. Do not remove the mold. When completely cold, unmold onto a serving plate, top down (the domed part will be on top).

Melt the 5 ounces chocolate in a double boiler. When slightly cooled, cover the *pane* with the chocolate, smoothing it with a small spatula. Spread the chocolate down to the ridge at the base of the *pane.* Before the chocolate sets, cover it completely with the finely chopped chocolate. The effect will be that of a small, round, rough loaf of bread—hence the name. Store the *pane,* covered loosely, in a cool place for 2 days before serving.

Pasqua a Napoli

EASTER IN NAPLES

*Easter
in
Naples*

Tortano
EASTER BREAD

Antipasto di Uova Sode, Salame, Carciofini, e Olive
STORE-BOUGHT ANTIPASTO

Timballo di Pasta
PASTA BAKED IN A CRUST

Pollo Farcito in Umido
BRAISED STUFFED CHICKEN

Piselli in Umido
PEAS IN A CASSEROLE

Carciofi in Umido
ARTICHOKES IN A CASSEROLE

La Pastiera
EASTER DESSERT

WINES
White: Greco di Tufo (Province of Avellino); serve cold
Dessert: Lacryma Christi, Bianco Amabile (Province of Napoli);
serve at cool room temperature or lightly chilled

Easter in Naples is the most important religious holiday and the occasion for a number of traditional dishes. In earlier times, with the memories of the Mardi Gras carnival (*Martedì Grasso*) long dulled by the rigors of the Lenten fast, Easter preparations in the kitchen took on the intensity of a battle plan, and weeks of planning and cooking would culminate in the grand finale of the Easter feast. Today the tempo is more relaxed, but Easter continues to be a time for families to get together, and Neapolitans like to celebrate the feast in a big way.

In the South, unlike in the North, where it is eaten frequently, *antipasto* is reserved for special occasions. From Rome to Palermo an Easter meal is sure to begin with a store-bought *antipasto* of eggs, *salame,* olives, and marinated vegetables such as eggplant, zucchini, sun-dried tomatoes, and tiny artichokes. Neapolitans like to serve their *antipasto* with *tortano.*

Easter
in
Naples

Tortano
EASTER BREAD

Tortano, the Neapolitan Easter bread, is traditionally made with lard and *cicioli* (bits of pork that remain after the lard has been clarified). Since not many people are willing to go to the trouble of making their own lard, *pancetta* is often substituted for the *cicioli*. But should you happen to be in Naples the week before Easter, you will find *cicioli* in the shops.

MAKES 1 9-INCH RING OF BREAD

9-inch (23 cm) ring mold,
greased with lard

1	thick slice (about 1 ounce) of *pancetta or* fatback, very finely chopped (30 grams)
5	tablespoons lard (75 grams)
1	pound (4 cups) flour (450 grams)
2	1/4-ounce envelopes active dry yeast (15 grams) *or* 1 ounce fresh yeast (30 grams)
1	cup plus 2 to 6 tablespoons warm water (280 to 340 ml)
2	ounces *caciocavallo* cheese (see page 423), finely chopped (about 1/2 cup) (60 grams)
2	ounces *provolone piccante* cheese (see page 425), finely chopped (about 1/2 cup) (60 grams)
1/4	cup freshly grated Parmesan cheese (35 grams)
1/4	pound Neapolitan *salame* without garlic, finely chopped (1 heaped cup) (110 grams)
1	egg yolk beaten with 2 teaspoons water

In a skillet, cook the *pancetta* with 2 tablespoons of the lard over medium-low heat until browned. When done, remove from the heat, add the rest of the lard, and allow to melt. Cool.

Put the flour in the large bowl of an electric mixer or mound on a wooden surface. Dissolve the yeast in 1/2 cup of the warm water and add to the bowl or place in a well in the center of the flour. Add enough warm water to make a soft dough, beating with the paddle attachment or mixing and kneading with your hands. Add the lard and *pancetta* to the dough, then the cheeses and *salame,* and beat thoroughly.

If you're using an electric mixer, remove the dough and knead it briefly by hand. Roll up the dough in a *salame* shape about 22 inches (55 cm) long and place in the prepared mold, seam down. Cover and put in a warm place to rise for 2 hours.

Preheat the oven to 350° (180) 15 minutes before you're ready to bake the bread. Bake the *tortano* for 50 minutes. Remove it from the oven and paint with the egg yolk. Return it to the oven and bake for 10 minutes more. Cool it on a rack for 15 minutes before turning it out. This bread is served hot or at room temperature. It is better hot. It can be prepared in advance and reheated for 15 minutes in a preheated 400° (200) oven. Leftover slices may also be reheated.

Timballo di Pasta
PASTA BAKED IN A CRUST

During Holy Week in Naples there is a custom known as *strusciare* that dates back to the time of the Spanish occupation. The literal translation of this word is "to drag," and it was originally used to describe the dragging motion made by the long trains of the women's dresses as they walked around the streets, gazed in shop windows, and met their friends. In many parts of Italy Catholics were obliged to make the Stations of the Cross at a different church on each day of Holy Week. In Naples, however, they were required only to *fare i sepolchri* (do the burials—i.e., visit a few churches and say their prayers before an urn containing the host, the wafer representing Christ buried). This was not nearly such a lengthy business and left a lot of time for the *strusciare.* Given the promenading and visiting undertaken by all self-respecting Neapolitans during Holy Week, it is fortunate that this time-consuming (but not complicated) *timballo di pasta,* yet another of those rich pasta dishes covered with pastry so beloved in the South, could be prepared ahead of time.

SERVES 6 TO 8

9-inch (23 cm) springform
pan, buttered

FOR THE *RAGUNCINO* (LITTLE RAGOUT):

2	tablespoons unsalted butter (30 grams)
2	tablespoons olive oil
1-1/2	medium onions, finely chopped
1	small carrot, finely chopped
	a 3-inch piece of celery, finely chopped
2	ounces *pancetta,* finely chopped (about 1/2 cup) (60 grams)
2	ounces ham, finely chopped (about 1/2 cup) (60 grams)
1/4	pound ground veal (110 grams)

1-1/2   teaspoons tomato paste dissolved in 1 tablespoon
        water
  3/4   cup dry white wine (185 ml)
    2   teaspoons unsalted butter mixed with
        1 tablespoon flour (10 grams)
  1/2   beef bouillon cube
        salt and freshly ground pepper, to taste
    1   cup water

FOR THE FILLING:

    1   ounce dried *porcini* mushrooms (30 grams) *or*
        1/3 pound fresh mushrooms, cleaned and finely
        chopped (150 grams)
    3   ounces sweet or hot sausage (90 grams),
        approximately
    2   tablespoons unsalted butter (30 grams)
    1   tablespoon olive oil
    2   chicken livers
    1   cup frozen tiny peas (135 grams)
        salt and freshly ground pepper to taste

FOR THE MEATBALLS:

  1/4   pound ground veal (110 grams)
  1/3   cup fine dry bread crumbs (40 grams)
    1   egg
2-1/2   tablespoons freshly grated Parmesan cheese
        (20 grams)
    3   tablespoons finely chopped parsley
        salt and freshly ground pepper to taste
    2   tablespoons unsalted butter (30 grams)
    2   tablespoons olive oil

FOR THE PASTA:

    1   gallon water (4 liters)
        salt
  2/3   pound *penne* (300 grams)
  2/3   cup freshly grated Parmesan cheese (90 grams)

continued

FOR THE *PASTA FROLLA* (PASTRY):

    3-1/4 **cups flour (375 grams)**
      3/4 **cup (6 ounces) unsalted butter (180 grams)**
      1/3 **cup sugar (75 grams)**
        4 **extra-large egg yolks**

          freshly ground black pepper to taste
        1 **egg yolk beaten with 1 teaspoon water**

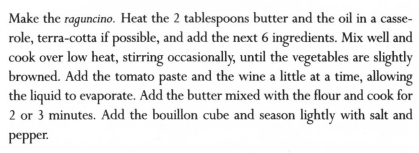

Easter
in
Naples

Make the *raguncino*. Heat the 2 tablespoons butter and the oil in a casserole, terra-cotta if possible, and add the next 6 ingredients. Mix well and cook over low heat, stirring occasionally, until the vegetables are slightly browned. Add the tomato paste and the wine a little at a time, allowing the liquid to evaporate. Add the butter mixed with the flour and cook for 2 or 3 minutes. Add the bouillon cube and season lightly with salt and pepper.

Add the water and simmer, covered, for an hour or more, adding more water if necessary and stirring every now and then. The *raguncino* must be dense but fluid. The *raguncino* may be prepared in advance and refrigerated, but bring it to room temperature before using it.

Make the filling. If you're using dried mushrooms, soak them in warm water for an hour. Drain and chop.

Prick the sausage all over and cook in 1 tablespoon of the butter and the oil in a small frying pan over medium heat for 10 minutes. Remove the sausage and cook the livers in the same pan over medium-high heat for 3 or 4 minutes. Remove them from the pan and dice. Slice the cooled sausage and reserve. Pour the fat remaining in the pan into a small saucepan and add the peas. Cook, covered, over the lowest heat for 10 minutes.

In a small frying pan, cook the mushrooms with the remaining tablespoon of butter for a few minutes until they absorb their liquid and add to the peas. Add the sausage and livers with 3 or 4 tablespoons *raguncino*. Season with salt and pepper. Simmer for 5 minutes and reserve. This filling can be prepared in advance, but refrigerate it and then bring it to room temperature before using it.

Make the meatballs. Mix together the first 6 ingredients and make meatballs the size of cherries. Heat the butter and oil and fry the meatballs over medium heat until lightly browned. Cool, cover tightly, and refrigerate until needed.

Cook the pasta. Boil the water with salt and cook the *penne* until *al dente*. Drain and pour a cup of cold water over it to stop the cooking. Mix the pasta with half the Parmesan and the remaining *raguncino*.

Preheat the oven to 350° (180).

Make the *pasta frolla* (see page 420). Roll out a little more than half the pastry and cut a round to line the bottom of the pan. Cut strips for the sides, pressing with the fingers to make the pastry adhere top to bottom. Put a third of the dressed pasta on the bottom of the pan. Spread half the filling and half the meatballs over the pasta. Sprinkle on half the remaining Parmesan. Cover with another third of the *penne,* the rest of the filling and meatballs, and sprinkle on the rest of the Parmesan. Cover with the remaining third of the pasta and grind black pepper over all.

Roll out a circle for the top of the *timballo* and cover the pasta, crimping the edges to seal. Make a chimney (steam vent) in the center and decorate the crust with pastry leaves or other shapes made with the remaining pastry. Paint the top of the *timballo* with the egg yolk.

Bake the *timballo* for 1 hour and 10 minutes or until lightly browned. Place on a rack and let sit for 15 minutes. Remove the sides and allow the *timballo* to rest for another 10 minutes before serving it.

NOTE: It's best to prepare the pasta and the pastry the day you serve the *timballo,* but if you're preparing all the elements in advance add 1/2 tablespoon oil to the cooled pasta. Assemble the *timballo* and refrigerate it, but bring it to room temperature before baking.

Pollo Farcito in Umido
BRAISED STUFFED CHICKEN

Lamb at Easter is traditional in almost all Western European countries, and Italy is no exception. But in Naples chicken is considered a luxury and is permitted as a variation. This is a festive bird filled with a succulent stuffing of veal, liver, and Swiss chard.

SERVES 6

6	ounces boneless veal, ground twice (170 grams)
1	chicken liver, very finely chopped
7	ounces Swiss chard *or* spinach, half pureed in a food processor, half finely chopped by hand (200 grams)
1	egg
6	tablespoons freshly grated Parmesan cheese (50 grams)
	pinch of hot red pepper flakes (optional)
	salt and freshly ground pepper to taste
1	4-pound roasting chicken (1.800 grams)
2	tablespoons olive oil
1	tablespoon freshly squeezed lemon juice
1/4	cup dry white wine (60 ml)
	small Swiss chard leaves and thin lemon slices for garnish

Mix together the veal, chicken liver, chard, egg, and Parmesan. Season with pepper flakes if desired, and add salt and pepper. Mix thoroughly with your hands.

Salt the chicken's cavity and stuff it loosely with the prepared mixture. Truss the chicken, tie it with twine, or sew the opening. Rub the chicken all over with salt and pepper.

Heat the oil in a heavy casserole with a tight-fitting lid. Add the chicken and the lemon juice. Turn the heat to very low and brown the chicken gently, turning often. After about 45 minutes, when the chicken is lightly browned, add the wine.

Continue cooking the chicken, covered, for 1-1/2 to 2-1/4 hours or until the juices run clear when the chicken is pierced with a kitchen needle. Allow the chicken to rest for 15 minutes, then remove the trussing or twine, removing the stuffing (in one piece if possible), and cut the chicken into serving pieces.

Slice the stuffing and place it in the center of a serving platter with the chicken pieces around it. Garnish the plate with small leaves of Swiss chard and thin lemon slices. Serve hot. This chicken is also good cold.

Piselli in Umido

PEAS IN A CASSEROLE

In the South peas and artichokes are just coming into season at Easter, and tiny sweet peas, considered the first "fruit" of the garden, are a welcome sign that winter is finally at its end. In this recipe the peas are sautéed in oil; spring onions and chopped *pancetta* are added to the pot, giving the peas a delicate flavor.

SERVES 6

> 1/4   cup olive oil (60 ml)
> 7   spring onions *or* scallions, finely chopped
> 1/2   pound *pancetta,* unsmoked bacon, *or* lean
>   fatback, finely chopped (about 1-3/4 cups)
>   (225 grams)
> 4-1/2   pounds fresh peas, shelled (2 kilograms), *or*
>   2 pounds frozen tiny peas (900 grams)
>   salt and freshly ground pepper to taste

Heat the oil in a saucepan and sauté the onions over low heat for 3 minutes. Add the *pancetta* and cook over low heat until lightly browned but not crisp. Add the peas and season with salt and pepper. Cover and cook over the lowest heat until the peas are done, 20 or more minutes. Serve the peas hot.

Carciofi in Umido
ARTICHOKES IN A CASSEROLE

In the following recipe artichokes are cooked in the same way as the peas and are perhaps even more delicious.

SERVES 6

10 medium artichokes, cleaned (see page 420)
2 tablespoons olive oil
2 large onions, finely chopped
    salt to taste
1/4 pound *pancetta or* fatback, finely chopped
    (1 scant cup) (110 grams)
2/3 cup hot water (160 ml), approximately
    freshly ground black pepper to taste

Cut the artichokes into 8 slices and leave them in the acidulated water until needed.

Heat the oil in a 12-inch sauté pan and sauté the onion with salt and a few tablespoons of water over medium-low heat for 2 minutes. Add the *pancetta* and cook over low heat for 5 minutes, stirring. Do not brown the *pancetta*. Drain the artichokes and add them to the onion with 1/3 cup of the hot water. Cover the pan and cook the artichokes over medium heat for 20 minutes, adding the remaining hot water if the liquid has cooked away and stirring occasionally. Taste for seasoning and add pepper. Serve hot.

La Pastiera
EASTER DESSERT

*Easter
in
Naples*

Pastiera is the most famous of all Neapolitan desserts and a very ancient recipe, long considered one of the principal culinary delights of Naples. In 1500 the Marchese Giovan Battista del Tufo listed it among the glories of Naples in his book *Ritratto o Modello delle Grandezze Delitie e Meraviglie della Noblissima Città di Napoli.* Neapolitans wax poetic on the subject of this dessert, which celebrates spring and rebirth, and they love to recount the legend attached to its own birth:

One spring the siren Partenope (the mythological founder of Naples) left her amethyst throne and flew down to the gulf between Posillipo and Vesuvius. Inspired by the gentle breezes and warm sun, she sang a song so beautiful that the people were enchanted and decided to give her seven gifts to symbolize the seven wonders of the world. Seven of the most beautiful maidens presented her with flour (wealth), *ricotta* (abundance), eggs (rebirth), sugar (sweetness), wheat boiled in milk (the fusion between animal and vegetable life), orange water (the perfume of Campania), and spices (homage). Partenope accepted these gifts and mixed them together to make the first *pastiera.*

Every Neapolitan family has its own *pastiera* recipe; they are all very similar and vary only in the proportions and whether or not pastry cream is added. The most important ingredient is wheat, which has been soaked in cold water for preferably two weeks. (Many Italian specialty shops sell it presoaked in cans.) The soaked wheat is combined with *ricotta,* candied citrus peel, citron, and eggs, then baked in a pastry crust. It tastes a little like a cheesecake, creamy, sweet, and with a slight taste of orange. Most Neapolitans prepare their *pastiera* on Holy Thursday, although it is not eaten until Easter Sunday. (It will keep for a week in the refrigerator.) Traditionally *pastiera* is served in the *ruota* (wheel) in which it is baked, but in this recipe it is served unmolded.

SERVES AT LEAST 12

11-inch cheesecake pan with
1¹/₂- to 2-inch sides, heavily
buttered and floured

1-1/2   cups milk (375 ml)
2-1/2   tablespoons sugar (35 grams)
         pinch of salt
         zest of 1/2 large lemon
    1   cup (1/2 pound) wheat, soaked in water for 2
         weeks (see note) (available in cans in Italian
         specialty shops) (225 grams)

FOR THE PASTRY CRUST:
    1   pound (4 cups) flour (450 grams)
  3/4   cup plus 1 tablespoon sugar (180 grams)
    1   cup (1/2 pound) unsalted butter, cut into pieces
         (225 grams)
    5   egg yolks
         grated zest of 1 orange

FOR THE FILLING:
1-1/3   pounds *ricotta* cheese (600 grams)
    1   cup plus 2 tablespoons sugar (250 grams)
    5   egg yolks
  1/3   cup candied orange peel in tiny dice (50 grams)
  1/2   cup candied citron in tiny dice (80 grams)
  1/2   teaspoon (or more to taste) orange extract *or*
         1 tablespoon orange water
         grated zest of 1 lemon
    3   egg whites at room temperature

         confectioners' sugar

The day before baking, put the milk, sugar, salt, lemon peel, and soaked
wheat in a heavy saucepan over a Flame Tamer. Bring slowly to a simmer
over the lowest heat. Cook the wheat, stirring frequently to prevent
scorching, until the milk is almost completely evaporated and the wheat
soft. This should take an hour or more. Cool, discard lemon peel, and
refrigerate.

continued

Make the crust. Put the flour, sugar, butter, egg yolks, and orange zest in the large bowl of an electric mixer with the paddle attachment. Wrap a tea towel around the bowl to prevent the flour from scattering and mix rapidly. (The dough can also be made in a food processor fitted with the steel blade.) Divide the dough into 2 parts, one slightly larger. Refrigerate the smaller part and roll out the larger part to fit the prepared pan. Gently press the pastry down into the pan, patching by simply pressing another piece of pastry on top if necessary. Trim the pastry evenly with a sharp knife. Refrigerate until the filling is ready. Preheat the oven to 350° (180).

Make the filling. Beat the *ricotta* in an electric mixer with the sugar until smooth and creamy. Add the egg yolks one at a time. Add the candied orange peel, candied citron, orange extract, and grated lemon zest. Add the reserved wheat and mix well. (If you're in doubt about the quantity of orange extract, taste the filling now and add more if desired.)

Beat the egg whites until stiff but not dry and fold them into the *pastiera* filling. Pour the filling into the prepared crust. Roll out the remaining pastry and cut 6 strips 1-1/2 inches wide. Lattice them on top of the pie.

Bake the *pastiera* for 1 hour and 30 to 45 minutes or until the filling seems firm and the pastry is "blond" (a light nut brown). Cool the *pastiera* on a rack.

When it's completely cold, run a sharp knife around the edges and turn the dessert out into a large pan with sides, such as a large round pizza pan. Immediately turn it back onto a serving platter. Cover it tightly with plastic wrap and refrigerate overnight before serving. This dessert is even better a day later. Dust with confectioners' sugar before serving.

This dessert will keep for a week to 10 days in the refrigerator. Bring it to room temperature before serving.

NOTE: If you prepare the wheat at home, you will need 6 ounces wheat (170 grams). Soak in cold water for 2 weeks, changing the water every 2 days. The day you make the *pastiera,* drain and weigh the amount needed.

CAMPANIA

La Vigilia in Piedimonte a Palazzo Gaetani

CHRISTMAS EVE IN PIEDIMONTE AT PALAZZO GAETANI

Pizza di Scarola
ESCAROLE PIE

Calascione di Piedimonte
TWO-CRUST PIZZA PIEDIMONTE

Baccalà Bollito con Salsa di Aglio, Olio, Limone, e Prezzemolo
BOILED DRIED SALT COD WITH GARLIC, OIL,
LEMON, AND PARSLEY SAUCE

Insalata di Rinforzo
FORTIFYING SALAD

Struffoli
RING OF TINY FRIED PASTRIES

WINES
White: Falerno Bianco (Caserta); serve very cold
Dessert: Moscato di Baselice (Benevento); serve chilled

Piedimonte d'Alife, at the foot of the Matese mountains, is a picturesque hill town with a superb view overlooking the whole province of Caserta. This part of Italy, close to Naples, suffered greatly during the Second World War. There is a magnificent 18th-century palace in the town that served as the American headquarters during the American occupation of Italy. Part of it was burned by the Germans, but it has now been restored and is something of a tourist attraction. Every year Michi Ambrosi de Magistris and her sister Antonella Litteri, who now own the palace with their cousins, come here for Christmas with their families. They have vivid memories of growing up in Piedimonte—of the vegetable garden, the chickens, rabbits, and sheep, and the round brick underground ice room in which snow, brought in by mule in the winter, was packed in straw and used to keep the ice creams and sherbets cool in summer.

In Italy the big Christmas meal is eaten on Christmas Eve. The dinner is meatless, a reminder of earlier times when the eve of a major feast demanded abstinence. Although Michi and Antonella are obviously well-to-do, their dinner is no different from what the rest of the village eats that night. It starts, as it did when they were children, with two double-crust pizzas and is supposed to end with 37 kinds of dried fruit! Actually the fruits are usually the centerpiece of the Christmas table. When a cousin from Piedimonte was explaining to me about the 37 kinds of dried fruits, we all tried to name them—impossible! But all kinds of nuts and three or four kinds of raisins count, so it is not totally implausible.

Pizza di Scarola
ESCAROLE PIE

This pizza has a rich crust made with butter. It makes a memorable lunch dish served with a tomato and basil salad. Leftovers are good cut up and served cold.

*Christmas
Eve
in
Piedimonte
at
Palazzo
Gaetani*

SERVES 8

10-inch cake pan with 2-inch
sides (26 by 5 cm) , buttered

FOR THE FILLING:

3	pounds escarole (1.350 grams)
	salt to taste
1/4	cup olive oil (60 ml)
1	garlic clove, peeled
1/2	teaspoon (or to taste) hot red pepper flakes
1/3	cup capers, rinsed and dried (60 grams)
1	cup black Gaeta olives, pitted (200 grams)
1/4	pound salt-packed anchovies, cleaned (see page 419) and cut into pieces (110 grams)
	freshly ground pepper to taste

FOR THE CRUST:

1	pound (4 cups) flour (450 grams)
1	cup (1/2 pound) unsalted butter, cut into pieces (225 grams)
2	1/4-ounce envelopes active dry yeast (15 grams) *or* 1 ounce fresh yeast
1/4	cup warm water (60 ml)
1	teaspoon salt
3/4	teaspoon freshly ground black pepper
1	egg yolk beaten with 1 tablespoon cold water

Make the filling. Separate the escarole leaves and wash thoroughly. Cook in boiling salted water until *al dente*. Drain, cool, and squeeze to remove all liquid.

Heat the oil in a 12-inch (30 cm) skillet and brown the garlic. Discard when browned and add the escarole, pepper flakes, capers, and olives. Cook over low heat, stirring occasionally, for 10 minutes. Add the anchovies and mix. Remove from the heat and taste for seasoning. Cool and reserve.

Make the crust. Put the flour in a large bowl or on a wooden surface and make a well in the center. Put the butter in the well. Dissolve the yeast in the warm water and pour it into the well. Add the salt and pepper. Mix all together, adding enough additional warm water, 2 or 3 tablespoons, to make a soft dough. (The dough can be made in an electric mixer; use the paddle attachment.) Put the dough in a bowl, cover, and put in a warm place, free of drafts, to rise for an hour.

When the dough has risen, divide it into 2 parts, one slightly larger. Line the bottom of the prepared pan with the larger part, pressing with your fingers to line the pan. Put in the filling. Lightly flour a wooden or marble surface and roll out a circle for the top crust. Drape the crust over the rolling pin and unroll it onto the pie. Trim the edges, leaving a 1/2-inch overhang. Fold this under to seal to the bottom crust and crimp the edges decoratively. Paint the pizza with the egg yolk. Set aside, covered, in a warm place for an hour.

Fifteen minutes before the pizza is ready to bake, preheat the oven to 375° (190). Bake the pie for 1 hour. Cool for at least 20 minutes before serving, if you're serving it hot, which is rarely done. Usually it is served at room temperature.

Calascione di Piedimonte
TWO-CRUST PIZZA PIEDIMONTE

Named after the local town, this pizza is completely different from the preceding recipe. The filling is richer, but it has a butterless, thick bread crust that is similar to a Neapolitan pizza crust, so it should be served hot.

SERVES 6 TO 8

11-inch (28 cm) cake pan,
oiled

FOR THE CRUST:

2	**tablespoons active dry yeast**
1/4	**cup warm water**
1	**pound (4 cups) flour (450 grams)**
2-1/2	**tablespoons olive oil**

FOR THE FILLING:

3/4	**cup freshly grated Parmesan cheese (105 grams)**
7	**ounces Swiss cheese, grated (1-1/2 cups) (200 grams)**
1/4	**pound *provolone* cheese, grated (1 heaped cup) (110 grams)**
1/4	**pound ham *or prosciutto or salame* without garlic *or* all 3, finely chopped (1 scant cup) (110 grams), *or* 1/2 pound *ricotta* cheese (for Christmas) (225 grams)**
1/2	**pound *mozzarella* cheese, finely chopped (225 grams)**
7	**large eggs**
	salt and freshly ground black pepper to taste
1	**egg yolk beaten with 1 tablespoon cold water**

Make the dough for the crust. Dissolve the yeast in the warm water. Put the flour, oil, and yeast in the large bowl of an electric mixer. Mix, using the paddle attachment, and add warm water as necessary, about 3/4 cup, to make a smooth dough. Cover and place in a warm place, free of drafts, for an hour.

Make the filling. Mix together the Parmesan, Swiss cheese, *provolone,* and ham. Mix and add the *mozzarella.* Add the eggs, one at a time, mixing. Season with salt and a generous amount of pepper.

When the dough has risen, divide it in half and roll out a circle to fit the prepared pan. Line the pan with the dough and pour in the filling, smoothing it. Roll out a circle for the top crust and cover the pizza, leaving a 1-inch overhang. Trim evenly and roll up bottom and top crust together to form an edge, pressing to seal. Make 4 small slits in the center of the crust to allow steam to escape. Cover the pizza with a cloth and place in a warm place, free of drafts, for an hour.

Fifteen minutes before the time is up, preheat the oven to 350° (180). Cook the *calascione* for 1 hour and 10 minutes. Remove it from the oven and paint rapidly with the egg yolk. Put the pizza back in the oven, turn the heat up to 425° (220), and cook for 10 minutes longer. Cool on a rack for 15 minutes. Turn the pizza out onto the rack and cool, if desired, or serve hot or tepid, preferably on a wooden platter.

continued

ANOTHER PIZZA FILLING

These pizzas can also be prepared with the following filling, using either crust.

4 pounds Swiss chard, the tender smaller leaves only
(1.800 grams)
salt
1 cup oil-packed black olives, pitted (200 grams)
8 oil-packed anchovy fillets, drained and chopped
1 heaped tablespoon rinsed and dried capers
1 tablespoon wine vinegar
1 garlic clove, finely chopped
3 tablespoons olive oil

Cook the Swiss chard in boiling salted water for about 8 minutes. Drain, squeeze out the water, and chop. Mix with all the rest of the ingredients and fill the crust. Bake as directed in the recipes.

Baccalà Bollito con Salsa di Aglio,
Olio, Limone, e Prezzemolo
BOILED DRIED SALT COD WITH GARLIC, OIL, LEMON, AND PARSLEY SAUCE

For centuries cod was preserved throughout Europe either by salting it in barrels or by drying it in the sun. It used to be one of the most inexpensive foods available, and every country bordering on the Mediterranean boasts innumerable *baccalà* recipes. Now, like many simple foods, it has become something of a luxury, but it is still very much a Christmas dish in Italy and is invariably served on Christmas Eve.

SERVES 6 TO 8

- 2-1/4 pounds dried salt cod, soaked in cold water for 24 hours (1 kilogram)
- 4 garlic cloves, crushed
- 1/2 cup plus 1 tablespoon finely chopped parsley
- 6 tablespoons freshly squeezed lemon juice (100 ml)
- 3/4 cup plus 1 tablespoon olive oil (200 ml)
- 3/4 teaspoon (or more to taste) hot red pepper flakes
  salt to taste
  parsley sprigs for garnish

After 24 hours' soaking the cod should be soft. Drain and rinse. Put the fish in cold water in a large saucepan and bring to a simmer. Let the fish simmer for 10 minutes, no more, or it will become tough. Cool to tepid in the water.

Mix together the garlic, parsley, and lemon juice. Add the oil slowly, beating with a fork. Add the pepper flakes and salt to taste.

To serve, peel the cod and cut it into pieces. Arrange it on a platter garnished with parsley and serve the sauce in a sauceboat.

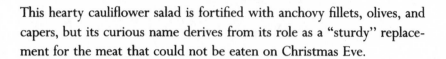

Insalata di Rinforzo
FORTIFYING SALAD

This hearty cauliflower salad is fortified with anchovy fillets, olives, and capers, but its curious name derives from its role as a "sturdy" replacement for the meat that could not be eaten on Christmas Eve.

SERVES 6 TO 8

3-1/2	pounds cauliflower, cleaned (1.600 grams)
1/2	cup green olives, pitted (100 grams)
1/2	cup black olives, pitted (100 grams)
5	tablespoons capers packed in salt, rinsed (55 grams)
7	salt-packed anchovies, cleaned (see page 419), *or* 14 oil-packed anchovy fillets, drained
1/2	cup extra-virgin olive oil (125 ml)
1/4	cup (or to taste) white wine vinegar (60 ml)
	pinch of salt
	a handful of finely chopped parsley (optional)

Divide the cauliflower into flowerets and cook in boiling salted water for 6 to 10 minutes, until tender but still firm. Drain and cool completely.

When the cauliflower has cooled, put it into a large salad bowl and add the olives and capers. Cut all but 2 of the anchovy fillets into small pieces and add to the bowl, reserving the 2 whole fillets.

Mix the olive oil and vinegar together with a pinch of salt and pour the dressing over the cauliflower. Mix thoroughly, tossing gently.

If desired, add the parsley just before serving. Garnish the salad with the 2 anchovies, crossed over the center of the dish.

This dish can be prepared in advance and refrigerated, but bring it to room temperature before serving. Red peppers packed in vinegar, rinsed and cut into strips, are a tasty and colorful addition.

Struffoli
RING OF TINY FRIED PASTRIES

No self-respecting Neapolitan would sit down to Christmas dinner without the promise of *struffoli*. In Naples and throughout Campania *struffoli* is the ultimate Christmas dessert, having the same significance in southern Italy as a turkey at American Thanksgiving. The literal translation of the name is "wads of cotton," and *struffoli* are, in fact, little wads or balls of fried pastry flavored with grated orange peel, dipped in honey, and decorated elaborately with candied cherries and slivers of citron, candied orange peel, and angelica. *Struffoli* have been eaten in southern Italy for thousands of years and are strangely similar to those extravagantly sweet, sticky honey balls served throughout the Middle East. Michi Ambrosi de Magistris gave me this recipe.

SERVES 6 TO 8

FOR THE *STRUFFOLI*:

- 1 pound (4 cups) flour (450 grams)
- 5 tablespoons unsalted butter, cut into pieces (75 grams)
- 2 tablespoons sugar
- 3 large egg yolks
- 1 tablespoon plus 1 teaspoon baking powder
  grated zest of 2 oranges
- 1/2 cup (or more) dry white wine (125 ml)
  olive oil for frying, about 1 quart (1 liter)

TO FINISH THE *STRUFFOLI*:

- 1-1/3 cups (1 pound) honey (450 grams)
- 1 tablespoon sugar
  grated zest of 3 oranges
  candied cherries, slivers of citron and candied orange peel, and strips of angelica for garnish

continued

Make the *struffoli.* Put the flour, butter, sugar, egg yolks, baking powder, and orange zest in the large bowl of an electric mixer. Add enough wine to make a dough neither too damp nor too crumbly, about 1/2 cup to begin with. Add more as necessary. Divide the dough into 5 parts. Roll out each part into a rectangle about 10 to 14 inches long and about 3 inches wide. Fold the near third of the dough toward the middle and the far third over that, as for puff pastry. Roll out again, fold as before, and roll out the pastry again into rectangles.

Using no flour, or as little as possible, shape cylinders the thickness of a little finger. Cut into 1/2-inch pieces. Heat the oil to hot but not smoking in a deep frying pan over medium-high heat and fry the *struffoli* in batches until lightly browned. The oil may bubble up. Drain the *struffoli* on paper towels.

Put the honey in a large stainless-steel pan and bring to a boil over low heat, stirring. Add the sugar and the *struffoli,* mixing gently until the sugar is melted. Remove from the heat and add the orange zest, mixing carefully. Allow to set for 1 minute and then spoon onto a large round platter in a ring shape. Wet your hands with cold water and give the *struffoli* a compact ring shape. Leave to cool completely. Cover the platter with plastic wrap and leave the *struffoli,* unrefrigerated, for 3 or 4 days before serving.

When you're ready to serve, decorate with candied cherries in the center and slivers of citron, candied orange peel, and angelica. This recipe can be doubled easily. Slice the *struffoli* with a knife and serve it on small plates with knives and forks.

CAMPANIA

Buffet Invernale

A WINTER BUFFET

*A
Winter
Buffet*

Involtini di Pasta
PASTA WRAPPED IN EGGPLANT

Brioscia Rustica con Verdure
BRIOCHE WITH VEGETABLES

Parmigiana di Carciofi
ARTICHOKES PARMESAN

Polipi Affogati
DROWNED OCTOPUS

Fesa Salmonata
COLD VEAL IN GREEN SAUCE

Caponata alla Napoletana
COLD VEGETABLE SALAD

La Spiritosa
MARINATED CARROTS

Crostata di Noci Cate
WALNUT TART

Coviglia di Cioccolato con Meringhe
FROZEN CHOCOLATE CREAM WITH MERINGUES

Babà alla Napoletana
NEAPOLITAN BABA

WINES

White: Biancolella (Ischia); serve very cold
Red: Gragnano Rosso (Napoli); serve cool
Dessert: Fiano Passito (Avellino); serve cool

Neapolitans delight in doing things up in a big way. An English lady visiting Naples in the 19th century was quite awed by their lavish centerpieces and beautiful tables. She wrote back to England that she had been to a dinner where the centerpiece was a cage of spun sugar with real birds inside—evidence of the skill of the *monzùs* of that time. A beautiful display has always been important in Naples, and in that era one could rent a pineapple for an exotic arrangement of fruit, because it was too expensive to buy!

The show, of course, is only part of a meal in Naples. Neapolitans take pleasure in repeating the same desserts and pasta *timballi* for the holidays. They enjoy the comfort of pasta, tomato sauce, and eggplant, and they're extremely inventive in creating a pasta, bean, and mussel soup. They can talk for hours about food, recounting in detail how the table looked and what was eaten at parties they have given or been to.

Many Neapolitan dishes are made purposely large so that leftovers will be on hand. In the summertime, in fact, it is so hot that they will cook only once, in the morning.

The recipes that make up this winter buffet come from several Neapolitan friends, all of them practiced and enthusiastic party givers. A typical Neapolitan buffet dinner consists of a large number of dishes—fish, vegetables, pasta, and at least one rich dessert—and while meat may be served, it will not be the centerpiece of the meal. Almost all the dishes can be prepared in advance—some even benefit by it.

Involtini di Pasta
PASTA WRAPPED IN EGGPLANT

Eggplant is served less often in Naples than farther south; but this dish, which can be prepared in advance, is an old Neapolitan favorite and a regular part of the local pasta repertoire.

SERVES 12 TO 15

15- by 10½-inch (38 by 27 cm) ovenproof glass dish

30	lengthwise 1/4-inch-thick peeled eggplant slices
	salt
5	tablespoons olive oil (75 ml) plus oil for frying, about 2 cups (500 ml)
3	pounds ripe fresh tomatoes (1.350 grams)
	freshly ground pepper to taste
	hot red pepper flakes to taste (optional)
8	fresh basil leaves plus basil for garnish
1-1/2	pounds fresh pasta (675 grams)
1	cup plus 3 tablespoons freshly grated Parmesan cheese (160 grams)

Put the eggplant slices in a large bowl of salted cold water. Leave for at least 4 hours and up to 12 hours. Rinse and pat dry. In batches, fry in hot olive oil in a skillet over medium-high heat until lightly browned. Drain on paper towels.

Make the sauce. Pass the tomatoes through a food mill into a saucepan (or process in a food processor fitted with the steel blade until you have a coarse puree). Simmer for 15 minutes and add salt and pepper, plus pepper flakes if desired. Remove the sauce from the heat and add the basil and 5 tablespoons olive oil. Reserve. Preheat the oven to 350° (180).

Cook the pasta in boiling salted water until *al dente*—only a few minutes for fresh pasta. Drain and dress with 1 cup of the Parmesan. Reserve 2/3 cup tomato sauce and dress the pasta with the rest. If desired, add more basil.

Lay out the eggplant slices on a work surface. Divide the pasta among the slices and roll up. Spread 1/4 cup sauce on the bottom of the prepared dish. Place the eggplant rolls in the dish in a single layer, close together, seams down. Spoon the rest of the tomato sauce over the rolls and sprinkle them with the remaining Parmesan. Bake for 30 minutes. Serve hot, garnished with basil.

Brioscia Rustica con Verdure
BRIOCHE WITH VEGETABLES

This dish is a good example of how the Neapolitans have taken a French brioche and changed it to suit themselves, adding Parmesan, *provolone,* and bits of ham or *salame,* and serving it, surrounded with vegetables, as a first course. In this recipe the vegetables are mushrooms and peas, but you can substitute almost any combination of vegetables.

A
W i n t e r
B u f f e t

SERVES 8

2-quart (2 liters) ring or
bundt pan, buttered

FOR THE *BRIOSCIA* (BRIOCHE):

1	**tablespoon plus 2 teaspoons active dry yeast *or***
	1 scant ounce fresh yeast
1/4	**cup warm milk (60 ml)**
2-2/3	**cups flour (300 grams)**
3	**eggs at room temperature**
1/2	**cup (1/4 pound) plus 3 tablespoons unsalted butter at room temperature, cut into pieces (150 grams)**
1	**heaped teaspoon sugar**
1/2	**cup freshly grated Parmesan cheese (65 grams) at room temperature**
1/2	**cup freshly grated *provolone* cheese (65 grams) at room temperature**
1-1/2	**ounces *prosciutto or* boiled ham *or salame* without garlic (scant 1/2 cup), finely chopped (45 grams)**
	salt and freshly ground pepper to taste

FOR THE VEGETABLES:

- 1-1/2 pounds fresh mushrooms (675 grams)
  salt and freshly ground pepper to taste
- 2-1/2 tablespoons unsalted butter (40 grams)
- 1-1/2 tablespoons finely chopped onion
- 5 cups frozen tiny peas (675 grams)

FOR THE SAUCE:

- 2 cups milk (500 ml)
- 1/2 cup flour (60 grams)
- 1 14-ounce can Italian plum tomatoes, drained and
  seeded (1 cup) (400 grams)
  salt and freshly ground pepper to taste
- 1/4 cup unsalted butter (60 grams)
- 1 cup heavy cream (250 ml)

Make the brioche. Dissolve the yeast in the milk. Put the flour, eggs, butter, and sugar in the large bowl of an electric mixer. Add the milk with the yeast and beat the mixture, using the paddle attachment, until the mixture is elastic and comes away from the sides of the bowl, about 10 minutes.

Add the Parmesan, *provolone, prosciutto,* salt, and pepper. Put the dough into the prepared pan, cover, and put in a warm place to rise for about an hour. The dough will come almost to the top of the pan. Fifteen minutes before the dough is ready, preheat the oven to 350° (180).

Bake the brioche for 45 minutes. Cool for 15 minutes on a rack before turning it out. The brioche may be prepared in advance, cooled, and wrapped in foil. To serve, heat it in the foil in a 375° (190) oven for 15 minutes.

Prepare the vegetables. Wash and slice the mushrooms. Put them into a skillet and cook over moderate heat until all their liquid has evaporated. Add salt, pepper, and 1 tablespoon of the butter and cook for 1 minute. Reserve. Put the remaining butter in a small saucepan and cook the onion over medium-low heat until transparent. Add the frozen peas, cover

continued

tightly, and cook over the lowest heat for about 25 minutes or until the peas are cooked, stirring occasionally. Reserve.

Make the sauce. Put the milk, flour, tomatoes, salt, and pepper in a blender or a food processor fitted with the steel blade. Blend for 1 minute. Melt the butter in a saucepan and add the milk mixture and the cream. Bring to a simmer, stirring, and simmer for 5 minutes. If serving later, cover the surface with plastic wrap.

To assemble the dish, preheat the oven to 375° (190) and put the brioche in the center of an ovenproof dish. Add 3 or 4 tablespoons sauce to the mushrooms and to the peas. Arrange the vegetables in the center and around the brioche. Cover with foil and bake for 20 minutes. Heat the sauce gently, slice the brioche, and serve it with vegetables around the slice and sauce on top. Pass the remaining sauce in a sauceboat.

Any leftover brioche can be heated wrapped in foil and used as bread or for aperitifs.

Parmigiana di Carciofi
ARTICHOKES PARMESAN

Artichokes and tomatoes seem an odd combination, but they make a good marriage. Italian cooks are so tirelessly inventive in finding different ways to use tomatoes, and tomatoes are so much a part of the Italian kitchen, that it's hard to believe the tomato is not a native Italian but a recent immigrant from America.

SERVES 8 TO 10
9- by 13-inch (23 by 30 cm)
ovenproof glass dish, oiled

FOR THE SAUCE:

- 1 small onion, finely chopped
- 1 28-ounce can Italian plum tomatoes with juice (800 grams)
  salt and freshly ground pepper to taste
  pinch of sugar
- 6 basil leaves, chopped

FOR THE ARTICHOKES:

- 12 artichokes, cleaned (see page 420)
  flour for dredging
  olive oil for frying, about 1-1/2 to 2 cups (350 to 500 ml)
  salt to taste

  a handful of fresh basil leaves, washed and dried
- 1 cup freshly grated Parmesan cheese (135 grams)
  freshly ground pepper to taste
- 3/4 pound *mozzarella* cheese, very thinly sliced* (330 grams)

* If the *mozzarella* is not fresh, grate it coarsely instead of slicing it.

continued

Make the sauce. Put the onion in a 10-inch frying pan, add 2 or 3 tablespoons of water to prevent burning, and cook over medium-low heat until transparent, about 7 minutes. Add the tomatoes and cook over medium-high heat, stirring occasionally, for 15 minutes or until the sauce has thickened. Mash the tomatoes with the back of the spoon as they cook. Add salt, pepper, and a pinch of sugar if the sauce is too tart. Add the chopped basil and cook for 1 minute. Reserve.

Drain and dry the artichokes and cut each into 10 pieces. Dredge in flour a few pieces at a time, shaking in a sieve to remove excess flour. Heat 3/4-inch oil in a skillet until hot but not smoking and fry the artichokes until browned, about 4 minutes per side. Salt while hot and drain on paper towels. Preheat the oven to 375° (190).

Assemble the dish. Put 1/4 cup sauce on the bottom of the prepared dish. Put a layer of basil leaves over the sauce and arrange one third of the artichokes on top. Sprinkle on a third of the Parmesan and grind pepper on top. Add half the *mozzarella.* Spoon half the remaining sauce over the cheese, add another layer of basil, top with another third of the artichokes and a third of the Parmesan, grind more pepper over, and add the rest of the *mozzarella.* Spoon on the remaining sauce, the rest of the basil, and the remaining artichokes and Parmesan.

Bake the dish for 50 minutes or until crispy. Serve hot or tepid. This dish freezes well.

Polipi Affogati
DROWNED OCTOPUS

The scarcity of meat in Naples is compensated for by the amazing variety of fish available, octopus being among the most plentiful. In the 19th century it was sold on the streets already cooked. This plebeian, everyday dish, so called because the octopus are "drowned" in tomatoes and garlic, is a great Neapolitan favorite. A few years ago it would have been unheard of to serve such a dish to guests. But today there is a growing interest in local dishes, and the once humble octopus is now very welcome on even the most formal occasion.

SERVES 8

9½-inch (24 cm) saucepan,
preferably terra-cotta

> 2-1/2   **pounds ripe fresh tomatoes, peeled and seeded (1.100 grams), *or* 1 2-pound can Italian plum tomatoes, drained (900 grams)**
> 4   **garlic cloves, peeled**
>   **salt and freshly ground black pepper to taste**
> 3/4   **cup olive oil (185 ml)**
> 5   **pounds baby octopus, cleaned (see page 419) (2.250 grams)**
> 2   **large handfuls of parsley, finely chopped**

Cut up the tomatoes and put into the saucepan with the garlic, salt, pepper, and olive oil. If each octopus weighs more than 3 or 4 ounces, cut in half lengthwise. Add the octopus to the pot, cover the pot with foil, and tie it with string to hold it in place. Put a lid over the foil. Cook the octopus for 45 minutes over low heat. Do not remove the foil and lid until the end of the cooking time.

Remove the lid and foil. If the sauce seems too thin, remove the octopus to a platter and simmer for 5 or 10 minutes to thicken the sauce slightly. Add the parsley and put the octopus back into the sauce. Simmer for 5 minutes and serve hot, in the pan.

NOTE: If you're preparing this dish in advance, add the parsley and simmer for 5 minutes when you're ready to serve.

COLD VEAL IN GREEN SAUCE

A Winter Buffet

This recipe comes from Ada Parasiliti, a Sicilian who runs the best cooking school in Milan. This is one of her favorite dishes. It's prepared a day or two in advance, looks particularly attractive on a buffet table, and, since it is served cold, is ideal for large parties.

SERVES 10 TO 12

> 1 veal eye of round, 2 to 2-1/2 pounds (about 1 kilogram)
> white wine vinegar
> salt
> 1/2 small onion, coarsely chopped
> 2 heaped tablespoons capers, rinsed and dried
> 2 large handfuls of parsley, washed and dried
> scant 1/2 cup white wine vinegar (100 ml)
> 1 cup olive oil (250 ml)
> artichoke hearts packed in oil and parsley sprigs for garnish

Soak the meat in equal parts vinegar and water to cover for 24 hours. Drain. Put the meat on to boil in equal parts fresh water and vinegar to barely cover, and add salt as for pasta water. Simmer until tender, about an hour. Cool the meat in its liquid and wrap in foil. Refrigerate for 1 or 2 days.

When you're ready to serve the meat, make the sauce. Put the onion, capers, and parsley in a blender. Add half the vinegar and, with the motor running, add the oil slowly, scraping down the sides as necessary. Add salt to taste and more vinegar as desired.

Slice the meat thinly. Put a round layer of meat on a serving platter. Spoon some sauce over and add another layer of meat, making a slightly smaller concentric circle. Spread the sauce over the meat and repeat the layers until all the meat has been covered with the sauce. Cover tightly and refrigerate until ready to serve.

At serving time, take an artichoke in one hand and with the other open the leaves one by one until the hearts look like roses. Garnish the dish with the artichoke "roses," 3 in the center and others around the dish. Tuck parsley around the edge of the dish.

A
Winter
Buffet

Caponata alla Napoletana
COLD VEGETABLE SALAD

This traditional, earthy Neapolitan salad is often served on its own as an *antipasto.* In her book on Neapolitan food, *Cucina Napoletana,* Jeanne Carola recommends covering the salad with chopped ripe tomatoes and rounds of toasted dried bread that have been dipped in a mixture of vinegar and water and covered with anchovy-wrapped olives. With these additions the dish is transformed into a complete meal.

SERVES 8

1-1/2	pounds cauliflower (675 grams)
	salt
1-1/2	pounds escarole (2 heads) (675 grams)
1	cup black Gaeta or spicy olives, pitted (200 grams)
1/3	cup spicy green Sicilian olives, pitted (70 grams)
1/2	cup capers, rinsed and dried (80 grams)
4	salt-packed anchovies, cleaned (see page 419), *or* 8 oil-packed fillets, drained and cut into pieces freshly ground pepper to taste
6	tablespoons white wine vinegar (100 ml)
1/2	cup plus 1 tablespoon olive oil (140 ml)

Wash the cauliflower and break it into flowerets. Cook in boiling salted water until *al dente.* Cool and put in a large salad bowl.

Wash the escarole, discarding the tough outer leaves. Dry and cut into bite-size pieces. Add to the cauliflower. Add the olives, capers, anchovies, salt and pepper to taste.

Beat together the vinegar and oil and pour the dressing over the salad. Toss to mix thoroughly. Cover tightly and refrigerate for at least 2 hours or overnight before serving.

La Spiritosa
MARINATED CARROTS

Use small, young carrots for this recipe, which is a variation of one that appears in *Cucina Napoletana* by Jeanne Carola. The flavor improves if the carrots are made a day or 2 before serving.

SERVES 6 TO 8

> 2 **pounds carrots (900 grams)**
> **salt to taste**
> 6 **tablespoons white wine vinegar (100 ml)**
> 3/4 **teaspoon hot red pepper flakes**
> 2 **tablespoons dried oregano**
> 2 **bay leaves (optional)**
> 4 **garlic cloves, sliced**
> 1/2 **cup plus 2 tablespoons olive oil (150 ml)**

Peel the carrots and cut them into 2-inch-long sticks about 1/3 inch thick. Cook in boiling salted water until tender but *al dente*. Drain.

Pour the vinegar over the hot carrots and mix. Add all the other ingredients and toss to mix thoroughly. Leave the carrots overnight, if possible in a cool place, not refrigerated.

WALNUT TART

Michi Ambrosi's winter walnut tart has a dense, nutty flavor. It's all the more rewarding served with whipped cream or vanilla ice cream, topped with a little of the rum and orange sauce used to make the filling. The orange sauce can be made well ahead as it keeps for months.

A Winter Buffet

SERVES 6 TO 8

9-inch (24 cm) tart tin,
buttered and floured

FOR THE CRUST:

- 2 cups plus 2 tablespoons all-purpose flour (250 grams)
- 2/3 cup potato flour (100 grams)
- 1/3 cup plus 2 tablespoons sugar (100 grams)
- 1 teaspoon baking powder
- 1/2 cup (1/4 pound) plus 2-1/2 tablespoons unsalted butter (150 grams)
- 1 egg yolk
  grated zest of 1 small lemon

FOR THE FILLING:

- 3 cups chopped shelled walnuts (360 grams)
- 3/4 cup sugar (165 grams)
- 2 tablespoons *Salsa d'Arancia* (recipe follows) *or* aromatic honey such as orange blossom
- 3/4 cup heavy cream (185 ml)
  softly whipped cream or vanilla ice cream for serving

Make the pastry for the crust. In an electric mixer or a food processor fitted with the steel blade, mix all crust ingredients together until they mass. Line the prepared tin with three quarters of the pastry, pressing it in with your hands. (Should the pastry tear, simply press a piece of pastry on top.) Trim away excess pastry and crimp the edges. Refrigerate the prepared crust and extra pastry while you make the filling. Preheat the oven to 350° (180).

Make the filling. Put the walnuts, sugar, and Orange Sauce in a saucepan and cook over medium heat, stirring, for about 15 minutes or until the sugar has browned. Cool slightly and add the cream. Pour the filling into the pastry shell. Crumble the remaining pastry and sprinkle the crumbs evenly over the filling.

Bake the tart for 1 hour and 10 minutes or until the crust is lightly browned. Serve at room temperature accompanied by softly whipped cream or vanilla ice cream.

Salsa d'Arancia
ORANGE SAUCE

1-3/4	cups freshly squeezed orange juice (425 ml), about 7 oranges
2-1/4	cups sugar (500 grams)
5	ounces white rum (150 ml)

In a saucepan, cook the juice and sugar together over low heat for 30 minutes. Add the rum and simmer for 30 minutes. Cool. When cool, the sauce must be the consistency of fluid marmalade. If it's not thick enough, cook it a little longer; if it's too thick, add a little orange juice.

This sauce keeps for months and is excellent over ice cream. Do not refrigerate; store in a dark, cool place.

Coviglia di Cioccolato con Meringhe
FROZEN CHOCOLATE CREAM
WITH MERINGUES

Coviglia is the Neapolitan name for a *semifreddo* made from egg yolks, sugar, beaten egg whites and cream, and whatever flavor you choose to use (coffee, nuts, berries, chocolate, etc.). A *semifreddo* is not hard to master, and with a few decorative touches it makes a stunning conclusion to a meal. In this recipe the chocolate *coviglia* is served and covered with small meringues. There's no question that this is a sinfully rich dessert, just right for a special occasion.

SERVES 8 TO 10

7- or 8-cup (1.5 liters)
domed mold, pastry bag, star tip

FOR THE *COVIGLIA* (FROZEN CREAM):

- 1/2 **pound good-quality semisweet chocolate (225 grams)**
- 3 **egg whites**
- 1-1/2 **cups heavy cream (350 ml)**
- 4 **egg yolks**
- 6 **tablespoons sugar (90 grams)**
- 2 **tablespoons white rum**

FOR THE MERINGUES:

- 2 **egg whites at room temperature**
  pinch of salt
- 1 **teaspoon freshly squeezed lemon juice**
- 1/2 **cup plus 2 tablespoons sugar (140 grams)**

Make the *coviglia*. Melt the chocolate in the top of a double boiler. Stir until smooth and set aside to cool.

Whip the egg whites until stiff but not dry. Reserve. Whip the cream until stiff but not dry. Reserve.

Beat the egg yolks with the sugar until pale and lemon-colored. Add the rum and cooled chocolate. Working quickly, fold in the egg whites, first a tablespoon and then the rest. Fold in the cream thoroughly.

Dampen the mold and line it with plastic wrap. Spoon the cream into the mold and put it in the freezer.

Make the meringues. Preheat the oven to 200° (95). Beat the egg whites with a pinch of salt and the lemon juice and, when the whites are frothy, add the sugar a little at a time. Beat the whites for 15 minutes or until glossy. Spoon the meringue into a pastry bag fitted with a star tip. Butter and flour a cookie sheet and pipe out small rosettes on it.

Bake the meringues for 4-1/2 hours. Turn off the oven and leave the meringues in the oven overnight. If you're not using them at once, store them in an airtight tin.

When you're ready to serve the *coviglia,* turn it out onto a round platter and leave at room temperature to soften for about 30 minutes, depending on how warm the room is. When softened, cover the surface with the small meringues, placed close together. Serve at once.

Babà alla Napoletana
NEAPOLITAN BABA

This sponge cake soaked in rum is the Neapolitan version of the well-known French *baba au rhum* and very likely first made its appearance in the 19th century, at a time when the *monzùs* were returning home armed with the recipes they had learned to prepare in France. Since then *Babà alla Napoletana* has become the pride of Naples and one of *the* essential Neapolitan party desserts.

SERVES 14 TO 16

10-inch ring mold 2½-quart
capacity (26 cm, 2½ liters),
buttered

FOR THE *BABÀ*:

2	1/4–ounce envelopes active dry yeast (15 grams) *or* 1 ounce fresh yeast
1/4	cup warm milk (60 ml)
2-2/3	cups flour (300 grams)
1/2	cup (1/4 pound) plus 4-1/2 tablespoons unsalted butter, at room temperature, cut into pieces (180 grams)
6	eggs at room temperature
2-1/2	tablespoons sugar (40 grams)
	pinch of salt
	grated zest of 1 small lemon

FOR THE RUM SYRUP:

2-2/3	cups sugar (600 grams)
1/2	cup freshly squeezed lemon juice (125 ml)
2	cups water (500 ml)
	grated zest of 1 small lemon
1-1/2	cups good-quality white rum (375 ml)

2 cups heavy cream, whipped, for garnish and serving (500 ml)
black cherries packed in syrup (Fabbri, if possible) and angelica "leaves" for garnish

Dissolve the yeast in the warm milk. Add 1 tablespoon of the flour, cover, and leave to proof in a warm spot for 5 minutes.

In the large bowl of an electric mixer, put the rest of the flour, the proofed yeast, half the butter, 3 of the eggs, the sugar, and salt. Beat with the paddle attachment until well mixed.

Add the remaining eggs, one at a time, letting each one be absorbed before adding the next. Add the rest of the butter and the lemon zest. Beat for 10 minutes, or until the batter is smooth and elastic. Cover the bowl with a clean cloth and set aside in a warm, draft-free place to rise for an hour.

When the dough has risen, gently spoon it into the prepared mold. Cover and set aside to rise again until the dough comes to the top of the mold.

Fifteen minutes before baking, preheat the oven to 425° (220).

Bake the *babà* for 15 minutes. Lower the heat to 375° (190) and bake for 15 minutes longer. Immediately turn the *babà* out onto a rack and cool for 10 minutes. Put back into the mold.

While the *babà* is cooling, make the syrup. Put the sugar, lemon juice, water, and zest in a saucepan and bring to a boil; simmer for 10 minutes. Remove from the heat and add the rum. Poke holes in the *babà* with a kitchen needle and spoon the hot syrup over it, letting it be absorbed each time before adding more. The *babà* must absorb almost all the syrup. If you're serving it later, leave a little of the syrup to pour over at the last moment. Keep the *babà* in its mold until serving time.

Decorate the *babà* with rosettes of soft whipped cream at its base, interspersed with black cherries in syrup and angelica "leaves." Or you can use fresh fruit, whipped cream, and toasted almonds.

Un Grande Buffet Estivo

A BIG
SUMMER BUFFET

A
B i g
S u m m e r
B u f f e t

Riso Estivo
SUMMER RICE

Pizza alla Campofranco di Michi
MICHI'S PIZZA CAMPOFRANCO

Parmigiana di Melanzane alla Napoletana
NEAPOLITAN EGGPLANT PARMESAN

Pasta Campagnola
COUNTRY PASTA

Un Altro Vitel Tonnato
ANOTHER TUNA VEAL

Alici Marinate
MARINATED FRESH ANCHOVIES

Zucchine Scapece
MARINATED ZUCCHINI (*page 178*)

Peperoni Gratinati
BAKED PEPPERS

Mozzarelline, Insalata di Pomodori, Basilico, e Olive Nere
TINY FRESH MOZZARELLA BALLS AND TOMATOES
WITH BLACK OLIVES AND BASIL

Pizza di Fragole
STRAWBERRY PIE

Sorbetto a Strati
LAYERED ICES

Semifreddo al Limone di Michi
MICHI'S FROZEN LEMON CREAM

WINES
White: Lacryma Christi (Napoli); serve cold
Rosé: Rosato di Massalubrense (Napoli); serve chilled
Dessert: Sanginella Spumante (Campania); serve cold

Michi Ambrosi de Magistris lives with her husband and eight children in the heart of Naples, where everything is at her fingertips—the best vegetable markets, the best cheese shops, and a butcher who "can do anything." Her apartment is on the top two floors of a *palazzo* overlooking the entire sweep of the Bay of Naples. Michi is an indefatigable party giver, and with the assistance of a few friends she put together this menu for the kind of party she likes to have on her own terrace at the height of the summer, when the days are hot and still but the evenings mercifully cool.

*A
B i g
S u m m e r
B u f f e t*

Riso Estivo
SUMMER RICE

A patriotic red, white, and green rice salad (the colors of the Italian flag), this is the perfect standby for a summer buffet dinner. It even looks refreshing, as the rice is mixed with arugula and turns a beautiful green. Michi always serves the rice alongside a large platter of tiny fresh *mozzarella* balls and one of ripe tomatoes with black olives and basil.

SERVES 6 TO 8

10-inch ring mold, 2¹/₂-quart
capacity (26 cm, 2¹/₂ liters),
oiled

1	**pound Arborio rice (450 grams)**
	salt
5	**tablespoons olive oil (75 ml)**
2	**tablespoons freshly squeezed lemon juice**
	freshly ground pepper to taste
1/2	**cup coarsely grated *pecorino* cheese (65 grams)**
1	**cup green olives packed in brine, pitted and cut into pieces (200 grams)**
5	**tablespoons mayonnaise (75 ml)**
1	**pound arugula, coarse stems removed, washed and dried (450 grams)**
	freshly squeezed lemon juice and olive oil to dress the arugula (optional)
	ripe fresh tomatoes for garnish

Pour the rice into a saucepan of boiling salted water, stir, and allow the water to return to a full, rolling boil. Lower the heat—the water should be at a steady but not vigorous boil—and cook the rice, stirring once or twice, for 17 minutes. Drain and dress with the 5 tablespoons oil and 2 tablespoons lemon juice. Spread on a large platter to cool.

When tepid, add pepper, *pecorino,* olives, and mayonnaise. In a food processor fitted with the steel blade, chop two thirds of the arugula very finely and add to the rice. The rice will be a beautiful green. Put the rice into the prepared mold, pressing with the back of a spoon—the rice must be firmly packed—and refrigerate until ready to use, up to 4 hours in advance.

When you're ready to serve the rice, turn it out onto a round platter. Dress the remaining arugula with salt, oil, and lemon juice if desired and put the arugula into the center of the mold. Surround the base with slices of tomato.

Pizza alla Campofranco
PIZZA CAMPOFRANCO

The word *pizza* is thought to have come from the Romans. *Pizza Margherita*, the pizza whose fame has spread throughout the world, was invented for Margherita, Queen of Naples, in 1880. No summer buffet in Naples could be without its pizza. In this recipe it is made with a rich brioche dough that is baked, then both filled and covered with *mozzarella,* tomato sauce, and basil and baked for another 15 minutes. The result is surprisingly light and delicious. (The following recipe can be served instead.)

continued

SERVES 8 TO 10

10-inch cake pan with 2-inch
sides (26 by 5 cm), buttered

FOR THE CRUST:

- 2 **1/4-ounce envelopes active dry yeast (15 grams)** *or*
  1 ounce fresh yeast
- 1/3 **cup warm milk (80 ml)**
- 1 **teaspoon sugar**
- 1 **pound (4 cups) flour (450 grams)**
- 1 **cup (1/2 pound) unsalted butter at room**
  temperature, cut into pieces (225 grams)
- 5 **eggs at room temperature**
- 1/3 **cup freshly grated Parmesan cheese (45 grams)**
  salt and freshly ground pepper to taste

FOR THE TOMATO SAUCE:

- 2 **tablespoons olive oil**
- 1/2 **medium onion, finely chopped**
- 2 **pounds plum tomatoes, peeled, seeded, and cut**
  into pieces, *or* **canned Italian plum tomatoes,**
  drained for 10 minutes (900 grams)
  salt to taste

TO COMPLETE THE PIZZA:

- 14 **ounces** *mozzarella* **cheese, very thinly sliced or**
  coarsely grated (about 3 cups) (400 grams)
- 3 **tablespoons freshly grated Parmesan cheese**
  (30 grams)
- 10 **fresh basil leaves, chopped, plus basil for garnish**
  freshly ground pepper to taste

Make the crust. Dissolve the yeast in the warm milk and add the sugar and 1 tablespoon of the flour. Cover the bowl and set aside for 10 minutes to proof.

A
Big
Summer
Buffet

Put the rest of the flour, the butter, eggs, Parmesan, salt, and pepper in the large bowl of an electric mixer. Add the proofed yeast to the bowl, wrap a tea towel around the bowl to prevent the flour from scattering, and beat the mixture, using the paddle attachment, for about 10 minutes. The dough will become elastic and come away from the sides of the bowl.

Put the dough in the prepared pan and set aside, covered, in a warm, draft-free place to rise for 2 hours. Fifteen minutes before the 2 hours are up, preheat the oven to 350° (180). Bake the brioche for 45 minutes. Cool on a rack for 10 minutes and then turn out onto the rack.

While the pizza is rising, make the tomato sauce. Heat the oil in a skillet, add the onion, and cook over low heat until the onion is transparent, occasionally adding a tablespoon of water to prevent burning. Add the tomatoes and cook over medium-high heat, stirring and mashing the tomatoes with the back of a wooden spoon, until the sauce is very dense, about 15 minutes. Add salt. Reserve.

When you're ready to serve the pizza, preheat the oven to 425° (220). Cut the pizza crust in half horizontally. Cover the bottom crust with half the *mozzarella,* 1-1/2 teaspoons of the Parmesan, and half the chopped basil. Spoon half the sauce over the filling and sprinkle 1 tablespoon of the Parmesan on top.

Put the other crust on top and add the remaining *mozzarella,* chopped basil, and tomato sauce. Sprinkle the remaining Parmesan over the top. Grind black pepper over all.

Bake the pizza for 15 to 20 minutes or until the *mozzarella* has melted. Serve the pizza hot, garnished with basil.

NOTE: The crust can be prepared in advance and wrapped tightly in foil.

Pizza alla Campofranco di Michi
MICHI'S PIZZA CAMPOFRANCO

A variation of the preceding recipe, the chief difference being that the filling is sealed in the uncooked pizza dough, left to rise, and then baked.

SERVES 8

8- to 8¹/₂-inch pan with
4-inch sides (20 by 10 cm),
springform if available,
buttered

FOR THE FILLING:

1	**tablespoon olive oil**
1	**1-pound can Italian plum tomatoes, drained (450 grams)**
	salt and freshly ground pepper to taste
1/4	**pound *prosciutto*, julienned (1 scant cup) (110 grams)**
1/2	**pound *mozzarella* cheese, coarsely grated (225 grams)**
8	**or 9 basil leaves, chopped, plus basil sprigs for garnish**

FOR THE CRUST:

1	**tablespoon active dry yeast *or* 1 ounce fresh yeast scant 1/2 cup warm milk (100 ml)**
2-2/3	**cups flour (300 grams)**
1/2	**cup (1/4 pound) plus 2-1/2 tablespoons unsalted butter at room temperature, cut into pieces (150 grams)**
4	**eggs at room temperature**
2	**ounces Parmesan cheese, grated (about 1/2 cup) (60 grams)**
	salt and freshly ground pepper to taste
1	**teaspoon sugar**

Start the filling. Heat the olive oil in a small frying pan. Gently squeeze the drained tomatoes to remove their liquid without tearing the tomatoes. Cook the tomatoes in the oil over high heat, turning once, until the remaining liquid has evaporated. Cool and reserve.

Make the crust. Dissolve the yeast in the warm milk. Put the flour, butter, eggs, Parmesan, salt, pepper, and sugar in the large bowl of an electric mixer. Add the yeast mixture. Wrap a tea towel around the bowl to prevent the flour from scattering and beat the mixture, using the paddle attachment, for about 10 minutes or until the dough is elastic and comes away from the sides of the bowl.

Put half the mixture in the prepared pan. Put in the tomatoes, sprinkle with salt, and grind black pepper over. Put the *prosciutto* over the tomatoes and spread the *mozzarella* over the *prosciutto*. Sprinkle the chopped basil over the filling and grind pepper over. Spread the remaining dough on top of the filling, pressing it into the corners to seal the top and bottom together. Cover with plastic wrap and a towel and put in a warm, draft-free place to rise for 2 hours.

Fifteen minutes before the rising time is up, preheat the oven to 350° (180). Bake the pizza for 45 minutes. Cool on a rack for 10 minutes before removing the sides. Cool for another 5 minutes before removing the bottom. Serve the pizza hot.

NOTE: This pizza can be prepared in advance and reheated, wrapped in foil, for 20 minutes in a 375° (190) oven. Leftover pizza may be reheated in the same way.

Parmigiana di Melanzane alla Napoletana
NEAPOLITAN EGGPLANT PARMESAN

In spite of its name, which appears to indicate some connection either with the city of Parma or with its famous cheese, this is a traditional southern Italian dish that has been eaten for at least 200 years in Naples and farther south. Sicilians claim it is a Sicilian invention first made not with Parmesan but with *caciocavallo* cheese. They even maintain that *Parmigiana* bears no reference to Parma at all but is a corruption of the Sicilian word *Parmigiana*, meaning "shutter," and that the dish was so called because the overlapping slices of eggplant resemble the louvers of a shutter. Whatever its origins, it is much beloved throughout southern Italy and can be prepared well in advance and then reheated. It also freezes well, and all over the South leftover *Parmigiana di melanzane* is used to dress short pasta.

SERVES 8

9- by 13-inch (23 by 33 cm)
ovenproof glass dish, oiled

5	pounds eggplant, sliced lengthwise 1/2 inch thick (2.250 grams)
	salt
	olive oil for frying
	flour for dredging
3-1/2	pounds ripe fresh tomatoes, peeled, seeded, and cut into pieces (1.600 grams), *or* 3 1-pound cans Italian plum tomatoes, drained (1.350 grams)
	pinch of sugar
1	cup freshly grated Parmesan cheese (135 grams)
	freshly ground pepper to taste
3/4	pound *mozzarella* cheese, thinly sliced (335 grams)
	a handful of fresh basil leaves, washed and dried
3	eggs

Layer the eggplant in a colander, salting each layer. Put a weighted plate on top and leave for about 2 hours. Rinse the slices and pat dry.

Heat olive oil to a depth of 1/2 inch in a large frying pan. Flour the eggplant slices and toss in a sifter to remove excess flour. Fry the slices in batches, adding oil as necessary, over medium-high heat, turning once, until lightly browned. Drain on paper towels.

Cook the tomatoes in a large sauté pan without oil over medium-high heat, mashing them with the back of a wooden spoon. Add a pinch of sugar and cook the sauce for 15 minutes or until thickened. Add salt to taste. Preheat the oven to 350° (180).

Assemble the dish. Put one third of the eggplant slices over the bottom of the prepared dish. Sprinkle 3 or 4 tablespoons of Parmesan over the eggplant and grind black pepper over. Add half the *mozzarella,* half the sauce, and half the basil. Add another third of the eggplant slices, 1/4 cup of the Parmesan, more pepper, and the rest of the *mozzarella,* basil, and tomato sauce. End with the remaining third of the eggplant. Beat the remaining Parmesan with the eggs and pour evenly over the eggplant.

Bake for 30 minutes or until lightly browned and bubbly. Serve hot or at room temperature.

Pasta Campagnola
COUNTRY PASTA

This baked pasta and tomato dish is sometimes called *cotti e crudi*. It *must* be made with ripe summer tomatoes, so if all you can find are those hard, pink, plastic-packed so-called tomatoes from the supermarket, put this recipe off until another season. This is Letizi Maione's recipe.

SERVES 6 TO 8

9- by 13-inch (23 by 33 cm)
ovenproof glass dish, oiled

	salt
4	**pounds small, round ripe fresh tomatoes, preferably all the same size (1.800 grams)**
1/2	**cup plus 2 tablespoons olive oil (150 ml)**
	a large handful of fresh basil leaves, washed and dried plus basil for garnish
3	**garlic cloves, finely minced**
	freshly ground black pepper to taste
	dried oregano to taste
1	**pound *sedanini or mezze zite,* broken into 2-inch pieces, *or pennette* (450 grams)**
1/2	**cup plus 1 tablespoon freshly grated *pecorino* cheese (75 grams)**
2	**tablespoons fine dry bread crumbs**

Preheat the oven to 350° (180). Heat salted water for the pasta.

Put the tomatoes into the prepared dish to make sure they fit. If they don't, add or subtract tomatoes as necessary. Cut the tomatoes roughly in half, making the bottom halves as close to the same height as possible. (The bottom of the tomatoes will be on top of the dish.) Reserve the bottom halves and cut up the stem halves into a large bowl, discarding the hard green stems. To the bowl add all but 3 tablespoons of the olive oil, the basil, torn into pieces with your hands, the garlic, salt, pepper, and oregano. Mix well and reserve.

Cook the pasta in the boiling salted water for 5 minutes. Drain and add to the bowl, mixing. Put half the pasta on the bottom of the prepared dish. Sprinkle over half the *pecorino* and 1 tablespoon of the bread crumbs. Put the remaining pasta on top and sprinkle the rest of the cheese and bread crumbs over it. Put the tomatoes on top, cut side down, arranging them decoratively. Trickle the rest of the oil over the tomatoes and add salt and pepper. Bake for 35 to 40 minutes, until the tomatoes are done. Serve hot or cold, garnished with basil.

Un Altro Vitel Tonnato

ANOTHER TUNA VEAL

Here is a recipe known the world over. Neapolitans claim it as a local dish, but no one seems to have a convincing theory as to how it came to be. Whatever its origins, the illogical mixture of veal and tuna is inspired, and one of its assets is that it tastes even better when prepared a day ahead of time.

SERVES 8 TO 10

2	cups dry white wine (500 ml)
1	12-ounce can tuna packed in oil, drained (330 grams)
5	salt-packed anchovies, cleaned (see page 419), *or* 10 oil-packed anchovy fillets, drained
1/3	cup salt-packed capers, rinsed (60 grams)
1	quart water, approximately (1 liter)
2-1/2	pounds veal eye of round (1.100 grams)
1	egg at room temperature
1	egg yolk at room temperature
1	teaspoon dry mustard
2	tablespoons freshly squeezed lemon juice
1-1/4	teaspoons salt
	freshly ground pepper to taste
3/4	cup olive oil (185 ml)
2	dill gherkins, cut into pieces
	anchovies and capers for garnish

Into a casserole in which the meat will fit snugly put the wine, tuna, 4 of the anchovies or 8 fillets, 3 tablespoons of the capers, and enough water so that the liquid will almost cover the veal. Bring to a boil before adding the meat. Cover the pan and simmer the veal until tender, about 1-1/4 hours. Cool the meat in its broth. When cool, wrap tightly and refrigerate. Reserve 1 cup of the broth with the tuna, anchovies, and capers.

Make the tuna sauce. Put the egg, egg yolk, mustard, lemon juice, salt, and pepper in a blender and blend for 30 seconds. Pour in the oil in a steady trickle. When the mayonnaise has thickened, add the drained ingredients from the broth, reserving the liquid. Add the remaining anchovies or fillets, capers, and the gherkins, scraping down the sides as necessary. Pour the sauce into a bowl. If it's too thick, thin it with a few tablespoons of the reserved broth.

Slice the meat thinly, using an electric knife if possible. Dip the veal slices into the sauce and place on a large serving platter in layers. Spoon the remaining sauce over the veal. Lay thin strips of anchovies on top and scatter capers all over the meat. Cover tightly and refrigerate until serving time. Serve cold.

Alici Marinate
MARINATED FRESH ANCHOVIES

Today these anchovies are an "in" dish in Naples, whether eaten as an *antipasto,* a main course, or, as in this case, part of a buffet dinner. Anchovies are known as *blue fish* in Italy not only because their skin is silver-blue but also because they inhabit the blue waters closest to the coast. You won't find fresh anchovies at your local supermarket, but every now and then they turn up at the fishmonger's.

SERVES 4 TO 6

> 2 **pounds very fresh anchovies, cleaned (see page 419) (900 grams)**
> 1/2 **cup plus 1 tablespoon freshly squeezed lemon juice (140 ml)**
> 2 **garlic cloves, sliced**
> 1-1/2 **teaspoons (or to taste) salt**
> 1/4 **teaspoon (or to taste) freshly ground black pepper**
> 1-1/2 **teaspoons (or to taste) dried oregano**
> 2 **tablespoons (or to taste) olive oil**

Wash and dry the anchovies. Layer them in a plate with a rim and dress each layer with lemon juice, garlic slices, and the seasonings. Leave to marinate overnight in the refrigerator.

When you're ready to serve the anchovies, drain them and layer them in a clean dish. Trickle a little olive oil over each layer. Serve at cool room temperature.

Peperoni Gratinati
BAKED PEPPERS

Neapolitans eat almost as many peppers as they do tomatoes. This ubiquitous vegetable (also brought back from the New World) arrives at the table in many guises—served with pasta, stuffed, rolled in bread crumbs, and, as in this recipe, first roasted and then baked with a mixture of capers, olives, and anchovies. This dish can be prepared a day in advance.

SERVES 4 TO 6

- 2-1/2 **pounds bell peppers, a mixture of red and yellow (1.100 grams)**
- 3 **tablespoons capers, rinsed and dried (30 grams)**
- 1/2 **cup black olives, pitted and halved (100 grams)**
- 3 **salt-packed anchovies, cleaned (see page 419),** *or* **6 oil-packed anchovy fillets, drained**
- 5 **tablespoons olive oil (75 ml)**
- 3 **tablespoons fine dry bread crumbs**
- 1/2 **teaspoon (or to taste) hot red pepper flakes salt and freshly ground pepper to taste**

Roast the peppers on a cookie sheet in a 400˘ (200) oven for 20 minutes. Turn the peppers and roast for another 20 minutes or until the peppers are dark and blistered. Wrap each in foil and set aside until cooled. Peel, seed, and cut into strips about 1 inch wide. Set aside in a bowl. Preheat the oven to 350° (180).

Mix the peppers and their juice with the capers, olives, anchovies cut into pieces, 3-1/2 tablespoons of the oil, 2 tablespoons of the bread crumbs, the hot pepper flakes, salt, and pepper. Put the mixture in an oiled *gratin* dish and trickle the remaining oil over it. Sprinkle the remaining bread crumbs over the peppers.

Bake for 45 minutes. Serve at room temperature.

STRAWBERRY PIE

This is a confusing name for an old-fashioned Neapolitan dessert because in America the word *pizza* normally refers to a *mozzarella* pizza—but here it's a sweet crust filled with pastry cream and fresh strawberries. Pastry cream, called *crema pasticcera* by the Neapolitans, is a much loved, thick custard sauce that is frequently served on its own.

A
Big
Summer
Buffet

SERVES 6 TO 8

8-inch springform pan with
2¹/₂-inch sides (20 by 6 cm),
buttered

FOR THE *CREMA PASTICCERA* (PASTRY CREAM):

    2 **cups milk (500 ml)**
    5 **tablespoons sugar (75 grams)**
  1/4 **cup wheat starch *or* cornstarch (30 grams)**
    4 **egg yolks**
      grated zest of 1 lemon
  15 **ounces (3 cups) fresh strawberries, sliced 1/2-inch thick (425 grams)**
      confectioners' sugar for the berries (optional) and for dusting the finished pie

FOR THE PASTRY:

    3 **cups plus 2 tablespoons flour (360 grams)**
  3/4 **cup less 1 tablespoon sugar (155 grams)**
  1/2 **cup (1/4 pound) plus 4-1/2 tablespoons cool unsalted butter, cut into pieces (180 grams)**
    4 **egg yolks**
      grated zest of 1 lemon

  1/2 **cup cookie crumbs made from graham crackers *or* digestive biscuits**

Make the pastry cream. Put the milk, sugar, wheat starch or cornstarch, and egg yolks in a blender and blend for 1 minute. Pour into a small saucepan and cook over medium heat, stirring, until it thickens. Remove from the heat and add the lemon zest. Place plastic wrap directly on the surface of the cream. Cool. If you're making the cream in advance, refrigerate it until you're ready to use it.

If the strawberries are not sweet enough for your taste, add a few tablespoons confectioners' sugar. Preheat the oven to 350° (180).

Make the pastry. In an electric mixer or a food processor, fitted with the steel blade, put the flour, sugar, butter, egg yolks, and zest. Mix until the pastry masses. Divide the pastry into 2 parts, one slightly larger. Roll out the larger part and line the prepared pan, leaving a 1/2-inch overhang. Sprinkle half the cookie crumbs over the bottom of the crust and spoon half the cream over the crumbs. Put all of the strawberries on top and spoon the remaining pastry cream over the berries. Sprinkle the rest of the crumbs over the cream.

Roll out the remaining pastry into a circle for the top crust and fit it over the pie. Trim the crust and roll the bottom crust over the top, sealing top to bottom. Crimp the edges and cut a strawberry or other shape to decorate the pie. Make holes in the top with a kitchen needle.

Bake for 55 minutes or until the pie is lightly browned. Cool completely on a rack before removing the sides and bottom of the pan. Dust with confectioners' sugar before serving. Refrigerate any remaining pie.

Sorbetto a Strati
LAYERED ICES

Neapolitans adore ice cream and ices. Before the days of refrigeration Neapolitans had snow brought down from the mountains nearby and stored in grottoes or holes covered with straw and leaves. Every day, during the summer months, donkeys would carry a load of well-wrapped snow to Castellammare, where it was taken by boat to Naples. It was considered such a necessity that, if for some reason the snow did not arrive, the carriers were fined.

Fruit ices with a sugar syrup base have always been a great favorite, and in Naples they are made with every imaginable kind of fruit. *Sorbetto a strati* is a Neapolitan specialty often served at a party or on a special occasion. Different-flavored fruit ices are frozen in separate layers in the same mold, and the base is decorated with flowers or fresh fruit before serving.

To make this marvelous striped Neapolitan delicacy, start with a sugar syrup, which can be prepared in advance and kept in a cool place. The proportions are 2 parts sugar to 1 part water. Bring to a boil and simmer for 10 minutes. Cool before using. Any kind of mold can be used, but a springform pan lined with plastic wrap is easiest for serving. Make the fruit ices according to the following proportions. Fill the mold with a layer of fruit ice and wait until it is firmly frozen before adding the next layer to prevent the colors from mixing with each other. Shortly before serving, remove the sides of the mold and turn the layered ices onto a platter. Decorate the dessert extravagantly with flowers or fresh berries. (Roses and nasturtiums make particularly attractive decorations.)

STRAWBERRY

> 3-1/3 **cups (1-2/3 pounds) fresh strawberries, pureed (750 grams)**
> 1 **cup sugar syrup (250 ml)**
> 1/4 **cup freshly squeezed lemon juice (60 ml)**

LEMON

2-2/3 cups freshly squeezed lemon juice (650 ml), about
10 lemons
grated zest of 2 lemons
1 cup sugar syrup (250 ml) (plus 2 or 3 more
tablespoons if the lemons are very sour)

TANGERINE

2 cups freshly squeezed tangerine juice (500 ml),
about 8 tangerines
grated zest of 6 tangerines
1 cup sugar syrup (250 ml)
1/2 cup freshly squeezed lemon juice (125 ml)

PEACH

2 cups pureed ripe fresh peaches, about 1 pound 6
ounces (630 grams)
1/4 cup freshly squeezed lemon juice (60 ml)
1 cup sugar syrup (250 ml)

APRICOT

2 cups pureed ripe fresh apricots, about 1-2/3 pounds
(750 grams)
1/4 cup freshly squeezed lemon juice (60 ml)
1 cup sugar syrup (250 ml)

FIG

2 cups pureed peeled ripe fresh figs, about 1 pound
6 ounces (630 grams)
1/4 cup freshly squeezed lemon juice (60 ml)
1 cup sugar syrup (250 ml)

continued

A
B i g
S u m m e r
B u f f e t

PEAR

2 cups ripe fresh pears, about 1-1/3 pounds (600 grams), pureed with 3 tablespoons freshly squeezed lemon juice
1 cup sugar syrup (250 ml)
3 tablespoons Poire William liqueur

For each ice, mix the ingredients and then process in an ice cream machine according to the manufacturer's directions.

FOR LEMON ICE: Mix the ingredients and set aside for an hour to allow the juice to absorb the flavor of the zest. Strain and process in an ice cream machine according to the manufacturer's directions. If you're using lemon ice, put it in the middle. It melts faster than the others.

Semifreddo al Limone di Michi
MICHI'S FROZEN LEMON CREAM

This is Michi Ambrosi's own special recipe. At its base is a layer of sponge cake known in Italy as *pan di Spagna;* next comes a lemon-flavored cream, and finally the dessert is covered entirely with whipped cream.

SERVES 8 TO 10

9-inch cake pan with 2-inch sides (24 by 6 cm), buttered and floured; 12-inch cheesecake pan with 2-inch sides (30 by 5 cm)

FOR THE *PAN DI SPAGNA* (ITALIAN SPONGE CAKE):

- **4 eggs, separated, at room temperature**
- **2/3 cup sugar (150 grams)**
- **1 cup less 2 tablespoons flour (100 grams)**

FOR THE LEMON CREAM:

- **1 14-ounce can condensed milk (400 grams)**
- **3/4 cup freshly squeezed lemon juice (185 ml) grated zest of 3 large lemons**
- **3/4 cup egg whites, from about 4 or 5 large eggs (225 grams), at room temperature**
- **2 cups heavy cream (500 ml) plus 3/4 cup heavy cream for icing (185 ml)**
- **1 lemon for garnish sugar**

continued

333

Preheat the oven to 325° (160).

Make the *pan di Spagna,* preferably the day before using it to facilitate slicing. Beat the egg yolks and sugar together until thick and lemon-colored. Beat the whites until stiff but not dry and fold them into the yolks. Sift the flour over the eggs and fold it into the batter. Pour the batter into the prepared cake pan. Bake for 45 to 50 minutes or until a straw inserted in the middle comes out dry. Cool on a rack for 10 minutes before turning it out. Cool completely and wrap in foil until ready to use.

When you're ready to finish making the dessert, dampen the cheesecake pan and line it with plastic wrap. Slice the *pan di Spagna* thinly and line the pan, reserving half for the top.

Make the lemon cream. Put the condensed milk in a bowl and mix in the lemon juice and zest. Whip the egg whites until stiff but not dry. Whip the 2 cups cream until stiff but not dry. Fold the cream into the condensed milk mixture; fold in the egg whites. Carefully spoon the mixture into the pan lined with cake. Cover with the remaining slices of cake. Cover the pan with plastic wrap and place in the freezer for 2 hours before serving. If you're freezing it for a longer time, allow it to soften before serving.

To serve, whip the 3/4 cup heavy cream until fairly stiff. Frost the dessert with the whipped cream. Slice the lemon very thinly and dip the slices in sugar. Arrange the lemon slices around the base of the frozen lemon cream.

Una Cena Autunnale a Napoli

A FALL DINNER
IN NAPLES

A
F a l l
D i n n e r
i n
N a p l e s

Vermicelli alla Monteroduni
MONTERODUNI FAMILY PASTA

Arrosto di Braciolette
MEAT CROQUETTES

Finocchi al Forno
BAKED FENNEL

Pizza di Amarene
BLACK CHERRY PIE

WINE
Red: Maranese (Napoli); serve cool

Almost all the recipes for the next three menus are from the Marchesa Nunziante Diana, who comes from a very old Neapolitan family and has a great interest in Neapolitan food. She has collected the heirloom recipes from her extended family, giving some of them the name of the *monzù* who created them. The following three menus are from her family recipes, except for the desserts, which were given to me by other Neapolitan friends.

Vermicelli alla Monteroduni
MONTERODUNI FAMILY PASTA

Marchesa Diana's niece, a member of the Pignatelli di Monteroduni family, told me that the last time the family met, the younger members had all prepared this pasta, quite by coincidence. As is to be expected in an Italian family, all had varied the dish slightly to suit themselves. Marchesa Diana declares this version to be the original.

SERVES 6 AS A FIRST COURSE

- 3-1/2 **tablespoons lard (50 grams)**
- 1/2 **medium onion, finely chopped**
- 1/2 **pound sweet or hot sausage meat, crumbled (225 grams)**
- 1/2 **cup canned tomato paste, Cirio if possible (100 grams)**
- 1 **pound *vermicelli* (450 grams)**
  salt to taste
- 3/4 **cup freshly grated Parmesan *or pecorino* cheese (105 grams)**
  freshly ground pepper to taste

Heat the lard in a saucepan and cook the onion with 1 or 2 tablespoons water over medium-low heat until it begins to brown slightly. Add the sausage meat and cook over moderate heat, stirring occasionally, for 5 minutes. Add the tomato paste, stirring, and cook for 2 minutes.

Cook the *vermicelli* in boiling water until *al dente*. Drain and salt the pasta lightly. Dress with the cheese and sauce. Grind black pepper over the pasta and serve at once. This recipe doubles easily.

Arrosto di Braciolette
MEAT CROQUETTES

In her book on Neapolitan food Jeanne Carola mentions that a friend of hers told her that his father always used this dish as a test when hiring a prospective cook. If the cook knew how to work the meat properly in the mortar, pounding it until it had the consistency of cream, he knew his trade and would be hired. In this age of the food processor we no longer need years of experience to prepare these delicate, appetizing veal croquettes.

MAKES ABOUT 25 CROQUETTES,
SERVING 6

Skewers

1	pound boneless veal, ground twice (450 grams)
2	heaped cups stale bread crumbs
	enough milk to cover the bread crumbs
3/4	cup freshly grated Parmesan cheese (105 grams)
2	large handfuls of parsley, finely chopped with 1 garlic clove
2	ounces *prosciutto,* finely chopped (1/2 cup) (60 grams)
1/4	cup unsalted butter, melted (60 grams)
	salt and freshly ground pepper to taste
30	or more strips of homemade-type bread, 3-1/2 inches by 1 inch (9 by 2.5 cm)

Puree the meat in a food processor fitted with the steel blade and put it into a bowl. Pour enough milk over the bread crumbs to cover them and soak for 30 minutes. Drain and squeeze the bread as dry as possible. Add the crumbs to the meat with the Parmesan, parsley, garlic, and *prosciutto.* Add 2 tablespoons of the melted butter to the meat and season the meat with salt and pepper. Process again in the food processor in batches.

Form croquette-shaped meat rolls, about 3-1/2 inches long and 1 inch wide. Skewer a piece of bread and then a croquette, both crosswise, alternating meat and bread, beginning and ending with bread on each skewer. Put the skewers on a heavily buttered baking sheet. Pour the remaining butter over the croquettes.

When you're ready to cook the croquettes, preheat the oven to 425° (220). Bake for 30 minutes; the bread should be browned. If not, bake a few minutes longer. Serve hot.

Finocchi al Forno
BAKED FENNEL

The distinctive taste of fennel is blended here with a béchamel and Parmesan sauce. This recipe can be prepared completely in advance and baked when needed. Quantities can be doubled without any problem; it makes an excellent first course.

SERVES 4 (6 AS ACCOMPANIMENT TO CROQUETTES)

12- by 7-inch (30 by 18 cm) ovenproof dish, buttered

>   3 **pounds bulb fennel (1.350 grams)**
>   **salt**
>   1/4 **cup unsalted butter (60 grams)**
>   1/3 **cup flour (40 grams)**
>   2 **cups milk (500 ml)**
>   **freshly ground pepper to taste**
>   1/2 **cup freshly grated Parmesan cheese (60 grams)**

Wash the fennel; remove and discard the stems and tough outer leaves. Quarter the fennel or cut into 6 pieces if very large. Cook in boiling salted water for 10 to 15 minutes or until tender. Drain well. Preheat the oven to 375° (190).

Melt 3 tablespoons of the butter in a saucepan. Blend together the flour, milk, salt, and pepper in a blender or a food processor fitted with the steel blade for 30 seconds. Pour the milk over the melted butter and, stirring constantly, bring to a boil. Simmer for 5 minutes, stirring. Remove from the heat and add all but 2 tablespoons of the Parmesan.

Put the fennel in the prepared dish and pour the cream sauce on top. Dot with the remaining tablespoon of butter and sprinkle the reserved Parmesan over the sauce. Bake for 45 minutes or until browned on top. Serve hot.

Pizza di Amarene
BLACK CHERRY PIE

Here is another of those sweet pies called *pizza* but with no hint of cheese. Cherry tartlets are sold in all the pastry shops in Naples, but this double-crust pie is suitable for making at home. Before the advent of the modern pastry shop, such a dessert would traditionally have been made by nuns.

SERVES 6 TO 8

10-inch (26 cm) tart tin,
buttered

FOR THE CUSTARD:

    1-1/2 **cups milk (375 ml)**
      1/4 **cup wheat starch *or* cornstarch (30 grams)**
        4 **egg yolks**
      1/4 **cup sugar (55 grams)**
           grated zest of 1 lemon
      1/2 **cup finely chopped peeled almonds (80 grams)**

FOR THE PASTRY:

    2-2/3 **cups flour (300 grams)**
      1/2 **cup plus 2 tablespoons cold unsalted butter, cut**
           into pieces (150 grams)
      2/3 **cup sugar (150 grams)**
        3 **large egg yolks**

      1/2 **pound fine-quality black cherry jam (225 grams)**
        1 **egg yolk beaten with 1 teaspoon water**
           confectioners' sugar

Make the custard. Put the milk, wheat starch or cornstarch, egg yolks, and sugar in a blender or a food processor fitted with the steel blade and blend for 30 seconds. Pour the milk into a saucepan and add the lemon

continued

zest. Cook over medium heat, stirring constantly, until thickened, after it simmers for about 2 minutes. Remove from the heat and place plastic wrap directly on the surface. Cool completely. Add the almonds and refrigerate, covered, until needed.

Make the pastry. Preheat the oven to 350° (180). Mix together all the pastry ingredients rapidly by hand, in an electric mixer with the paddle attachment, or in a food processor fitted with the steel blade until they mass together. Divide the pastry into 2 parts, one slightly larger. Roll out the larger piece into a circle to fit the tart pan and fit it into place, leaving a small overhang. Pour half the custard into the shell, spoon the cherry marmalade over the custard, then add the rest of the custard.

Roll the remaining pastry into a circle and fit it over the top of the pie. Cut away the excess pastry and roll the edges under to seal the top to the bottom crust. Crimp decoratively and paint the top crust with the egg yolk.

Bake for 50 minutes or until lightly browned. Cool for 15 minutes before removing the pan's sides. Cool completely before removing the bottom part of the pan. Sprinkle with confectioners' sugar before serving.

CAMPANIA

Cena Invernale

WINTER DINNER

Pasticetti alla Genovese
GENOVESE SAVORY PASTRIES

Bue Braciato alla Genovese
GENOVESE BRAISED BEEF

Scarola con Uva Passa e Pinoli
ESCAROLE WITH RAISINS AND PINE NUTS

Mantecato di Castagne con Croccante
CHESTNUT ICE CREAM WITH PRALINE

WINE
Red: Taurasi DOC (Avellino); serve at room temperature

Here is a menu that takes advantage of the cold season of the year. This is the kind of nourishing, hearty fare guaranteed to keep away winter's chills.

Actually no one in Genoa has ever heard of the two recipes labeled *Genovese*. But in the 17th century there was a lot of trade between Naples and Genoa; a lot of *trattoria*s in Naples were owned and run by Genovese, so many dishes in the south of Italy are called by the name of this northern Italian city.

Pasticetti alla Genovese
GENOVESE SAVORY PASTRIES

These salty little pastries filled with ham, peas, and *mozzarella* make a very pleasant beginning for dinner on a cold winter's evening. They should be served hot and presented wrapped in a folded white napkin. When you're preparing them in advance, you can either refrigerate them until it's time to bake them or bake them in advance and reheat them at the last minute. The filling can be varied with leftover roast meats or *salame*. This is an unusual recipe; I have never encountered it outside this family.

MAKES 12 PASTRIES,
SERVING 8 TO 10

12 3-inch (8 cm) tart tins,
buttered

FOR THE BÉCHAMEL:
- **1-1/2 cups milk (375 ml)**
- **2 tablespoons flour (20 grams)**
- **salt and freshly ground pepper to taste**
- **freshly grated nutmeg to taste**
- **1 tablespoon unsalted butter (15 grams)**
- **1/4 cup freshly grated Parmesan cheese (35 grams)**

FOR THE FILLING:
- **1 tablespoon unsalted butter (15 grams)**
- **2/3 cup fresh or frozen peas (90 grams)**
- **salt and freshly ground pepper to taste**
- **3 ounces boiled ham, chopped (3/4 cup) (90 grams)**
- **1/3 pound *mozzarella* cheese, coarsely grated (1-1/4 cups) (150 grams)**

continued

FOR THE PASTRY:

   2-1/2 cups flour (280 grams)
     1/2 cup plus 1 tablespoon sugar (125 grams)
     **1/2 cup (1/4 pound) plus 2 tablespoons unsalted
         butter, cut into pieces (140 grams)**
       3 large egg yolks

       1 egg, beaten

*Winter
Dinner*

Make the bechamel. Put the milk, flour, salt, pepper, and nutmeg in a blender and blend for 30 seconds. Melt the butter in a saucepan and add the milk. Simmer, stirring, for 5 minutes, until thickened. Remove from the heat and add the Parmesan. Place plastic wrap directly on the surface, cool, and refrigerate until needed.

Make the filling. Melt the butter in a small saucepan and add the peas, salt, and pepper. Cover and cook over very low heat, stirring occasionally, until the peas are done, about 15 minutes. Cool. Add the cooled peas, ham, and *mozzarella* to the cold béchamel. Taste for seasoning and refrigerate.

Make the pastry. Mix together the flour and sugar and mound on a pastry board. Make a well in the center and put in the butter and the egg yolks. Mix all together rapidly. When the pastry holds together, wrap it in plastic wrap and refrigerate for 30 minutes. Preheat oven to 375° (190).

Divide the pastry into 2 parts. Roll out one part and cut 12 4-inch (10 cm) rounds, using a cookie cutter or a cardboard pattern. Line the tart tins with the pastry. Divide the filling among the tins. Roll out the remaining pastry and cut 12 top crusts. Place these over the pastries, pressing the edges to seal and crimping decoratively. Paint with the egg and make holes in the crusts with a toothpick.

Bake for 40 to 45 minutes or until nicely browned. Cool on a rack for 5 minutes before turning out. Serve hot.

Bue Braciato alla Genovese
GENOVESE BRAISED BEEF

Beef is not eaten very often in southern Italy, nor is it particularly noted for its quality or tenderness. Since it is a scarce commodity, beef is reserved for special occasions and usually braised, having been larded with strips of fat before cooking to improve its flavor. Italians like to use the pan juices that collect during cooking (together with a generous amount of Parmesan) to dress a dish of pasta that is served separately as a first course.

SERVES 8 OR MORE

1	beef eye of round or heel of round, about 3 to 3-1/2 pounds (1.350 to 1.600 grams)
1/4	pound fatty *pancetta,* cut into larding strips and chilled (110 grams)
1	ounce dried *porcini* mushrooms (30 grams)
2	tablespoons olive oil
1-1/2	medium carrots, finely chopped
1	large celery stalk, finely chopped
1	large onion, finely chopped
2	ounces *prosciutto,* finely chopped (1/2 cup) (60 grams)
	a handful of parsley, finely chopped
3/4	cup dry red wine (185 ml)
	salt and freshly ground pepper to taste
1	quart hot meat broth, approximately, *or* 1 quart hot water and 3 meat bouillon cubes (1 liter)

Make holes in the meat with a larding needle and lard with the *pancetta* strips. Soak the mushrooms in cold water for 30 minutes. Drain and chop.

Pour the oil into a heavy casserole large enough for the meat to fit snugly. Add the mushrooms, carrots, celery, onion, *prosciutto,* parsley, and any remaining *pancetta,* finely chopped. Lay the meat on the bed of vegetables

continued

and pour 1/2 cup of the wine over it. Cover the casserole and cook over medium heat, turning the meat occasionally, until the wine has evaporated.

Add the remaining wine, salt, and pepper. Let the meat cook slowly over low heat, still covered, until the meat and vegetables are a dark brown. Add enough hot broth to come halfway up the meat, cover again, and simmer for 2 hours or more, turning the meat occasionally. Test the meat after 1-1/2 hours to see if it is tender. If the sauce is too thin at the end of the cooking time, remove the meat and boil the sauce to thicken it.

Let the meat rest before slicing it. Strain or puree the sauce. Arrange the meat slices in a serving dish, pour some of the sauce over it, and serve the rest in a sauceboat.

If the dish is prepared in advance, leave the meat unsliced until you're ready to serve. Then slice it thinly, put it in an ovenproof dish, and pour some of the sauce over it. Cover with foil and heat in a preheated 375° (190) oven for 15 minutes.

Any leftover sauce is good with pasta. Dress the cooked pasta with Parmesan first and then toss with the sauce.

Scarola con Uva Passa e Pinoli

ESCAROLE WITH RAISINS AND PINE NUTS

Neapolitans have a particular love for leafy vegetables and are jokingly referred to as *mangiafoglie* (leaf eaters) by the rest of Italy. Escarole grows in huge quantities all over Campania and is eaten both on its own and with meat. This recipe offers an unusual play of flavors and textures.

SERVES 6 TO 8

> 3 **pounds escarole, washed and the leaves separated**
> **(1.350 grams)**
> **salt**
> 2 **garlic cloves**
> 1/2 **cup less 1 tablespoon olive oil (110 ml)**
> 1/2 **teaspoon (or more to taste) hot red pepper flakes**
> 3 **tablespoons pine nuts (45 grams)**
> 3 **tablespoons raisins, soaked in warm water until**
> **plump and drained (30 grams)**

Cook the escarole in a large pan of boiling salted water until *al dente,* about 10 minutes. Drain thoroughly. Squeeze out the excess water when the escarole has cooled enough to be handled.

Crush the garlic. Heat the oil in a skillet large enough to hold the escarole and brown the garlic. Add the red pepper flakes and the escarole to the skillet and simmer for 20 minutes, mixing occasionally. Taste for salt. Add the pine nuts and raisins. Simmer for 10 minutes longer. Serve hot.

Mantecato di Castagne con Croccante
CHESTNUT ICE CREAM WITH
PRALINE

The number and variety of ices and ice creams in Naples is quite staggering. There is *il mantecato, il sorbetto, il gelato, la cremolata, il parfait, lo spumone, la cassata gelata, la granita, la ghiacciata, il semifreddo, la coviglia, il pezzo duro*—and that's not all. Each one has its own rules of preparation and its own special flavors. *Mantecato* is the richest of all, made from a base of egg yolks, sugar, and heavy cream. As befits such an extravagant concoction, it is the custom to present this ice cream decorated with additional whipped cream, marrons glacés, and candied violets—and it looks spectacular. If you don't want to go to the bother of making your own chestnut puree, substitute one that is ready-made, but the commercial product will be presweetened, so eliminate the sugar syrup called for in the recipe.

SERVES 8 TO 10

6- to 8-cup domed or other
decorative mold

	vegetable oil
1	**lemon**
1-3/4	**cups sugar (400 grams)**
3/4	**cups shelled hazelnuts (120 grams)**
1/2	**cup water (125 ml)**
2	**cups unsweetened chestnut puree (see directions below) (480 grams)**
2	**tablespoons unsweetened cocoa powder**
5	**egg yolks**
1	**cup milk (250 ml)**
2	**cups heavy cream (500 ml)**

1   **teaspoon vanilla extract**
    marrons glacés, candied violets, and whipped
    cream for garnish

Prepare the praline. Oil a marble surface or a large platter and place the lemon nearby. In a small, heavy saucepan, heat 1/2 cup of the sugar and cook over medium heat until golden brown, taking care not to burn the caramel. Add the hazelnuts and mix, stirring, until all are coated with caramel. Turn out onto the oiled surface and press flat with the lemon.

Leave to harden. When you're ready to use the praline, chop very coarsely.

Put the mold in the freezer while you prepare the ice cream. Heat 1 cup of the sugar with the water, swirling until the sugar has melted. Simmer for 5 minutes. Cool. When the syrup has cooled, add it to the chestnut puree along with the cocoa.

Beat the egg yolks with the remaining sugar. Scald the milk and add it to the yolks. Put the milk and yolks in a saucepan and cook the custard until it is slightly thickened and coats the back of a metal spoon. Add it to the chestnut puree mixture along with the cream and vanilla. Cool and process in an ice cream machine, following the manufacturer's instructions.

Remove the mold from the freezer and put a layer of ice cream on the bottom. Sprinkle chopped praline over the ice cream. Add another layer of ice cream and more praline, reserving 3 tablespoons, then add a final layer of ice cream. Cover tightly and freeze until serving time, preferably overnight.

When you're ready to serve, turn the ice cream out onto a serving platter. Allow it to soften for at least 30 minutes. Sprinkle the reserved praline on top of the ice cream. Make soft rosettes of whipped cream at the base, interspersed with halved marrons glacés and candied violets.

continued

To make chestnut puree: Peel 1-1/2 pounds (675 grams) fresh chestnuts. Put them in boiling water for 4 or 5 minutes, drain, and peel away the inner skin. Work quickly as this becomes difficult as they cool. Rubber gloves will help you avoid burning your fingers. Put the peeled chestnuts back into the saucepan with milk to cover and bring to a boil. Simmer for 10 to 20 minutes or until tender when pierced with a needle. Drain the chestnuts and puree in a blender, food processor fitted with the steel blade, or food mill. They will keep, tightly covered, for several days in the refrigerator.

Cena in Famiglia in Primavera

A FAMILY DINNER
IN LATE SPRING

A
F a m i l y
D i n n e r
i n
L a t e
S p r i n g

Uova a Nevole
LITTLE RICOTTA CREPES

Galantina di Tonno del Monzù Umberto Selo
MONZÙ UMBERTO SELO'S TUNA GALANTINE

Insalata di Crescione
WATERCRESS SALAD

Spumone di Crema con Panna e Fragole
SPUMONE WITH STRAWBERRIES AND CREAM

WINE
White: Campi Flegrei (Napoli); serve cold

A light meal to celebrate the end of winter and the arrival of spring.

This family dinner, with recipes from Marchesa Nunziante Diana, has two of the family *monzù*'s best dishes, one of which even carries his name. To have a dish known by your name was (and is) a great honor for a *monzù*. These dishes are full of Neapolitan character—sophisticated and elegant, they would be served for an important family occasion.

Uova a Nevole

LITTLE RICOTTA CREPES

Loosely translated, *uova a nevole* means "eggs of cloud." These delightful crepes are light and delicate, and they seem to melt in your mouth. The dish can be prepared in advance; if you wish, it can be baked in cream rather than in a tomato sauce, although the latter is more authentically Neapolitan.

This is an unusually delicate dish, usually served in the evening for company. It would also make a good first course for a company lunch.

MAKES 24 TO 26 CREPES,
SERVING 6 TO 8

Crepe pan with 4-inch
(10 cm) bottom

FOR THE *CRESPELLE* (CREPES):

> 1/2 **cup milk (125 ml)**
> 1/2 **cup flour (60 grams)**
> **salt and freshly ground pepper to taste**
> 4 **eggs**
> **unsalted butter for the crepe pan, about 1/4 cup**
> **(60 grams)**

FOR THE FILLING:

> 1 **cup milk (250 ml)**
> 1/3 **cup flour (40 grams)**
> **salt and freshly ground pepper to taste**
> 3 **tablespoons unsalted butter (45 grams)**
> 1/2 **cup heavy cream (125 ml)**
> 1/4 **cup freshly grated Parmesan cheese (35 grams)**
> 1/2 **pound *ricotta* cheese (225 grams)**
> 3 **ounces *prosciutto,* chopped (3/4 cup) (90 grams)**

continued

FOR THE TOMATO SAUCE:

- **1 tablespoon unsalted butter (15 grams)**
- **1 tablespoon olive oil**
- **2 tablespoons finely chopped onion**
- **1 1-pound can Italian plum tomatoes with juice (450 grams) *or* 1-1/2 pounds ripe fresh tomatoes, peeled and seeded (675 grams)**
  salt and freshly ground pepper to taste

1/2 cup freshly grated Parmesan cheese (65 grams)

Make the crepes. Put the milk, flour, salt, and pepper in a blender or a food processor fitted with the steel blade and blend for 30 seconds. Add the eggs and blend again, taking care that the flour is absorbed. Pour the mixture into a bowl.

Heat the crepe pan over medium heat and add a dab of butter just to grease the bottom. Stir the batter and pour in a large spoonful of the mixture, rotating the pan so that the batter covers the bottom of the pan. Turn the *crespella* and cook briefly on the other side. Turn out the crepe onto a sheet of foil. Make all the crepes in this way, buttering the pan when necessary. Cover the crepes tightly and refrigerate until needed.

Make the filling. Put the milk, flour, salt, and pepper in a blender or a food processor fitted with the steel blade and blend for 30 seconds. Melt the butter in a saucepan and add the milk and cream. Bring to a simmer and cook, stirring, for 5 minutes. Remove from the heat and add the Parmesan. Cool and add the *ricotta* and *prosciutto*. Cover and refrigerate until needed.

Make the tomato sauce. Heat the butter and oil and sauté the onion in a saucepan over low heat until transparent. Add the tomatoes—if fresh, cut into pieces—and simmer the sauce for 15 minutes or until thickened, mashing with the back of a wooden spoon if you're using canned tomatoes. Add salt and pepper. Reserve.

Assemble the dish. Butter a large ovenproof dish or 2 small ones. Lay the crepes out on a work surface with the first-cooked side down. Divide the

A Family Dinner in Late Spring

356

filling among them. Roll up and place in the dishes, seam down. If you're preparing them in advance, cover and refrigerate at this point. Or they can be frozen.

When you're ready to serve, preheat the oven to 375° (190). Spoon the tomato sauce over the *crespelle* and sprinkle the Parmesan over the sauce. Bake for 30 minutes or until crusty around the edges. Let rest for 5 minutes before serving.

MONZÙ UMBERTO SELO'S TUNA GALANTINE

There is a recipe for a galantine made with fish in *Cuoco Galante* by Vincenzo Corrado, published in Naples in 1793. At that time Neapolitans had a great interest in everything French, and perhaps this is a French recipe adapted to use local ingredients and to suit the Neapolitan palate. This tuna galantine recipe is particularly interesting because it bears the name of a very well-known *monzù* whose dish it was. Umberto Selo cooked for Marchese Nunziante Diana's family, one of the oldest in Naples.

SERVES 6 TO 8

Cheesecloth or thin white
cloth about 24 inches square
(60 cm)

FOR THE GALANTINE:

- 1 **pound fresh tuna, skin and bones removed (450 grams)**
- 1 **pound large shrimp, peeled and deveined (450 grams)**
- 1/4 **cup shelled unsalted pistachios, peeled (40 grams)**
- 2 **salt-packed anchovies, cleaned (see page 419) and cut into pieces**
- 3 **eggs, separated**
- 5 **to 6 tablespoons fine dry bread crumbs**
  salt and freshly ground pepper to taste

FOR THE COURT BOUILLON:

- 2-1/2 quarts water (2-1/2 liters)
- 2 cups dry white wine (500 ml)
- 2 parsley sprigs
- 1/2 teaspoon peppercorns
- 1-1/2 teaspoons salt
- 1 onion, quartered
- 1 thin lemon slice
- 1 clove

FOR THE MAYONNAISE:

- 1 large egg at room temperature
- 1 teaspoon dry mustard
- 1/2 teaspoon salt
  freshly ground pepper to taste
- 1 tablespoon freshly squeezed lemon juice
- 3/4 cup olive oil (185 ml)
- 3 or 4 tablespoons capers, rinsed and dried (50 grams)

  cherry tomatoes stuffed with shrimp salad, parsley, and shrimp for garnish

Chop the tuna finely in a food processor fitted with the steel blade and put into a bowl. Reserving 5 shrimp, chop the rest in the food processor and add to the tuna. (You should have a slightly rough puree.) Add the pistachios. Puree the anchovies in the food processor and add to the tuna with the egg yolks and reserved whole shrimp.

Beat the egg whites until frothy and fold them into the tuna. Add enough bread crumbs to make the mixture hold together and season with salt and pepper. Form a ball with the mixture. (The mixture will be soft.) Dampen a piece of thin white cloth and place the ball of tuna on it, pull up the cloth around it, and tie it tightly to make a round ball, slightly flattened on top. Refrigerate until needed.

continued

Make the court bouillon. Put all the ingredients into a saucepan in which the fish will fit and bring to a boil. Simmer for 20 minutes. Lower the ball of fish into the simmering liquid, cover, and simmer gently for 1 hour. Cool the tuna in the broth for 1 hour. Remove and place a weight on top—not too heavy; a can of tomatoes or a small cutting board will do. When completely cooled, refrigerate until serving time. (Also cook the shrimp for garnish in the court bouillon, just until pink.)

Make the mayonnaise. Put the egg, mustard, salt, pepper, and lemon juice in a blender or a food processor fitted with the steel blade. Blend for 30 seconds. Add the oil in a steady trickle; it may not take all of the oil. When the mayonnaise has thickened, pour it into a bowl and add the capers.

Slice the galantine into thin wedges, like a pie, without separating the slices. Put it in the center of a round platter with the extra shrimp on top, surrounded by the cherry tomatoes and parsley. Pass the mayonnaise in a sauceboat.

Insalata di Crescione
WATERCRESS SALAD

In spring wild watercress is sold in Italian markets. It is perfect with this meal. The watercress should be rinsed once with vinegar in the water to eliminate any visitors, and it should be dressed only with salt and olive oil. Of course garden-grown watercress is good too.

Spumone di Crema con Panna e Fragole
SPUMONE WITH
STRAWBERRIES AND CREAM

Neapolitans love to tell you that ice cream not only tastes good but *is* good for you, that it helps your digestion, that it is, in fact, a necessity for a healthy diet. Of all the ice creams made in Naples *spumone* is the best known. The charm of *spumone* is its contrasting textures. The first layer is composed of a hard ice cream, the next layer a *semifreddo,* a lighter, more creamlike filling. In this recipe the *semifreddo* is flavored with strawberries, and the finished *spumone* is covered with fresh strawberries.

SERVES 10

2¹/₂-quart (2¹/₂ liters) *spumone*
mold

FOR THE ICE CREAM:
>   3 **cups milk (750 ml)**
>   **peel of 1 small lemon**
>   6 **egg yolks**
>   1 **cup sugar (225 grams)**

FOR THE *SEMIFREDDO* (FROZEN CREAM):
>   3 **eggs, separated**
>   1/2 **cup sugar (110 grams)**
>   2 **tablespoons white rum**
>   1-1/3 **cups strawberries, pureed (2/3 pound)**
>   **(300 grams)**
>   1-1/4 **cups heavy cream (300 ml)**
>   **extra strawberries for garnish**

continued

Put the mold in the freezer.

Prepare the ice cream. Scald the milk with the lemon peel. Put the egg yolks in a bowl and beat them with the sugar until thick and lemon-colored. Slowly add the hot milk to the yolks and then pour the mixture back into the saucepan. Cook over low heat, stirring constantly, until the custard coats the back of a metal spoon and is slightly thickened. Do not boil. Cool, stirring occasionally.

When the custard is cold, discard the peel and process the custard in an ice cream machine, following the manufacturer's instructions. Line the cold mold with the ice cream, freezing or softening the ice cream as necessary. Press it with the back of a spoon to make the ice cream adhere. Freeze until hard before adding the *semifreddo*.

Prepare the *semifreddo*. In a bowl, beat the egg yolks and sugar until thick and lemon-colored. Add the rum and strawberry puree. Whip the cream until fairly stiff. Beat the egg whites until stiff but not dry. Fold the cream and then the egg whites into the *semifreddo*. Spoon—do not pour—into the center of the *spumone*. Cover and freeze overnight.

Turn out the *spumone* on a large platter. Soften for 30 minutes before serving. Surround it with strawberries or, if available, cover completely with wild strawberries placed stem down on the surface of the *spumone*.

A Napoli da Nino

AT NINO'S IN NAPLES

Pasta con le Zucchine
PASTA WITH ZUCCHINI

Calamari alla Napoletana
NEAPOLITAN SQUID

Carciofi Gratinati
BAKED ARTICHOKES

Crema con Croccante
FROZEN CREAM WITH PRALINE

WINE
White: Monte Somma (Napoli); serve cold

Nino del Papa is an architect who lives in Naples. His great passion in life is cooking, and best of all he likes to prepare quick, simple food. Not for him the interminable time it takes to make the famous Neapolitan *ragù*. This is a weekly rite in the kitchens of Naples; a *ragù* is not something made casually, and it cannot be left unwatched but must be guided, stirred, and fussed over for 4, 5, or even 6 hours. Nino still remembers crying with frustration as a child as he waited for a dinner that took anywhere from 4 to 8 hours to prepare. After waiting at the table for hours, the cook was still frying something at seven o'clock. Perhaps this is why he is now so fond of the quick and simple. In fact, all the recipes in this menu are both simple and speedy—and typical of what's eaten today at good Neapolitan tables.

Pasta con le Zucchine
PASTA WITH ZUCCHINI

Zucchini is eaten with pasta throughout Italy. In Naples it occasions great rivalry—everybody has his or her own version, and the dishes can be quite elaborate. This recipe is extremely simple, and the key to its success is that both the zucchini and the basil be absolutely fresh.

SERVES 6 AS A FIRST COURSE

> 3 pounds garden-fresh zucchini (1.350 grams)
> salt
> olive oil for frying
> 1 cup freshly grated Parmesan cheese (130 grams)
> a large handful of fresh basil leaves plus extra
> basil for garnish
> 1 egg
> 5 tablespoons heavy cream (75 ml)
> freshly ground pepper to taste
> 1 pound *vermicelli or spaghetti* (450 grams)

Slice the zucchini crosswise 1/8 inch thick and sprinkle with salt. Leave in a colander for an hour. Drain and pat dry.

Fry in 1 inch of olive oil in a skillet over medium heat until lightly browned. Layer the zucchini in a large, shallow dish, sprinkling each layer with Parmesan and basil. Keep the zucchini warm in a warm oven.

Beat the egg with the cream in a large bowl that will hold the pasta. Add salt and pepper.

Cook the pasta until *al dente* and add it to the dish with the zucchini. Mix together thoroughly and pour into the bowl with the cream, mixing again. Serve at once, garnished generously with basil and accompanied by the pepper mill.

Calamari alla Napoletana
NEAPOLITAN SQUID

Nino, a true Neapolitan, cares more for fish than for meat. He loves to tell you his mother's rule for fish: the first day it does not even need salt, the second day you add salt, the third day you add salt and oil, the fourth day you add lemon, and the fifth day you throw the fish away. But her rule doesn't apply to squid, since it must be *freschissime* and never more than 2 days old. Here it is cooked in oil with tomatoes, olives, and, of course, lots of garlic.

SERVES 6

8-inch (21 cm) saucepan,
terra-cotta if available

2	**pounds fresh squid, cleaned (900 grams)**
1/3	**cup olive oil (80 ml)**
2	**garlic cloves, finely chopped with 2 tablespoons parsley**
1-1/2	**pounds ripe fresh tomatoes, peeled, seeded, and cut in pieces (675 grams), *or* 3 cups drained canned Italian plum tomatoes***
1	**scant cup black Gaeta olives, pitted (180 grams) salt and freshly ground pepper to taste**
1/2	**teaspoon hot red pepper flakes (optional) chopped parsley for garnish**

Rinse the cleaned squid in cold water. Drain and cut the squid into strips a little narrower than 1/2 inch. If some of the squid are small, just halve them lengthwise. Rinse again in cold water and drain. Reserve.

* Terra-cotta pans vary, so reserve some of the tomatoes' juice in case you need more liquid.

Heat the oil in the saucepan and add the chopped garlic and parsley. Cook over low heat for 5 minutes. Add the squid and cook over medium heat until they emit their liquid. Cook, stirring, until the liquid is almost completely evaporated.

Add the tomatoes, well drained, and the olives. Season with salt and pepper, plus the pepper flakes if desired. Cook, uncovered, over medium heat for 20 to 30 minutes (only about 25 minutes if you're planning to reheat it) or until tender, stirring occasionally.

Serve the squid in the terra-cotta pan. If you prepare this dish in advance, reheat it gently. Sprinkle with extra parsley before serving.

Carciofi Gratinati
BAKED ARTICHOKES

This quite simple artichoke dish should be made with the smallest artichokes you can find.

SERVES 6

10	small artichokes, cleaned (see page 420)
1	lemon
3/4	cup olive oil (185 ml)
3	garlic cloves
	salt to taste
3/4	cup black Gaeta olives, pitted (125 grams)
1/4	cup capers, rinsed and dried (40 grams)
6	tablespoons finely chopped parsley
2-1/2	tablespoons fine dry bread crumbs

Rub the artichokes with the lemon. Cut the artichokes in half and then cut each half into 4 wedges. If you're not using them at once, put them in acidulated water. Preheat the oven to 375° (190).

Heat the oil with the garlic in a large sauté pan. When the garlic has browned, discard it and add the artichokes, drained and dried. Cover and cook over medium heat for 15 to 20 minutes or until *al dente*. Salt lightly. Add the olives, capers, and parsley, mixing well. Put the mixture in an oiled ovenproof dish and sprinkle the bread crumbs over it.

Bake for 20 to 30 minutes or until lightly browned. Serve hot.

Crema con Croccante
FROZEN CREAM WITH PRALINE

This recipe is almost embarrassingly simple, but it is eaten all the time in and around Naples. It is almost cloyingly sweet but quite irresistible for anyone even the slightest bit partial to Italian ice cream. Neapolitans sometimes like to serve it with a hot chocolate sauce, but this really does seem to be gilding the lily. If you prefer, you can use nougat instead of almonds and chocolate.

SERVES 6 TO 8

10- by 5-inch (25 by 13 cm)
loaf pan, dampened and lined
with plastic wrap

FOR THE *CROCCANTE* (PRALINE):

	vegetable oil
1	**lemon *or* orange**
1/3	**cup sugar (75 grams)**
1/2	**cup unpeeled shelled almonds (80 grams)**

FOR THE CREAM:

4	**egg yolks**
2/3	**cup sugar (150 grams)**
2	**tablespoons white rum**
2	**egg whites**
1-2/3	**cups heavy cream (400 ml)**
1/2	**cup (3 ounces) coarsely chopped good-quality semisweet chocolate (100 grams)**
	extra praline and chopped semisweet chocolate for garnish (optional)

continued

Oil a marble surface or a cookie sheet with vegetable oil and place the lemon nearby. Cook the sugar in a small, heavy-bottomed pan over medium heat until it's a tawny golden brown, stirring. Add the almonds and stir over low heat for 1 minute. Turn out onto the oiled surface and flatten with the lemon. Leave to harden. The praline can be stored in an airtight tin. When you're ready to use it, chop it very coarsely.

By hand or in a mixer, beat the egg yolks with the sugar until thick and lemon-colored. Add the rum and set aside. Beat the egg whites until stiff but not dry and fold them into the yolks. Beat the cream until stiff but not dry and fold into the egg mixture. Spoon one third of the cream into the prepared mold and sprinkle half the praline and half the chocolate over it. Spoon in another third of the cream and sprinkle the remaining praline and chocolate over it. Spoon the remaining cream over and cover the dessert with plastic wrap. Freeze overnight.

Turn the mold out onto a serving platter and soften it in the refrigerator for 30 to 40 minutes before serving. If desired, decorate the cream at the base with extra chocolate and praline.

Una Colazione Semplice a Sorrento

A SIMPLE LUNCH IN SORRENTO

A
Simple
Lunch
in
Sorrento

Pasta, Fagioli, e Cozze
PASTA, BEANS, AND MUSSELS

Palline di Ricotta in Salsa
LITTLE RICOTTA BALLS IN TOMATO SAUCE

Broccoli con Acciughe
BROCCOLI WITH ANCHOVIES

Torta di Mele di Sorrento
APPLE PIE

WINE
Rosé: Sorrento Rosato; serve chilled

In addition to being an architect, Nino del Papa recently bought a hotel in Sorrento because he wanted to run his own restaurant. Called La Cocumella, the hotel was once an old convent with a beautiful garden filled with flowers and orange and lemon trees. It has an idyllic setting overlooking the Bay of Naples, one of the most beautiful views in southern Italy. Sorrento is a busy port with boats going back and forth to Naples and Capri, and it still has the bustling atmosphere of a working port. The seafood is fresh and plentiful, and there are local fruits and vegetables everywhere. For a lunch served on the terrace of his hotel, Nino chose this menu.

Pasta, Fagioli, e Cozze
PASTA, BEANS, AND MUSSELS

This is a fisherman's soup. At one time its ingredients consisted of anything left unsold from the catch of the day mixed with pasta and beans to make an unforgettable rib-sticking soup laced with garlic. Nino has his own version using mussels, and the result is unusual and satisfying. If you want to prepare the recipe ahead of time, do not add the mussels until the last minute.

SERVES 6 TO 8

1	**pound dried navy, white kidney, *or borlotti* beans (450 grams)**
2-1/2	**quarts water (2.5 liters)**
1/3	**cup olive oil (80 ml), plus 1-1/2 tablespoons**
4	**garlic cloves**
1	**4-inch celery stalk, chopped**
	salt to taste
1/2	**teaspoon (or to taste) hot red pepper flakes**
1	**tomato (a canned plum tomato will do)**
1	**teaspoon tomato paste diluted in 1/3 cup water (80 ml)**
3	**pounds mussels, washed and scrubbed (1.350 grams)**
1/2	**pound *tubetti, ditalini, or* other small pasta (225 grams)**

Soak the beans in water to cover overnight. Drain and rinse. Put the beans in a pan, terra-cotta if available, and add the water. Bring to a boil and simmer for 1-1/4 hours or until tender. Reserve.

In a small saucepan, heat 1/3 cup oil over medium heat and add 3 garlic cloves. When the garlic has browned, add the celery and sauté for 1

continued

minute. Add the salt, pepper flakes, tomato, and diluted tomato paste. Simmer for 8 minutes. Reserve.

Prepare the mussels. In a pan large enough to hold the mussels, heat the 1-1/2 tablespoons oil with the remaining garlic clove. Add the mussels, cover, and cook over medium-high heat, shaking the pan occasionally, until the mussels open. Remove from the heat and discard any mussels that have not opened. Put a colander in a bowl and put the mussels in the colander. When they have cooled, remove the mussels from their shells over the colander and put the mussels in another bowl, discarding the shells. Pour the juice over the mussels, avoiding the sandy deposit. Reserve the mussels and juice.

When you're ready to serve the soup, add the contents of the saucepan to the beans. Remove 1 cup of beans and puree the rest in a blender or a food processor fitted with the steel blade. Return the cup of beans to the puree and heat. Add the pasta and cook until *al dente*. Add the mussels and their juice and simmer for 1 minute. Serve the soup hot.

A
Simple
Lunch
in
Sorrento

Palline di Ricotta in Salsa
LITTLE RICOTTA BALLS IN TOMATO SAUCE

Fresh *ricotta,* which in the south of Italy is nearly always made from sheep's milk, was once made only during lambing season, in the spring and fall. Now it's available any season of the year. *Ricotta* literally means "recooked," for after the *pecorino* cheese has been made from the sheep's milk the remaining whey is cooked again, then drained in loosely woven grass baskets to make *ricotta.* It's a wonderful cheese to cook with, very light and with very little fat. These little cheese balls cooked in a tomato sauce are very tasty.

SERVES 6

2	tablespoons olive oil
2	garlic cloves
2	pounds ripe fresh tomatoes, peeled, seeded, and cut into pieces (900 grams)
3/4	pound *ricotta* cheese, drained if watery (330 grams)
3	egg yolks
2/3	cup freshly grated Parmesan cheese (90 grams)
7	tablespoons finely chopped parsley
6	tablespoons fine dry bread crumbs
	salt and freshly ground pepper to taste
	chopped parsley for garnish (optional)

Heat the oil in a skillet and brown the garlic. Discard the garlic and add the tomatoes. Simmer, uncovered, for 20 minutes, mashing the tomatoes with the back of a spoon.

continued

While the sauce is cooking, prepare the *ricotta* balls. Put the *ricotta,* egg yolks, Parmesan, parsley, and bread crumbs in a small bowl. Mix with a fork and add salt and pepper to taste. Make balls the size of walnuts. Refrigerate if you're preparing the balls in advance.

When the sauce has cooked for 20 minutes, add the *ricotta* balls. Cook over medium heat for 20 minutes, turning once very carefully; they are fragile. Remove to a serving dish, again carefully, and serve hot, garnished with parsley if desired.

These *ricotta* balls can also be cooked in the oven. Put 2 tablespoons sauce on the bottom of an ovenproof dish and put in the uncooked *ricotta* balls. Spoon the sauce over them and cook for 20 minutes in a preheated 350° (180) oven. Serve hot.

Broccoli con Acciughe
BROCCOLI WITH ANCHOVIES

In southern Italy anchovies are often used to accentuate the flavor of a vegetable, and the farther south one goes the more frequently they appear. In this instance they are used to add a sophisticated edge to a dish of winter broccoli.

SERVES 6

    4 pounds broccoli (1.800 grams)
        salt
  1/2 cup olive oil (125 ml)
    2 garlic cloves
    7 salt-packed anchovies, cleaned (see page 419) *or*
        14 oil-packed anchovy fillets, drained

Separate the broccoli into flowerets more or less the same size after washing well in cold water. Cook until *al dente* in lightly salted boiling water. Drain.

Heat the oil in a skillet large enough to hold the broccoli. Add the garlic and, when browned, remove the pan from the heat. Cut the anchovies into pieces and add them to the hot oil, mashing with a wooden spoon. Return the pan to the heat and add the broccoli. Mix well, cover, and simmer for 20 minutes, stirring occasionally. Add hot water a little at a time if it begins to burn or dry out too much. Taste and add salt if needed.

Torta di Mele di Sorrento
APPLE PIE

Where else but the south of Italy could this engagingly different apple pie—made not just with apples but with raisins soaked in rum, almonds, and crushed *amaretti* cookies—come from? Served with heavy cream, this exotic rendition of an all-time home favorite makes a perfect dessert.

SERVES 6

8-inch (20 cm) springform
pan, buttered

FOR THE FILLING:

2	tablespoons unsalted butter (30 grams)
3/4	cup sugar (165 grams)
2-1/2	pounds Golden Delicious apples, peeled, cored, and thinly sliced (1.100 grams)
1/3	cup raisins, soaked in 2 tablespoons white rum for 30 minutes (60 grams)
1/4	cup coarsely chopped, lightly toasted, peeled almonds (40 grams)
1	scant cup *amaretti* cookies, pulverized (100 grams)
1/4	teaspoon (or to taste) ground cinnamon grated zest of 1 large lemon
2	eggs, separated

FOR THE PASTRY:

2-2/3	cups flour (300 grams)
1/4	cup sugar (55 grams)
6	tablespoons cool unsalted butter (90 grams)
1/4	cup cold lard (60 grams)
1	egg
1	tablespoon (or more) white rum
1	egg yolk beaten with 1 teaspoon cold water

Make the filling. Put the butter, sugar, and apples in an 8-inch saucepan. Cook over medium heat, stirring occasionally, until the apples' juices have been absorbed, about 20 minutes (timing depends on the quality of the apples). When the apples are ready, they will be soft and almost pureed. Set them aside to cool.

When cooled, add the other filling ingredients except the egg whites. Beat the whites until stiff but not dry and fold them into the apple mixture. Reserve. Preheat the oven to 350° (180).

Make the crust. Mix together rapidly all the pastry ingredients, using enough rum to make the pastry hold together. Refrigerate one third of the pastry and roll out the rest into a circle large enough to line the prepared pan. Fit the bottom crust into place and cut away the excess pastry, leaving a 1/4-inch overhang. Spoon the filling into the crust. Roll out the refrigerated pastry into a circle large enough to cover the pie. Fit it in place and roll the overhang of top and bottom crusts together. Crimp the edges and decorate the pie with leaves or an apple or other shapes made from the trimmed pastry. Paint the surface with the egg yolk beaten with water.

Bake for 50 to 60 minutes or until lightly browned. Cool on a rack for 15 minutes before removing the pan's sides. Cool completely before removing the bottom of the pan. Serve with a pitcher of cold heavy cream.

Cena sulla Terrazza Guardando Posillipo

SUPPER ON THE TERRACE OVERLOOKING POSILLIPO

Pizza Ripiena di Melanzane
EGGPLANT PIZZA

Pizza Ripiena con Piselli, Spinaci, e Prosciutto
PIZZA WITH PEAS, SPINACH, AND HAM

Polpettone Uso Galantina
COLD MEAT LOAF IN THE GALANTINE STYLE

Semifreddo di Fragole con Salsa di Fragole
FROZEN STRAWBERRY CREAM WITH
STRAWBERRY SAUCE

WINES
Rosé: San Giorgio (Benevento); serve chilled
Dessert: Moscato di Baselice (Benevento); serve chilled

It is particularly pleasant to sit on a terrace overlooking Posillipo. The name itself means "pain alleviating," and Posillipo is an enchanting residential area extending out along a cape that curves around the Bay of Naples. From here you can look back to Naples and out to Capri. In this almost unreal paradise even the simplest meal, beginning with a choice of two pizzas, becomes a memorable event.

The first pizza was explained to me at a dinner given by an Italian gastronomic club. One of the club members had given an extraordinary dinner in Capri in a grotto. She said the food was placed on a candlelit boat and the guests arrived in other boats—the wooden kind with oars, she said, so there would be no noise. The pizzas were rowed in still hot and were a great success. She had prepared most of the dinner herself—a lot of fish dishes, *caponatas*, salads, and *semifreddos*. The entire grotto was illuminated with candles, with Mozart playing in the background.

Pizza Ripiena di Melanzane
EGGPLANT PIZZA

This pizza has a rich crust made with butter and an egg yolk and is more what we would think of as a savory double-crust pie. Filled with eggplant, tomatoes, a layer of basil leaves, and lots of cheese, it is as filling as it is delicious.

SERVES 6 TO 8

10-inch (26 cm) pizza tin
with removable sides,
buttered

FOR THE FILLING:

- 2 **pounds eggplant, cut into 3/4-inch dice (900 grams)**
  salt
  olive oil for frying, about 3/4 cup (185 ml)
- 2 **scant cups drained canned Italian plum tomatoes (450 grams)**
- 1 **tablespoon unsalted butter (15 grams)**
- 3/4 **cup freshly grated Parmesan cheese (105 grams)**
- 1/2 **pound *mozzarella* cheese, coarsely grated (225 grams)**
  freshly ground black pepper to taste
  **a handful of fresh basil leaves, washed and dried,
  or 1 tablespoon dried oregano**
- 3 **salt-packed anchovies, cleaned (see page 419), or 6 oil-packed anchovy fillets, drained**

FOR THE CRUST:

- 2-2/3 **cups flour (300 grams)**
- 1/2 **cup (1/4 pound) unsalted butter, cut into pieces (110 grams)**
  salt and freshly ground pepper to taste
- 1/3 **to 1/2 cup milk (80 to 125 ml)**

- 1 **egg yolk beaten with 2 teaspoons water**

Layer the eggplant in a colander, salting each layer. Leave for an hour. Rinse and pat dry.

Heat the olive oil in a skillet and fry the eggplant slowly in batches over medium-high heat. Drain on paper towels. Cool completely.

Squeeze the drained tomatoes gently to remove their liquid. Melt the butter in a small frying pan and add the tomatoes. Cook over medium heat, mashing with a wooden spoon, for 10 to 15 minutes or until very dense. Add salt. Set aside to cool. Preheat the oven to 400° (200).

Make the crust. By hand or in a food processor, mix the flour, butter, salt, pepper, and enough milk to make a soft dough. Divide the dough into 2 parts, one slightly larger than the other. Roll out the larger part into a circle large enough to line the pan. Drape it over the rolling pin and unroll it over the pan, leaving a 1/4-inch overhang.

Sprinkle 2 tablespoons of the Parmesan over the bottom of the crust and put the eggplant on top. Sprinkle over another tablespoon of Parmesan. Put the *mozzarella* on this and grind black pepper over it. Sprinkle another tablespoon of Parmesan on the *mozzarella* and add a layer of basil leaves. Spoon the tomato sauce over this layer, then add the rest of the basil and the anchovies cut into pieces. Sprinkle over the remaining Parmesan and grind black pepper over all.

Roll out the remaining pasta into a circle to fit the pizza and unroll it on top. Trim the crust, leaving a 1/2-inch overhang, and roll it under the bottom edge. Crimp the edges to seal. Paint the crust with the egg yolk. Make holes in the center with a kitchen needle to vent the steam.

Bake for 1 hour. Cool for 5 minutes and remove the pan's sides. Cool on a rack. Turn out when cooled. The pizza can be prepared in advance and reheated in a 400° (200) oven for 15 minutes. Serve hot or tepid.

Pizza Ripiena con Piselli, Spinaci, e Prosciutto
PIZZA WITH PEAS, SPINACH, AND HAM

Another pizza with the same crust but a different filling.

SERVES 6 TO 8

10-inch (26 cm) pizza tin
with removable sides,
buttered

2	tablespoons unsalted butter (30 grams)
1	tablespoon finely chopped onion
1-3/4	cups fresh or frozen peas (240 grams)
	salt and freshly ground black pepper to taste
3/4	cup tomato puree (225 grams)
	crust from preceding recipe
1/2	cup freshly grated Parmesan cheese (60 grams)
3/4	cup (11 ounces) cooked, drained, and coarsely chopped spinach (300 grams)
1/2	pound *mozzarella* cheese, thinly sliced or coarsely grated (225 grams)
1/4	pound *prosciutto or* boiled ham, julienned (1 scant cup) (110 grams)
3	eggs
1	egg yolk beaten with 2 teaspoons water

Make the filling. Melt 1 tablespoon of the butter in a saucepan and sauté the onion over low heat until transparent. Add the peas, cover, and simmer until done, about 15 minutes if frozen, 10 minutes if fresh. Season with salt and pepper. Reserve.

Melt the remaining butter in a small frying pan and add the tomato puree. Simmer until very thick and dense, 10 to 15 minutes, depending on the tomatoes. Add salt to taste and cool completely.

Preheat the oven to 350° (180). Make the pastry and line the pan with the bottom crust.

Put the tomato sauce on the bottom of the crust and sprinkle a tablespoon of Parmesan over it. Grind black pepper over this layer. Add the spinach (squeeze out all liquid) and then the *mozzarella*. Sprinkle half the remaining Parmesan over the *mozzarella* and put the ham on top. Add the peas and sprinkle the remaining Parmesan over them. Beat the eggs with salt and pepper and pour them over the filling, spreading with a fork. Grind black pepper over the filling.

Roll out the top crust and fit it in place, sealing the edges with the overhang. Crimp and make holes in the center with a kitchen needle. Paint the crust with the egg yolk. Bake for 1 hour. Cool on a rack for 5 minutes, then remove the sides and turn out. Serve hot or tepid. The pizza can be prepared in advance and reheated in a preheated 400° (200) oven for 15 minutes.

Polpettone Uso Galantina

COLD MEAT LOAF IN THE GALANTINE STYLE

This is a lazy person's recipe for a veal loaf—utterly simple to make and perfect for summer eating. It can be embellished with gelatin, either coating the meat or chopped as a garnish.

SERVES 10

10- by 4-inch (26 by 10 cm)
loaf pan, buttered

1	cup fresh bread crumbs, soaked in milk to cover (60 grams)
1-2/3	pounds boneless veal, ground twice (750 grams)
2	ounces *pancetta,* coarsely chopped (1/2 cup) (60 grams)
1/4	pound good-quality *mortadella,* half coarsely chopped and half in tiny dice (1 scant cup) (110 grams)
1/4	pound boiled ham, half finely chopped and half in tiny dice (1 scant cup) (110 grams)
1/2	cup plus 1 tablespoon freshly grated Parmesan cheese (75 grams)
1/3	cup shelled pistachios, blanched and peeled (60 grams)
1	tablespoon unsalted butter, melted (15 grams)
5	eggs
	salt and freshly ground pepper to taste

Preheat the oven to 375° (190). Mix all the ingredients together and mix thoroughly with your hands. Put the mixture into the prepared pan and bang it once or twice on a hard surface to remove air pockets. Cover tightly with foil.

Prepare a pan larger than that holding the *polpettone* and fill it with very hot water. Put the *polpettone* in the bain marie and bake for 2 hours. Remove it from the oven and place on a rack. Put a small cutting board on top and weight it with canned goods. Cool and then refrigerate with the weight still on top.

When you're ready to serve the *polpettone,* slice it thinly and serve it cold or at room temperature, garnished with gherkins, cherry tomatoes, olives, or radishes.

Semifreddo di Fragole con Salsa di Fragole
FROZEN STRAWBERRY CREAM
WITH STRAWBERRY SAUCE

This rich but simple ice cream is best reserved for that brief season when perfectly ripe local strawberries are available.

SERVES 8 TO 10

7- to 8-cup (2 liters) mold

FOR THE FROZEN CREAM:

    5 **egg yolks at room temperature**
1/2 **cup sugar (100 grams)**
1-1/3 **cups strawberries, pureed (11 ounces)**
      (300 grams)
    2 **egg whites at room temperature**
      pinch of salt
1-1/2 **cups heavy cream (375 ml)**

FOR THE SAUCE:

    2 **scant cups strawberries, pureed (14 ounces)**
      (400 grams)
2/3 **cup sugar (150 grams)**
1/4 **cup orange liqueur (60 ml)**
      grated zest of 1 lemon

      strawberries and mint leaves for garnish

Make the frozen cream. Beat the egg yolks and sugar until light and lemon-colored. Add the pureed strawberries and mix. Beat the egg whites with a pinch of salt until stiff but not dry and fold them into the puree. Beat the cream until fairly stiff and fold it in. Spoon the strawberry mixture into the prepared mold, cover tightly, and freeze until ready to serve.

Make the sauce. Mix together all the ingredients and refrigerate until needed.

When you're ready to serve, turn out the ice cream onto a round platter. Soften at room temperature for 30 minutes. Cover the ice cream with strawberries or surround the base of the dessert with whole strawberries. Mint leaves, if available, make a lovely contrast at the base. Serve the sauce separately in a sauceboat or a pitcher.

Cena in Cosenza

DINNER IN COSENZA

Dinner
in
Cosenza

Pappardelle in Timballo
BAKED WIDE NOODLES

Cotolette di Maiale al Limone
LEMONY PORK CHOPS

Carciofi Ripieni
STUFFED ARTICHOKES

Crema di Castagne al Cioccolato
CHESTNUT CREAM WITH CHOCOLATE

WINES
Red: Ciró DOC (Catanzaro); serve at room temperature
Dessert: Moscato di Saracena (Cosenza); serve at cool room
temperature

Calabria is the toe of the Italian boot. In ancient times the land was productive and fertile, and it was in Calabria that the Greeks established many colonies, the most famous of which was Sybaris, a city whose very name signifies luxury and wealth. Alas, today Calabria is the second-poorest region in Italy after Basilicata. The terrain is spectacular but mostly mountainous and underpopulated. Stendhal wrote a journal of a trip taken through Calabria in the early 19th century. It later turned out that he had never actually visited the place—there were so many bandits on the roads in those days that he was too scared to go.

Calabrian cooking is based almost entirely on pasta and vegetables, and Calabrians will tell you that their most typical local meat dishes are those that contain the least meat. When meat does appear on the menu, it tends to be pork. Calabria is famous for its pigs, and Calabrian cooks know how to use every part of the animal, including the blood, from which they make *sanguinaccio*—the famous Calabrian sweet made of pork blood. Foxes are also considered a delicacy in Calabria, but this is not a common passion.

The Mollo family provided the recipes for this menu with the assurance that these dishes would have been the kind their ancestor, once mayor of Cosenza, would have served to Alexander Dumas *père* when he visited Calabria in his travels across Italy in 1854. (Unfortunately the actual menu was not kept.) Cosenza has experienced numerous earthquakes, and many times the damage from a previous earthquake has hardly been repaired before the next one has struck. Dumas had the misfortune to arrive in Cosenza just after it had been hit by a particularly bad one. Calabrians are known for their lavish hospitality, and since there was not a single *palatto* in the city still standing, the mayor decided to receive his honored visitor in what was left of his own garden. He had the table set with his finest china, crystal, and silver (which had somehow miraculously survived the earthquake), Persian rugs were placed on the grass, and a magnificent meal was served by servants in livery. Needless to say, Monsieur Dumas was impressed.

Pappardelle in Timballo
BAKED WIDE NOODLES

This *timballo*—layers of sausages, hard-cooked eggs, and cheese in a *ragù* sauce—can be served with or without a crust and is a popular dish in Cosenza today. It is a simplified version of the *timballi* once eaten all over the South that date back to the 18th century. Each town would have a slightly different version, depending on local tastes, but the *ragù* sauce that held all the ingredients would be the common denominator. Regardless of where it was made, the *timballo* sauce would be simmered gently for hours to ensure that it would *pipiare* (puff slowly).

Although this *timballo* is often served without the crust, the little extra work for the crust is worth the time. The crust, besides being more festive and showy, is a perfectly balanced marriage of sweet and spicy-salty. Together the two complement each other. In my house we always serve it in its crust.

WITHOUT CRUST, SERVES 6;
WITH CRUST, SERVES 8 TO 10

Without crust: 13^{1}/$_{2}$- by 9-inch (34 by 23 cm)
oval ovenproof glass dish, oiled.
With crust: 10^{1}/$_{2}$-inch round pan with 2^{1}/$_{2}$-inch sides
(26 by 6 cm), buttered.

FOR THE CRUST (OPTIONAL):
- 3-1/2 **cups flour (400 grams)**
- 2/3 **cup sugar (150 grams)**
- 1/2 **cup (1/4 pound) plus 1 tablespoon cold unsalted butter, cut into pieces (125 grams)**
- 5 **tablespoons cold lard or solid shortening, cut into pieces (75 grams)**

        1   egg
        2   tablespoons (or more) dry white wine
        1   egg yolk beaten with 1 teaspoon cold water

FOR THE *RAGÙ*:
        5   tablespoons olive oil (75 ml)
        4   garlic cloves
        2   medium onions, finely chopped
        2   ounces fatty *prosciutto or pancetta,* finely
            chopped (1/2 cup) (60 grams)
        1   pound boneless beef, coarsely chopped
            (450 grams)
      1/2   cup dry red wine (125 ml)
        2   16-ounce cans Italian plum tomatoes with juice,
            chopped (900 grams), *or* 3 pounds ripe fresh
            tomatoes, peeled, seeded, and coarsely chopped
            (1.350 grams)
        1   tablespoon tomato paste dissolved in 1/4
            cup water
            salt and freshly ground pepper to taste

      1/3   pound sausage (150 grams)
      1/4   cup dry red wine (60 ml)
        3   hard-cooked eggs
      2/3   pound *pappardelle* (300 grams)
        3   tablespoons unsalted butter (45 grams)
      3/4   cup freshly grated Parmesan cheese (105 grams)
        3   ounces *caciocavallo* cheese, cut into tiny dice
            (3/4 cup) (90 grams)
            freshly ground black pepper to taste

Make the crust if you're using it. Put the flour, sugar, butter, lard, egg, and wine in the large bowl of an electric mixer and mix rapidly, using the paddle attachment. Or use a food processor or your hands. Add more wine if necessary: the dough shouldn't be damp or crumbly. Divide the dough into 2 parts, one slightly larger. Roll out the larger part to 1/4-inch thickness in a circle large enough to line the prepared pan. Fit it into the pan and trim away any excess pastry. Refrigerate the crust while you make the filling.

continued

Make the *ragù*. Heat the oil in an 8-inch saucepan. Add the garlic and fry gently until browned. Discard the garlic and add the onion and *prosciutto*. Cook over medium-low heat, stirring occasionally, until the onion is transparent. Add the beef and, when browned, add the red wine. Allow almost all the wine to evaporate. Add the chopped tomatoes and the tomato paste. Season lightly and bring the sauce to a boil. Cover and simmer for 1 hour, stirring now and then. At the end of the cooking time the sauce should be abundant but not watery. If the sauce is too thick, add a little hot water; if too thin, uncover and cook until slightly thickened. Taste for seasoning. If you're preparing the dish in advance, cool the *ragù* before mixing it with the pasta. This sauce can be prepared up to 4 days in advance. Refrigerate until needed.

Prepare the sausages. Cover the bottom of a small frying pan with water. Prick the sausages and cook, turning often, until the water has evaporated. Pour the wine over them and continue cooking until the wine has evaporated. Cool the sausages completely. Remove and discard the casings and slice the sausages. Reserve. Preheat the oven to 350° (180).

Cut the eggs into 4 or 6 wedges. Cook the *pappardelle* in boiling salted water until *al dente*. (If you're using De Cecco egg pasta *pappardelle*, cook for 4 minutes only.) Drain and dress the pasta with the butter and half the Parmesan. If you're preparing the dish in advance, cool the pasta completely at this point before finishing the dish.

Mix the *pappardelle* with half the *ragù*. Put half the pasta in the prepared dish or on top of the bottom crust. Strew the sausages on top, lay over the egg wedges, and sprinkle over half the *caciocavallo*. Spread half the remaining sauce over the cheese and sprinkle half the remaining Parmesan over the sauce. Layer on the rest of the pasta and the rest of the *caciocavallo;* spread on the rest of the *ragù*. Sprinkle on the remaining Parmesan and generously grind black pepper over all. (Bring to room temperature if you've refrigerated it.)

If you're using the crust, roll out the top crust into a circle, drape it over the rolling pin, and unroll it on top of the filling. Trim, leaving a 1-inch overhang. Roll this under to seal it to the bottom crust, pressing so the crusts adhere. Crimp the edges and decorate the top, if desired, with the remaining bits of pastry. Paint the top with the egg yolk.

If you've used the crust, bake for 1 hour and 10 minutes or until nicely browned on top. Cool on a rack for 20 minutes, loosen the sides gently with a sharp knife, and turn out onto a large pizza pan with sides. Turn over again rapidly onto a serving platter.

Without crust, bake for 30 minutes. Allow to rest, covered with foil, for 10 minutes before serving.

NOTE: If there is leftover *timballo,* it can be reheated, wrapped in foil, in a preheated 375° (190) oven for 15 minutes or eaten at room temperature.

Cotolette di Maiale al Limone
LEMONY PORK CHOPS

*Dinner
in
Cosenza*

This modern Calabrian dish makes excellent use of the abundant lemons and *pecorino* cheese found all over the South.

SERVES 6

1/2	cup fine dry bread crumbs
1/2	cup freshly grated *pecorino* cheese (65 grams)
1/2	cup freshly grated Parmesan cheese (65 grams)
2	tablespoons finely chopped parsley
1	small garlic clove, finely chopped
1	tablespoon dried oregano
	salt and freshly ground black pepper to taste
6	pork chops, about 3-1/3 pounds (1.500 grams)
1/2	cup freshly squeezed lemon juice (125 ml)
1/4	cup olive oil (60 ml)
1/4	cup water (60 ml)
6	slices of lemon, rinds removed
	parsley and lemon slices for garnish

Preheat the oven to 400° (200). Mix together the bread crumbs, *pecorino*, Parmesan, parsley, garlic, and oregano. Add salt and grind black pepper generously over the mixture.

Dip the pork chops into the lemon juice and then into the breading mixture. Press the crumbs into the chops to make them adhere. When all are coated thoroughly, put them into an oiled ovenproof dish in one layer. Mix together the remaining lemon juice, oil, and water and spoon it over the chops. Put a slice of lemon on each pork chop.

Bake for 45 to 50 minutes or until browned. Run the dish under the broiler for 3 or 4 minutes to brown the center chops. Transfer the meat to a warmed serving platter, garnish with parsley and lemon slices, and serve hot.

Carciofi Ripieni
STUFFED ARTICHOKES

This dish is typically southern in its use of bread crumbs and *pecorino*. Globe artichokes can be used for this recipe, but in Calabria they prefer smaller artichokes.

SERVES 6 TO 8

8	globe artichokes or 10 to 12 smaller artichokes, cleaned (see page 420)*
1	large lemon, cut in half
3	ounces *pancetta,* finely chopped (3/4 cup) (90 grams)
2/3	cup fresh bread crumbs
3	tablespoons finely chopped parsley
1/2	cup freshly grated *pecorino* cheese (65 grams)
2	eggs
	salt and freshly ground black pepper to taste
6	tablespoons olive oil (100 ml)
	parsley sprigs for garnish

Rub the artichokes with the lemon halves and leave them in cold water with the lemon halves until needed. When you're ready to prepare the artichokes, remove the stems, cutting away evenly at the stem base so the artichokes will sit flat in the pan. Cut away the cleaned tender part of the stems and chop finely.

Put the chopped artichoke stems in a bowl with the *pancetta,* bread crumbs, parsley, and *pecorino.* Mix, add the eggs, season with salt and pepper, and mix well again. Drain and dry the whole artichokes and salt lightly all over. Using your fingers, gently open the centers of the

* If the artichokes do not have stems, use 1-1/2 times the stuffing mixture.

continued

artichokes to stuff them. Divide the mixture among them, pressing lightly to fill them completely.

Put 1/4 cup of the oil in a pan in which the artichokes fit snugly, trimmed part down. Pour the remaining 2 tablespoons oil on top of the artichokes. Add 1 inch of water to the pan. Bring to a boil, cover, and simmer for 25 to 30 minutes or until the artichokes are tender when pierced with a kitchen needle and the water has been absorbed. Meanwhile, preheat the oven to 375° (190). Remove the lid from the pan and place the pan in the oven. Bake for 25 minutes. Serve in the pan or transfer the artichokes to a heated serving platter. Garnish with the parsley.

Crema di Castagne al Cioccolato
CHESTNUT CREAM WITH CHOCOLATE

This is an elegant dessert for a *Gran Galá* (an important dinner). It comes from Anna Maria Monticelli, who decorates it in the classical way with whipped cream, marrons glacés, and candied violets.

SERVES 12

2-quart (2 liters) mold lined
with plastic wrap

  2-1/2 **pounds chestnuts (1.100 grams)**
   1/2   **cup milk (125 ml)**
   1/2   **pound good-quality semisweet chocolate**
         (225 grams)
     1   **cup (1/2 pound) unsalted butter at room**
         temperature (225 grams)

1/2 pound (2-1/2 cups) confectioners' sugar
     (225 grams)
1/2 cup good-quality dark rum (125 ml)
  1 cup heavy cream, whipped (250 ml)
     marrons glacés and candied violets for garnish

Remove the shells from the chestnuts. Bring a large pan of water to boil
and add the chestnuts. Boil over low heat for 25 to 35 minutes or until the
chestnuts are tender when pierced with a kitchen needle. Remove a
cupful of chestnuts at a time and peel away the skins using rubber gloves.
(Remove only a cupful at a time as chestnuts are impossible to peel when
cold.) Put the peeled chestnuts back into the pan and add the milk. Put
the chestnuts over low heat and mix with a wooden spoon until they have
absorbed the milk.

While the chestnuts are cooking, melt the chocolate in a double boiler. In
an electric mixer, beat the butter with the confectioners' sugar until light.
Add the chocolate to the chestnuts and add this mixture to the butter and
sugar. Add the rum and puree the mixture in batches in a food processor
fitted with the steel blade or a food mill. Spoon into the prepared pan and
refrigerate for a day.

When you're ready to serve, turn the mold out onto a serving dish and
frost with whipped cream. Make soft mounds of whipped cream at the
base interspersed with marrons glacés and candied violets.

EXTRA RECIPES

Collecting recipes is like collecting antiques—some of them don't (immediately) seem to fit into your rooms or, in this case, your menu; but after a little while you simply cannot imagine living without them. The following recipes are all a bit that way. In addition, they are typically southern Italian, quick to prepare, and come in useful for impromptu meals or on those days when one's imagination runs dry.

Le Zite della Nonna
GRANDMOTHER'S PASTA

Paola Pettini has a cooking school in Bari and has collected local recipes all her life. This is a simple pasta with tomatoes and olives, to serve on that evening when you have nothing in the kitchen and don't want to go shopping.

SERVES 6 TO 8

3	pounds ripe fresh tomatoes (1.350 grams)
1/2	medium onion, thinly sliced
	salt and freshly ground pepper to taste
1/2	pound (2 cups plus 2 tablespoons) spicy Italian olives, pitted and halved (225 grams)
	a handful of basil leaves, washed
1/2	cup olive oil (125 ml)
3	or 4 tablespoons fine dry bread crumbs
1-1/3	pounds *zite,* broken into 3 pieces (600 grams)

Preheat the oven to 400° (200). Wash the tomatoes and cut away the green stem end with a sharp knife. Cut the tomatoes in half crosswise and put them in an ovenproof dish, cut side up. Put a slice of onion on each tomato and season well with salt and pepper. Distribute the olives among the tomatoes. Chop the basil coarsely and strew it over the tomatoes. Trickle the oil over the tomatoes and sprinkle the bread crumbs on top. Cook the tomatoes in the oven for 1-1/4 to 1-3/4 hours or until the liquid from the tomatoes has evaporated. If the tomatoes seem dry, cover them with foil for the first 30 minutes of cooking time. Then remove the foil and continue cooking until done.

Cook the *zite* in boiling salted water until *al dente.* Dress the pasta with the sauce, adding more basil if desired.

Maltagliati ai Peperoni
PASTA WITH PEPPERS
IN THE NEAPOLITAN STYLE

An unusual pasta recipe from Letizia Maione's aunt, who was quite well known in Naples. She had a radio program and gave recipes to her listeners. Her recipes were very efficient—weights right, oven temperatures right, most unusual. In general, her recipes were typically Neapolitan, but always with a certain twist. Here the pasta is tossed with a cream sauce and topped with roasted peppers.

SERVES 6

2-1/4	pounds large bell peppers, a mixture of red and yellow (1 kilogram)
1/4	cup olive oil (60 ml)
1	garlic clove
6	tablespoons finely chopped parsley
	salt to taste
1	large onion, finely chopped
6	tablespoons unsalted butter (90 grams)
1/3	cup dry white wine (80 ml)
2	beef bouillon cubes
1-1/2	cups heavy cream (375 ml)
1	pound *maltagliati, pennette, or* other short pasta (450 grams)
	freshly ground pepper to taste

Roast the peppers in a preheated 400° (200) oven, turning as necessary, for about 40 minutes or until the skins are blackish and blistered. Wrap the peppers in foil and cool. When cooled, remove the skins, seeds, and stems and cut the peppers into 3/8-inch (1 cm) strips.

continued

Heat the oil in a sauté pan and brown the garlic. Discard the garlic when browned. Add the peppers, 1/4 cup of the parsley, and salt. Simmer the peppers for 1 minute. Remove from the heat and reserve.

In a skillet large enough to hold the cooked pasta, cook the onion over medium-low heat, adding a few tablespoons of water to prevent browning. When the onion is transparent, add the butter and cook the onion until lightly browned. Pour in the white wine and add the bouillon cubes, mashing with a wooden spoon to dissolve them. When the wine is reduced by half, add the cream and simmer for a few minutes to thicken.

Cook the pasta in boiling salted water until *al dente.* Drain and pour into the skillet with the cream and mix thoroughly for a minute. Pour into a warm serving dish and arrange the reserved peppers on top of the pasta. Sprinkle the remaining parsley on top and serve at once accompanied by the pepper mill.

Tagliolini alle Punte d'Asparagi
TAGLIOLINI WITH ASPARAGUS TIPS

Sicilians love to take the tenderest tips of the first spring asparagus, cook them in a little oil, roughly puree them, add cream and Parmesan, and serve with pasta. This recipe from Palermo can be used with other vegetables such as zucchini or peas and can be prepared in advance and reheated just before serving.

In Italy pasta was once served only at the middle-of-the-day dinner. Habits have changed, and this pasta would be served today to evening-dinner guests.

5-1/2 pounds fresh asparagus (2.025 grams)
   3 tablespoons olive oil
  1/4 cup unsalted butter (60 grams)
      salt and freshly ground pepper to taste
1-1/3 cups heavy cream (330 ml)
1-1/3 pounds fresh *tagliolini* (600 grams)
   1 cup freshly grated Parmesan cheese (135 grams)

Break off the top 2 inches of the asparagus tips and reserve. Remove and discard the tough parts of the stalks; break the remaining parts into 1-inch pieces. Heat the oil and 3 tablespoons of the butter in a skillet and add the asparagus pieces. Sauté slowly until the pieces are tender. Add salt and pepper. Puree the asparagus pieces in a blender or a food processor fitted with the steel blade, scraping down the sides as necessary. Reserve until ready to serve. At serving time, add the cream to the pureed asparagus and heat but do not boil.

Cook the pasta in boiling salted water until *al dente*. This takes only a few minutes with fresh pasta. While the pasta is cooking, sauté the reserved tips in the remaining butter in a skillet until *al dente*. When the pasta is done, drain and dress it with the Parmesan and half the sauce. Mix well and transfer it to a heated platter. Pour the rest of the sauce over the pasta and scatter the reserved asparagus tips on top. Serve hot and pass the pepper mill.

Puttanesca Cotta
COOKED PUTTANESCA PASTA

*Extra
Recipes*

The fame of *puttanesca* (the prostitute's pasta) is widespread. A quick, down-to-earth, hearty pasta sauce from Campania, it is one of the few completely authentic southern Italian dishes to have become well known in its own right. However, what exactly are the correct ingredients is a murkier issue. No one seems to disagree about the garlic, anchovies, and tomatoes, but whether a *puttanesca* should contain olives or capers, both, or neither seems to depend on who serves it. This recipe and the following one have both olives and capers.

SERVES 6 TO 8

3/4	cup olive oil (185 ml)
3	garlic cloves, finely chopped
1/2	teaspoon (or to taste) hot red pepper flakes
1-1/2	pounds ripe fresh tomatoes, peeled, seeded, and cut into pieces (675 grams)
1/4	cup capers, rinsed (40 grams)
3/4	cup black Gaeta olives, pitted (150 grams)
3	salt-packed anchovies, cleaned (see page 419), *or* 6 oil-packed anchovy fillets, drained dried oregano to taste a handful of parsley, finely chopped salt to taste
1-1/3	pounds *vermicelli or spaghetti* (600 grams) chopped parsley for garnish (optional) freshly ground pepper to taste

410

Heat the olive oil in a skillet and add the garlic. When browned, add the pepper flakes, tomatoes, capers, and olives. Cook over fairly high heat for 10 minutes. Add the anchovies cut into small pieces, oregano, and parsley. Cook for 2 minutes. Taste for seasoning and add salt if necessary.

Cook the *vermicelli* in boiling salted water until *al dente*. Drain and dress with the sauce. Garnish with parsley if desired. Serve at once and pass the pepper mill.

Puttanesca Cruda

UNCOOKED PUTTANESCA PASTA

This uncooked *puttanesca* sauce is extremely simple to prepare and can be refrigerated until needed.

SERVES 6 TO 8

3/4 **cup capers (120 grams)**
6 **garlic cloves, crushed**
3/4 **cup olive oil (185 ml)**
1 **tube anchovy paste, about 2 ounces (60 grams)**
1/2 **teaspoon hot red pepper flakes *or* Tabasco sauce to taste**
1-1/2 **cups (about 9 ounces) black Gaeta olives, pitted (300 grams)**
6 **or 7 large ripe fresh tomatoes, peeled, seeded, and cut into small pieces**
1-1/2 **pounds *spaghetti* (675 grams)**
1/4 **cup finely chopped parsley for garnish (optional)**

Rinse the capers under running water and soak in cold water for an hour. Drain and pat dry.

Put the garlic in the olive oil. Add the anchovy paste, whisking to amalgamate the oil and paste. Add the pepper flakes or Tabasco and the capers. Cut the olives into 4 pieces and add to the sauce with the tomatoes. Mix well and set aside for at least 1 hour and up to 4. Do not add salt.

When you're ready to serve, cook the pasta in boiling salted water (very lightly salted; the anchovy paste is salty) until *al dente*. Drain and dress with half the sauce. Arrange the pasta on a platter and pour the rest of the sauce on top. If desired, sprinkle the finely chopped parsley over the pasta just before serving. Serve at once.

Minestra di Natale
CHRISTMAS SOUP

This Christmas soup recipe comes from Silvia Cereo, who was born in Capri and lived there as a child. It is a local dish made in Benevento, reputed to be where witches live and known to be the home of Strega liqueur. Made with chicken and escarole, it is served in Italy as a first course. With a loaf of crusty bread and a glass of wine, however, this fragrant winter soup becomes a meal in itself.

SERVES 8

> 1 roasting chicken, about 3-1/2 pounds (1.600 grams)
> 3 quarts water (3 liters)
> 2 bay leaves
> 1 medium onion, quartered
> 1 tablespoon peppercorns
>   peel of 1 small lemon
> 1 chicken bouillon cube
>   salt to taste
> 2 pounds escarole (900 grams)
>   freshly grated Parmesan cheese for serving (optional)

Wash the chicken and put it in a stockpot with the water and all the ingredients except the escarole. Bring to a boil, cover, and simmer over the lowest heat for 2 hours. Cool and strain the broth. When the chicken is cool enough to handle, remove and discard the skin. Remove the meat from the bones and tear it into small strips. Return the meat to the broth, discarding the bones.

Discard the tough outer leaves of the escarole and wash it. Cut the escarole into lengthwise strips about 1 inch wide.

continued

When you're ready to serve the soup, heat the broth to boiling and add the escarole. Simmer until done, about 5 minutes, stirring occasionally. Remove the lemon peel and serve hot, passing grated Parmesan if desired, although this delicate soup should be served as is.

Pasta Svelta
QUICK PASTA

A simple sardine pasta from Signor Hassan of the oddly named Charleston Restaurant in Palermo, which serves only Sicilian food. The dish leaves the taste of the fish intact, and the marriage of flavors with the hot *linguine* is perfect. If sardines are not available, try smelts.

SERVES 4 TO 6

9- by 13-inch (23 by 33 cm)
ovenproof glass dish

> 2 **pounds fresh sardines, cleaned (see page 419)**
> **(900 grams)**
> 1/2 **cup plus 1 tablespoon olive oil (140 ml)**
> 1/4 **cup water (60 ml)**
> 1 **pound *linguine* (450 grams)**
> 6 **salt-packed anchovies, cleaned (see page 419), and**
> **cut into pieces, *or* 12 oil-packed anchovy fillets,**
> **drained and cut into pieces**
> 1 **cup finely chopped parsley, packed**
> **freshly ground black pepper to taste**

After cleaning the sardines you can peel them, if desired, by gently pulling away the skin, but it's not necessary. Rinse the fish under cold water and pat dry. Preheat the oven to 450° (230).

Put 1 tablespoon olive oil on the bottom of the ovenproof dish. Arrange the sardines over the bottom and sides in one layer. Pour 1/4 cup of the remaining olive oil and then the water over the sardines. Bake for 15 minutes.

Cook the pasta in boiling salted water until *al dente*. While the pasta is cooking, heat the remaining oil in a small saucepan with the anchovies, mashing them to a paste with a wooden spoon. Drain the pasta and mix it with the oil and anchovies. Pour it into the dish with the sardines and mix thoroughly, sprinkling the parsley over the pasta as you toss. Serve at once in the baking dish and pass the pepper mill.

LINGUINE WITH OLIVES, CAPERS, AND ANCHOVIES

This Neapolitan recipe is quick and delicious, made with pantry ingredients that don't require a large shopping expedition.

SERVES 4 TO 6

- 2/3 cup (1/4 pound) capers packed in salt (110 grams)
- 1/2 cup olive oil (125 ml)
- 3 garlic cloves, crushed
- 1 cup black Gaeta olives, pitted and halved (200 grams)
- 1 cup finely chopped parsley, packed
- 6 salt-packed anchovies, cleaned (see page 419), *or* 12 oil-packed anchovy fillets, drained
- 1 pound *linguine* (450 grams)
  freshly ground black pepper to taste

Rinse the capers under cold water and soak for an hour in fresh cold water. Drain and pat dry.

Heat the olive oil in a skillet and add the garlic. Cook the garlic slowly until browned. Discard the browned garlic and add the olives, capers, and parsley. Add the anchovies, mashing them with the back of a wooden spoon to dissolve them. Remove the sauce from the heat. Reheat before using.

Cook the *linguine* in boiling salted water until *al dente*. Drain and mix thoroughly with the hot sauce over the lowest heat. Serve at once and pass the pepper mill.

Pizzette Napoletane
SMALL NEAPOLITAN PIZZAS

Simple little *mozzarella* pizzas are always a hit, and these miniature ones never fail to please children of any age. They are usually served piled high on a platter, and someone is kept busy rushing back and forth to the kitchen to replenish the dish—because, as Italians say, one calls the other.

MAKES ABOUT 40,
SERVING ABOUT 8

FOR THE PIZZA DOUGH:
- 1 pound (4 cups) flour (450 grams)
- 2 1/4-ounce envelopes active dry yeast (15 grams) *or* 3/4 ounce fresh yeast
- 1-1/4 to 1-1/2 cups (or as needed) warm water (300 to 350 ml)
- 1/3 cup mashed potato

FOR THE TOMATO SAUCE:
- 3 tablespoons olive oil
- 1 medium onion, finely chopped
  salt to taste
- 1 2-pound can Italian plum tomatoes, drained (about 4 cups) (900 grams)
  freshly ground pepper to taste

TO FINISH THE *PIZZETTE*:
  olive oil for frying, about 2 cups (500 ml)
- 1/3 pound *mozzarella* cheese, coarsely grated (1-1/4 cups) (150 grams)
  dried oregano *or* chopped fresh basil *or* both
  freshly ground black pepper to taste
  a few tablespoons freshly grated Parmesan cheese

continued

Make a mound of the flour on a work surface, preferably wooden. Make a well in the center. Dissolve the yeast in 1 cup warm water and pour into the well together with the mashed potato. Beat with a fork, gradually incorporating the flour. Add extra warm water as needed to make a soft dough. Put the dough in an oiled bowl and set aside to rise in a warm place, covered, until doubled in volume, about 1 to 1-1/2 hours.

Make the tomato sauce. Heat the oil in a saucepan and add the onion and salt to taste. Cook the onion over medium-low heat until transparent, adding a tablespoon of water to prevent browning. Add the tomatoes and cook for 20 minutes over fairly high heat, stirring occasionally. The sauce must be dense. Season with salt and pepper and cool.

Make the *pizzette*. When the dough is ready, take a small ball of dough in your hands and flatten it to make a pizza about 3 inches (8 cm) in diameter with a raised edge, or roll out the dough with a rolling pin and make the slightly raised edge by hand. Make all the *pizzette*. (This is one of those recipes for which it's useful to have a kitchen friend.)

Heat the oil in an 11-inch skillet and fry the *pizzette* a few at a time until golden brown. Drain on paper towels. Preheat the oven to 425° (220) when you're ready to serve the *pizzette*. Fill them with a spoonful of sauce, with *mozzarella,* oregano, and a grinding of black pepper on top. Or use tomato sauce, basil, and Parmesan or whatever you like. Bake the *pizzette* for 5 minutes or until the *mozzarella* has melted. Serve very hot.

TECHNIQUES

How to Clean Fresh Sardines and Anchovies

Using kitchen scissors, cut off and discard the head. Open the fish along the stomach and remove and discard the entrails. Open up the sardine without separating the 2 parts of the body and remove the central bones and fins. Rinse under cold water and drain. If desired, the skin may be peeled away, but this is usually not called for.

How to Clean Salt-Packed Anchovies

With your thumbnail or a sharp knife, open up the bottom side of the anchovy. Remove and discard entrails and bones. Separate the 2 sides of the fish and remove and discard the fins. Rinse under cold running water and dry on paper towels.

How to Clean Octopus

Using scissors, cut away the eyes. Remove the small bony part in the middle of the tentacles underneath. Turn the head inside out and remove

the intestines. Turn the head back as before and peel away the transparent skin. Rinse thoroughly and leave in cold water until needed.

How to Clean Artichokes

Have ready a large bowl of cold water. Remove the outer leaves of the artichokes until you reach the inner yellowish leaves. Break off the green parts remaining and rub the cleaned part of the artichoke with a cut lemon. Remove the fuzzy choke with a small metal spoon. If there is a long stem, trim it to about 3 inches (8 cm) from the base. Cut away the stringy fibers from the stem and trim away the green part from the base of the artichoke. Rub the stem and base with lemon and put in the cold water along with the used lemon halves.

How to Make Pasta Frolla by Hand

Mix together flour and sugar and mound on a wooden pastry board or a marble surface. Make a well in the center and put the butter cut into pieces, the egg yolks, and the lemon zest in the well. Mix together rapidly, rubbing the mixture through the hands. Work just until all is blended.

IN A FOOD PROCESSOR
Put sugar, flour, butter, and zest in the bowl of the processor fitted with the steel blade. Add the yolks through the tube with the motor running. As soon as the dough masses, turn off the machine.

IN THE LARGE BOWL OF AN ELECTRIC MIXER
Use the paddle attachment. Put all the ingredients in the bowl. Wrap a tea towel around the bowl to prevent the flour from scattering and mix until the pasta masses around the paddle.

Roll out the *pasta frolla* with the help of a long spatula. (Mine is about 12 inches/30 cm long.) *Pasta frolla* should be touched as little as possible after mixing. It can be patched very easily. Simply place a piece of dough on top of the torn place and press gently. It is not necessary to dampen the pastry.

The dough can also be used for cookies. Roll out a little thicker and cut

Techniques

with a fairly large cookie cutter. Bake at 350° (180) for 10 to 13 minutes or until golden.

How to Salt Eggplant

There seem to be several schools of thought on salting and sweating eggplant—which is done to remove any bitter juices and excess moisture. The more usual way is to layer slices of eggplant in a colander, salting each layer as you go. Then a plate is placed on top with a weight on it. The eggplant slices are left to drain for at least an hour, but sometimes as long as overnight. They are then rinsed under cold water and patted dry with towels. Another approach, much easier if slightly eccentric, is to leave the eggplant slices in heavily salted cold water for at least 12 hours. They are then drained and fried immediately—you skip the drying step altogether.

How to Roast Peppers

In Italy peppers are often roasted directly on the flame of a gas stove; you hold the pepper on a fork and try hard not to burn your fingers. A much easier method is oven-roasting. Place whole peppers on a foil-lined baking sheet or pizza pan. Heat the oven to 400° (200) and roast the peppers for about 20 minutes on each side or until they are charred all over. Wrap them in the foil used to line the baking sheet and leave to cool, about 15 minutes. When the peppers are cool enough to handle, peel away the skin—it slips off easily—and remove and discard seeds and stems.

How to Preserve Peppers

Once the peppers are roasted, cleaned, and cut into 1/2-inch strips, they're ready to be preserved in olive oil. Layer the strips in a clean jar. On each layer, put slices of garlic, parsley leaves, a piece of dried hot red pepper or a fresh hot green pepper sliced into thin rings. Oregano and basil can be added. Cover the peppers completely with olive oil. These peppers keep well, refrigerated, but must be brought to room temperature for serving. The oil can be reused for another batch of peppers or to dress salads or soft cheeses. The peppers will keep in the refrigerator, covered, for a week.

How to Freeze Peppers

Put the cleaned roasted pepper strips in plastic containers, seal, and freeze. The peppers can be defrosted and added to pasta sauce, eaten as an hors d'oeuvre dressed with oil, garlic, and hot pepper flakes, and generally used wherever roasted peppers are needed.

How to Cook Pasta

Use 5 quarts of water for each pound of pasta, adding 1 teaspoon coarse salt for each quart. Bring the water to a rolling boil, drop in the pasta, stir with a wooden spoon so the pasta doesn't stick together, and, when the water boils again, lower the heat so that the pasta boils normally. The cooking time varies from 5 minutes to more than 15 minutes, depending on the quality of the pasta, the type of water, the altitude, and the weather! The only way to know when the pasta is done is to taste it—you'll learn by experience.

How to Puree Tomatoes

Many recipes call for tomato puree. I prefer that you make your own—from peeled and seeded fresh tomatoes or drained canned Italian plum tomatoes—rather than using canned puree. Simply put the tomatoes in a blender or food processor fitted with the steel blade and process until smooth or pass them through a food mill.

INGREDIENTS

ANCHOVIES

There are three kinds: fresh (very rarely available in America), salt-packed, and oil-packed. I usually use the salt-packed anchovies, but if they are unavailable the oil-packed anchovies or fillets can be substituted. The salt-packed variety keeps almost forever tightly covered in the refrigerator, so don't worry about buying a big tin.

ITALIAN CHEESES

All of these cheeses are available in the United States, but you may have to try an Italian specialty market for some of the more unusual ones.

- *Caciocavallo* is a compact cheese made of cow's milk in a rounded gourd shape with a topknot. The cheeses are tied together in pairs and left about 20 days to mature. If they're left longer than that, the cheese has a stronger taste and is known as *caciocavallo piccante*. This cheese is made almost exclusively in southern Italy, particularly in Molise, Abruzzi, and Campania.

- *Caciotta* is a sheep's milk cheese, usually made in winter. The usually handmade cheeses weigh about 1 kilogram (2-1/4 pounds). The cheese is eaten at all stages of maturity; when it's very fresh, it's particularly delicious—though almost rubbery. It's served with olive oil poured over it and with lots of freshly ground black pepper on top. It's usually ready to eat after 20 days, though sometimes aged longer.

- *Fior di latte* looks very much like *mozzarella* but has a completely different taste. It's not particularly good as a table cheese, but when cooked it can substitute for *mozzarella*.

- In Italy *mozzarella* is made only with buffalo milk, by law. The best *mozzarella* comes from Campania, and *mozzarella* is very much a part of Neapolitan food, from pizzas and *timballi* to pasta. Freshness is essential: a good *mozzarella* for the table is not more than a day old. It's delicious eaten simply on its own, in a Caprese salad, or with a trickle of olive oil.

- Parmesan: Look for true Parmesan, with the words *Parmigiano-Reggiano* stenciled in brown on the rind. Good Parmesan has a straw yellow color and should be moist. For grating at the table, the cheese should be a bit softer and more crumbly than cheese for cooking. To store, wrap the cheese in aluminum foil and keep it in a plastic container in the refrigerator. Always grate Parmesan fresh; it quickly loses its flavor once it's grated.

- *Pecorino,* sometimes called *pecorino Romano,* is made from sheep's milk and is probably one of the oldest of Italian cheeses; it was made in the shepherds' village of Rome. It is eaten all over the South but rarely found above Rome. It becomes "*piccante*" when it's mature, which is anywhere from six months to a year. We buy *pecorino* in the country around Rome from the shepherds. When it's young, the cheese is good on the table; the *piccante* version is best grated. Grate it as needed, using a food processor fitted with the steel blade. A perfectly seasoned *pecorino* will produce a tear in the middle when it's cut, known as *la lacrima*.

- *Provolone,* a cow's milk cheese, is eaten both young (*dolce*) and aged (*piccante*). The older *provolone* has a much stronger taste and is the one generally available in Italian-American markets.

- *Ricotta* means "recooked," and this sheep's milk cheese is made from the whey left after making *caciotta*. It's placed in reed baskets to allow the remaining liquid to seep out. When the forms of *ricotta* are turned out, they have a lovely woven design left by the imprint of the reeds. Freshly made *ricotta* is eaten with rum and sugar as a dessert or simply eaten on its own. It is used in pastries and ices, cakes, and pasta dishes of all kinds and is even fried. When fresh it is soft and moist but holds its shape when turned out of the reed basket. As it ages it tends to dry and become less soft. *Ricotta* is also made from goat's milk and, particularly north of Rome, from cow's milk. It's the cow's milk variety that's most often available in America, but sometimes, especially at Easter, you can find the real sheep's milk kind.

CITRUS FRUITS
Before you use their zest, wash lemons and oranges under cold running water with kitchen soap, then dry them thoroughly. If you suspect they have been subjected to heavy spraying and/or artificial coloring, use organic citrus fruits.

FLOUR
Except when cake flour is specified, the flour called for in these recipes is ordinary unbleached all-purpose flour.

OLIVE OIL
We use olive oil for everything. For frying purposes, a less expensive oil will do, but be sure the quality is good.

OLIVES

Southern Italians are particularly fond of olives. The recipes note whether a particular kind, such as Gaeta, is recommended, but you can always substitute. A readily available supermarket brand is Progresso's black olives, which are quite good. Spicy green Sicilian olives are also used in many of the recipes.

PANCETTA

Pancetta means "little belly," hog belly in this case, cured in a similar way to ham. (There is also *guanciale,* or cheeks of the hog, cured in the same way, but it's rapidly disappearing.) *Pancetta* has a distinctive taste, very different from our sweet smoke-cured bacon—American bacon is not a substitute. A better choice would be lean fatback or what we call in Georgia "streak of lean, streak of fat."

PARSLEY

I always use flat-leaf parsley.

PASTA

The De Cecco brand is universally available in America and is a very good pasta of consistent quality. La Molisana can occasionally be found. Braibanti is particularly good for long pasta, *spaghetti, vermicelli,* etc. Barilla is good, as is Buitoni. In general, look for pasta imported from Italy.

SALAME

The varieties of *salame* found all over the south of Italy are bewildering. They are of all sizes, all girths, with and without garlic or *peperoncino,* with large pieces of fat and lean meat, with finely ground meat, with and without fennel seeds or other aromatic herbs. Aside from the industrially produced *salame* available in America, in Italy you will always find local *salame* with its own character.

TOMATOES

In most recipes I've given a choice of fresh or canned tomatoes; when only fresh are specified, you can be assured that the recipe is greatly enhanced by fresh—and, in most cases, that it's a summer dish. For canned, always choose tomatoes labeled Italian plum tomatoes—they have the best flavor and texture for cooking.

WHEAT STARCH

Although it's not easily found in America, wheat starch is used almost exclusively in southern Italy. Cornstarch is a good substitute.

ZUCCATA

This long zucchinilike squash is found in Sicily. It is candied and used in sweets. *Zuccata* can be replaced by citron, although they're not the same thing.

EQUIPMENT

TERRA-COTTA POTS AND PANS

These are wonderful for cooking slow *ragùs* and roasts, anything that responds to gentle heat. Terra-cotta pans distribute heat well and hold it for some time after the heat has been turned off; I always use a Flame Tamer underneath the pot to reduce the heat a bit. It's important to season the pans before you use them. To season, first soak the pan in cold water to cover for 24 hours. Then rub the bottom of the pan with a peeled clove of garlic. Add a quart of water to the pan, bring it to a boil, discard the water, and your pan is ready to be used.

INDEX

Index

Index

Index

Index

Index

Index

Index

Index

Index